THE MAKING OF
A NATIONAL THEATRE

THE MAKING
OF A
NATIONAL THEATRE

by

GEOFFREY WHITWORTH

C.B.E

FABER AND FABER LTD
24 Russell Square
London

First published in mcmli
by Faber and Faber Limited
24 Russell Square London W.C.1
Printed in Great Britain
at the Bowering Press Plymouth

PREFACE

Some day, no doubt, the complete annals of the National Theatre will be written, based on the archives of the theatre itself, and prolonged from age to age. To this monumental work the present sketch has been conceived as a kind of preliminary chapter. While memories are still fresh, it is possible to recall the steps whereby the National Theatre idea was first imposed on a more or less unwilling public; and then, as an eye witness, to tell the story of the outstanding events which led to the actual foundation of the theatre.

In greater debt than I had anticipated to contemporary documents and correspondence, the book has assumed the nature of an anthology rather than of a continuous narrative. This I believe may be all to the good, for the reader will find himself in first-hand contact with the past, while such comment as I have permitted myself provides a personal perspective to what might otherwise have been a merely dry transcription. I must admit that some of my quotations are now somewhat 'dated', but when first written or delivered they would have appeared novel and even revolutionary to those who read or heard them. They serve at any rate to remind one of the mental background which nourished the Dream, and to me are fascinating as revealing the steps whereby the saturation of contemporary opinion with the *mystique* of a National Theatre was attempted and largely achieved. That nothing may now hinder the final consummation of our hopes is a matter for prayer and fasting.

The names of many friends and colleagues who have so kindly placed much valuable information and material at my disposal defy enumeration. To all of them I tender my sincere thanks. Although the book is officially sponsored neither by the Shakespeare Memorial Theatre Committee nor by the Joint Council of the National Theatre and the Old Vic, I have enjoyed the boon of access to their minutes and to various documents in their possession. Likewise I must acknowledge the assistance I have received in generous measure from Messrs. Bircham & Co., Solicitors to the S.M.N.T. Committee and to the Trustees. The extracts from Parliamentary Debates in 1913 and 1949 appear by consent of the Editor of *Hansard*; and for the inclusion of several reports and letters to that journal I am indebted to the Manager of *The Times*, and not least for the permission, endorsed by Mr. Winston Churchill himself, to reprint Mr. Churchill's speech at the Ellen Terry banquet in 1906. Pamela Countess of Lytton has also been most kind in placing at my disposal many important documents and letters. Mr. Bernard Shaw, a few months before his death, kindly agreed to the printing in full of the concluding scene from *The Dark Lady of the Sonnets*, while Mr. C. D. Medley, literary executor of Harley Granville-Barker, wrote that there would be no objection to my using the passages from his published writings which occur during the course of the book.

In the first chapter I have not scrupled to avail myself of the account of the early English drama as given by Mr. R. Farquharson Sharp in his valuable *Short History of the English Stage*, while the story of the National Theatre movement itself throughout the crucial first decade of the present century would have been far less complete were it not for the assistance of my old friend S. R. Littlewood who, among other details, supplied me with his rare copy of the pamphlet issued by the *Daily Chronicle* in 1906. I am also in deep debt to Mr. James Archer, to Mr. Alan Gomm, and to Mr. Philip Carr, for help in various ways, and for the loan of private correspondence. Miss Frances Briggs and Mr. Kenneth Rae, secretaries respectively of the British Drama League and the Joint Council of the National Theatre and the Old Vic, have been

PREFACE

good enough to answer a number of queries; and I must pass a vote of thanks to my wife both for her valued encouragement and for a retentive memory which has recalled many an incident which might otherwise have been overlooked.

In regard to the Plates, Mr. Arthur Coleman of Cheltenham has been at considerable pains to find the portrait of Richard Badger, instigator of the Statue scheme. In all other cases, the owners of copyright, where traceable, have been good enough to permit the free use of their photographs, and due acknowledgment to them will be found in the list of illustrations.

Finally, I must thank Mr. Brian O'Rorke for the loan of his photograph of the South Bank of the Thames, showing the site of the National Theatre-to-be.

CONTENTS

ILLUSTRATIONS

I

NO NEW THING

Listening to the House of Commons debate on the 21st of January 1949, when the National Theatre Bill was given its second reading, one felt that the result of the debate was a foregone conclusion. In spite of the financial difficulties in which the country found itself, no one demurred to the proposed expenditure by the State of a million pounds on a project which a few years before would have been the subject of bitter controversy. Party strife gave way to party concord, and any criticism which arose took the form of a complaint that the sum voted was not even larger, so that Scotland and Wales might have their national theatres too. All this will be narrated in its proper place. It is only mentioned now to stress the remarkable change which has lately become noticeable in public feeling in regard to the place of the drama in the life of the nation. For believe me, the acceptance of a national theatre scheme for London was by no means the simple matter that it seemed. Rather was it the unlooked-for culmination of long and often disheartening effort on the part of a few stubborn enthusiasts, fighting heavy odds over the space of a century or more.

Even so, the national status which our theatre occupies to-day is no new thing. The very roots of drama are buried in a past when the link between State and Stage was inextricably close. To understand how close, one has only to recall those communal rituals and religious ceremonials which were so vital a feature in the life of prehistoric man, and which survive to this day among savages. The coming of civilization did not destroy this alliance, and it is a difference not in kind but in quality which separates primitive drama from the tragic masterpieces of classical Greece. The Athenian theatre was essentially a national theatre. The city state was responsible for its organization, and the performances were conducted in a spirit of national festival. For a modern analogy you need go no further than the Passion Play of Oberammergau, where atmosphere and administration bear a striking resemblance to those of the Festival plays at Athens in the fifth century B.C.

With the fall of Greece, Rome took over many elements of Hellenic culture, albeit on a lower plane; and when in its turn the Roman Empire was due for catastrophe, state-provided circuses held only second place to state-provided bread as among the bribes offered by a dying Empire to its citizens in revolt. In their ultimate degradation these circuses, with their human sacrifice of trembling slaves and heroic Christians, were fit only to assuage the blood-lust of an audience of sophisticated savages. Only the work of respectable playwrights like Terence and Plautus survived the dark ages in manuscript form—relics of an earlier and more humane form of Latin drama.

During the medieval period, as a new Christian civilization spread throughout the western world, the Theatre came to life again, but not so much for its own sake as to satisfy the requirements of religious, social, and educational institutions. Owing little or nothing to classical tradition either in form or subject-matter, the plays were, like Gothic Architecture, a new creative discovery, and, as in earliest times, they were definitely inspired by the state religion of the time. As a method of religious instruction Miracle and Mystery Plays were promoted by the clergy, and performed in church. They were consciously didactic, and were meant to stimulate the imagination through the eye as the most effective means for reaching the understanding of an illiterate common folk. As their popularity grew, these plays were transferred from the church to the churchyards. And then, little by little, to open spaces in the towns, with the result that the performances began to lose their exclusively sacred character. Secular scenes were tacked on to scriptural plots; and even jugglers and strolling players were included among the actors. Eventually the ecclesiastics came to the conclusion that it was no longer suitable that the clergy should take part in these popular productions, and their appearance was forbidden by a papal bull early in the thirteenth century. As the plays grew more elaborate, and the cost of producing them increased, it was no wonder that they began to pass into the hands of the Trade Guilds, which, like the modern Trade Unions, had plenty of funds at their disposal. Coventry and York were famous among the centres which specialized in religious pageant plays, and their significance for our present purpose is that their background was institutional, and that they came to be financed by the community rather than by private enterprise.

The members of the guilds contributed a yearly rate, known as the Pageant Silver, to defray expenses. The prototype of the modern theatrical manager is to be found in the 'Pageant Master', who was elected from among the craftsmen to direct the proceedings. The plays were prepared with the utmost care, and their representation considered an event of great moment.

By the middle of the fifteenth century, what were known as 'Moralities' began to displace Mystery and Miracle Plays in public favour. In the 'Moralities', embodiments of the Virtues and Vices were substituted for the well-known characters of Holy Writ, and it is not surprising that before long new themes were sought, and that a shift to purely secular subjects began. Then as the plays grew more specialized, the players too became a distinct class, and their calling a separate one. Patronage was now a necessary condition of the actor's existence, and royal or noble favour was essential to success. The earliest royal patron of the drama was Richard III. While still Duke of Gloucester, he attached a company of players to his household, granting them permission to travel about his domains whenever he did not require their services at home. This did something to regularize the actor's calling, with the important consequence that amateur acting became quite the fashion. The pastime of 'amateur theatricals' was taken up, first by the gentlemen of the Inns of Court, and subsequently by those of higher degree, with as great a zest as any displayed to-day. Universities and schools caught the infection, and even the clergy began to interest themselves once more in the writing of plays. Our oldest English comedy, *Ralph Roister Doister*, was the work of Nicholas Udall, Headmaster of Eton, for performance by his boys. Such Tudor plays as those of John Heywood (Udall's contemporary), and Bishop Still's *Gammer Gurton's Needle* are farcical comedies of everyday life, with plots largely original and with a flavour distinctly popular.

The strife of opinion which accompanied the Reformation found a convenient outlet in the drama, and scurrilous attacks on Protestants or Papists were all too frequent. Many attempts were made to control the resulting disorders, and in 1556 actors were prohibited from roaming through the country as being likely disseminators of heresies and seditions. These were the 'rogues and vagabonds' which are often held up to us to-day as evidence of the low esteem in which the actor was held in older days. But this surely is an error. The fact that unauthorized companies of strolling players were frowned upon throws up in high relief the artistic and social prestige of the regular companies as by law established. With such a social and educational backing as we have indicated, it is impossible to believe that the drama as such was viewed as anything but a commendable influence and as a praiseworthy vehicle for the expression of the high renaissance spirit which was transforming the culture both of England and of Europe, and attracting to itself the best minds of the age.

When Elizabeth ascended the throne in 1586, the leading professional actors of the day were comprised in three or four companies, of which the Earl of Leicester's was the chief. Schoolboy companies were also employed for the elaborate and expensive Masques performed at lordly mansions or at the Court itself. It was a time, too, of professional theatre-building. In place of the inn-yard, new-fangled play-houses were constructed, such as the Globe, the Swan, and the Curtain. Here the style of production was simpler than in the case of the Masques and Court performances, not only because of the physical form of the new play-houses, but because the productions were now more and more dependent on the support of a paying public. Yet the dramatic impulse of the playwright remained aristocratic rather than proletarian. Glorious poetry was the order of the day, combined with a strain of rough and tumble that seemed no less genuinely inspired. By the same token, not seldom did freedom of speech transcend the limits of political propriety. Censorship became more drastic—'Art tongue-tied by Authority', as Shakespeare said; but that does not seem to have fettered his genius, and the institution of censorship served to weld more closely the connection between State and Stage. Queen Elizabeth was a confirmed patron of the drama, and seems to have welcomed the introduction of her Royal Person, both by symbol and by name, in several plays of the period—notably in the last scene of Shakespeare's *Henry VIII* and in a famous passage from *A Midsummer Night's Dream*.

This happy state of things continued unimpaired more or less right up to the Revolution; but with the execution of King Charles I complete disaster overtook the theatre, as it overtook so much else that had been valued in the life of the English people. It was now that the Rogues and Vagabonds came into their own. They were able to keep the flag flying in the remote parts of the country. But in London the established and reputable companies were put entirely out of business, and if one or two of them contrived to offer a clandestine performance now and then, it was at the risk of fines and imprisonment. Had the puritan régime lasted a few years longer than it did, the life-line which preserved the stage tradition from one generation to another might well have been broken. As it was, the Restoration came only just in time. One of the first acts of Good King Charles was to reverse the policy of the Protector in regard to the theatre. Soon after his entry into London, he openly granted two royal patents, the one to Davenant's company at Lincoln's Inn Fields, the other to Thomas Killigrew's at the Cockpit in Drury Lane. Davenant's players were known as the 'Duke of York's Company', and Killigrew's as the 'King's Servants'. They took an oath of loyalty to the Lord Chamberlain, were privileged to wear His Majesty's uniform, and ranked as 'Gentlemen of the Chamber'. In 1682 the two companies were united under the style of 'The King's Company', and were established in a new theatre built by Sir Christopher Wren on the site of the historic playhouse to be known then and to this day as 'The Theatre Royal, Drury Lane'. A new era of prosperity for the English theatre had begun.

And similar developments were taking place in Paris. There, also, two companies had been active under royal patronage: the Royal Players of the Hotel de Bourgogne and the even more famous troupe of the great Molière himself. Some years after Molière's death in 1680, Louis XIV amalgamated both companies, and provided them with a theatre in the rue Mazarin, financed them with a grant of £12,000 (an immense sum in those days), and thus inaugurated the Comédie Française, mother of the National theatres of Europe.

Why, you may ask, did a comparable opportunity in England fail to evolve on similar lines? For one thing, perhaps, the financial resources at the disposal of the Merry Monarch were inferior to those of the Roi Soleil. For another thing, and this was more important, the English estimate of the drama's worth to the nation was less exalted than that which obtained on the other side of the Channel. Charles was full of good will towards the arts, but favoured the frivolous and the licentious; so it was that the typical dramatists of the period were writers like Congreve and Vanbrugh, and it is small wonder that the more solid elements in the nation were not interested, and that the puritan remnant vehemently disapproved. Indeed, almost to our own day a large and politically powerful section of our people continued to show a mistrust of the stage and all its works. But in France they managed differently. Good manners if not good morals were the thing. The plays of Molière did not raise a blush, and were wholly free from the coarseness of idea and expression which here went on unchecked till, in 1698, Jeremy Collier's brilliant pamphlet: *A Short View of the Profaneness and Immorality of the English Stage*, cried shame on a bawdiness which has only raised its head again in present times.

In any case, the Restoration theatre, lacking at once the moral and economic background for a national establishment, was forced to rely on private enterprise which meant, in effect, not so much the enterprise of speculative adventurers as the disinterested patronage of the nobility. Unfortunately, the system was weak on the managerial side. The first management of Drury Lane, for instance, was frankly incompetent, and soon there were numerous desertions from the King's Company to a new playhouse in Lincoln's Inn Fields. By the beginning of the eighteenth century, in spite of the licence regulations, several other theatres had come into being under one pretext or another, and between Drury Lane and Covent Garden in particular arose a bitter rivalry which continued well on into the days of Garrick. Despite the unique prestige which that great actor brought to the theatre which he controlled, it is significant that the three most successful plays of the period, *She Stoops to Conquer*, *Douglas*, and *The Rivals*, received their first performance not at the 'Lane', but at the 'Garden'. Garrick, it must be admitted, was not infallible in his choice of plays, and the intrigue and competition between the various managements were as troublesome to him as to his colleagues. This competitive spirit led to riots and disorders,

engineered by the partisans of the different theatres, which, however regrettable in themselves, did provide a good advertisement
for the plays and kept the theatre well before the public eye.

But we must not be led away from the main theme of our study
by these seductive by-ways. Let Shakespeare himself lead us back
to the straight and narrow path, for from him, as we shall see,
more than from anyone else, derive those influences which, in a
final analysis, were to lead to that recognition of the drama as a
fine art which was to make possible the foundation of a National
Theatre.

The gradual growth of the Shakespeare cult deserves a book
to itself. At his death, he was regarded as but one among several
others 'of the tribe of Ben', and had it not been for the loyal
industry of two fellow-actors, Hemminge and Condell, editors of
the First Folio, his renown might never have reached the heights.
Ben Jonson, who certainly regarded himself as destined for the
premiership, was generous enough to contribute a tribute of
conventional verse to the folio, while a contemporary sonnet by
one William Basse suggests that there may have been some talk
of interment in Westminster Abbey. That honour, however, was reserved for Jonson twenty-one years later, Shakespeare
himself being buried at his home-town of Stratford-on-Avon, a
puritan stronghold where no organized remembrance could be
expected apart from the chancel tomb, an honourable position
which was allotted to him less, perhaps, on account of his poetry
than of his local eminence as a man of property and a lessee of
tithes.

But in London, at any rate, the memory of Shakespeare, poet
and playwright, was not forgotten. His plays continued to be
performed, and he is mentioned in *Fuller's Worthies* (1662), and
in other seventeenth-century biographies. After the Restoration,
however, the text of his plays was treated on the stage with scant
respect. Dryden had the temerity to re-write *Antony and Cleopatra*
and the *Tempest*, to better suit, as he thought, the taste of the

time; and all kinds of liberties were taken in production. But if the groundlings and the fashionable allowed themselves to be fobbed off with any kind of tinsel, there were some who demanded the pure gold. A serious school of literary criticism was coming to birth which firmly recognized his genius, and to what heights their estimate was raised is attested by the famous Preface with which Dr. Johnson embellished his edition of Shakespeare's plays published in 1765. On this James Boswell commented:

If it had no other merit but that of producing his Preface, in which the excellencies and defects of his immortal bard are displayed with a masterly hand, the nation would have had no reason to complain. A blind, indiscriminate admiration of Shakespeare had exposed the nation to the ridicule of foreigners. Johnson, by candidly admitting the faults of his poet, had the more credit in his bestowing on him deserved and indisputable praise; and doubtless none of his panegyrists have done him so much honour.

This shows, among other things, that Shakespeare was already well known on the Continent, if not universally appreciated. Did not Voltaire regard him as little better than a barbarian, a traitor to civilization and a Goth in the worst sense of the word? Here in England, however, the dawn of the Gothic revival was an asset to Shakespeare's repute, while the growing literacy of the nation favoured the recognition of his poetic and moral grandeur among the public at large. Pious citizens who on conscientious grounds would never enter a theatre, began to peruse his plays at home, and the time was not far distant when his works would be found together with the family Bible as a common object not only in the mansions of the great but in the humble habitations of the poor.

So much for Shakespeare the poet. As dramatist, one man above all others was responsible for his apotheosis: David Garrick. Anticipating at Drury Lane what Henry Irving was to do at the Lyceum a hundred years later, it was he who finally established Shakespeare as England's playwright-in-chief. And though he too was not proof against some egregious tamperings with the text, it was in Shakespeare that he found time and again the inspiration for the highest flights of his genius.

Towards the end of his career, in 1769, when Garrick organized at Stratford-on-Avon a great Jubilee Celebration as much to the glory of Shakespeare as to his own, a galaxy of rank and fashion crowded into the little town from London and the surrounding district. Dr. Arne acted as musical director, and for the pageant on the first day Garrick himself was director, librettist, and star performer all in one. Mr. Ivor Brown and Mr. George Fearon have given a full account of the proceedings in their amusing book, *Amazing Monument*. 'The second day', they explain, 'was to be the Great Day. It opened with the familiar gun-fire, bell-ringing and seranades; also with unfamiliar rain. However, there was no flinching. The public breakfast was well attended, and the entire company moved on to the Rotunda for the Jubilee's particular pleasure, the recitation by Garrick of his "Ode Upon Dedicating the Town Hall and erecting a Statue to Shakespeare". The actor stood with wand and medal beneath the elegant statue and recited the major part of his composition of which he was so proud'—and of which the following lines are typical:

> *Now swell at once the choral song,*
> *Roll the full tide of harmony along;*
> *Let rapture sweep the trembling strings,*
> *And fame expanding all her wings,*
> *With all her trumpet tongues proclaim*
> *The lov'd, revered, immortal name!*
> *SHAKESPEARE! SHAKESPEARE! SHAKESPEARE!*
> *Let th'enchanting sound,*
> *From Avon's shore rebound!*
> *Through the air*
> *Let it bear*
> *The precious freight the envious nations round!*

Bardolatry indeed. . . . But also something more; for on that occasion when first the Shakespeare glory was publicly proclaimed before the world, a seed was sown that would some day come to flower in a splended playhouse founded in his name, and destined to transform an obscure little Warwickshire township into a famous shrine of national, nay, international, pilgrimage.

II

GENESIS OF AN IDEA

Though Garrick's festival was not repeated, small-scale performances of Shakespeare's plays were given now and then in Stratford, and on the initiative of a London publisher, a Mr. Britton, was established in 1815 the 'Shakespeare Club' which survives to this day. From then onwards, there began a not unhealthy rivalry between Stratford and London in the matter of the Shakespeare cult, and as we shall see, the first National Theatre scheme was drawn up by another London publisher, Effingham Wilson by name, who himself drew inspiration from the purchase in 1847, on behalf of the nation, of Shakespeare's Birthplace by a body known as the Shakespeare Committee. This committee was still in being twenty years later, and at one of its London meetings, Tom Taylor (the author of *Still Waters Run Deep*) read a paper outlining a National Theatre plan. His claim to be first in the field was disputed by the aforesaid Effingham Wilson and the controversy became the subject of an article in the *Morning Advertiser* for December 1874, which leaves no doubt that it is to Mr. Wilson that we owe the first concrete suggestion for the establishment of a national theatre in a form consonant with the conceptions of to-day. This then proves to be an important landmark in our story, and I should like to quote the article in full, under its original title:

'HONOUR TO WHOM HONOUR IS DUE'

'We recently assigned' [says the *Morning Advertiser*] 'the chief credit of proposing a National Theatre to the late Lord Lytton. Doubtless it was a matter in which he took much interest. Many others have taken the subject up, notable amongst them Mr. Tom Taylor. We do not somehow much fancy the idea of a National Theatre under his supervision and guidance, any more than we should under the special patronage of Mr. Boucicault. But some time ago Mr. Tom Taylor did take up the subject very vehemently, and his advocacy drew forth the following statement from W. Wilson, the well-known publisher of the Royal Exchange, which was then, we remember, sent round to various journals, many of which published it. It is worthy of reproduction, now that the subject has cropped up again, as showing how many years it has occupied the attention of men of mark in literature. To Mr. Wilson certainly belongs the credit of being first in the field, and the letters addressed to him by the late Lord Lytton, Charles Dickens, Charles Kemble, and others, are extremely interesting.'

Then follows a reprint of the Wilson 'Statement', dated the 19th January 1864.

Sir,

The document read by Mr. Tom Taylor, at the last meeting of the Shakespeare Committee, signed by himself, Mr. Theodore Martin, and Mr. Shirley Brooks, appears to me to be but a reiteration of a plan proposed by me years since, when a very young man. I cannot, therefore, resist again placing before the public the plan in question.

The proposition was originally made in 1848, and discussed in two pamphlets written by me, entitled *A House for Shakespeare; a Proposition for the Consideration of the Nation.* The first pamphlet (a reprint from an article in *Hood's Magazine*) was published by Mr. Hurst, of King William Street, Strand; and the second, six months afterwards, by Mr. Mitchell, of Red Lion Court, Fleet Street.

The plan was warmly and cordially approved by many of those eminent in Literature and Art, from some of whose opinions I extract the following:

From The Right Hon. Lord Lytton: 'I thank you very much for your able and interesting pamphlet. I think it would indeed be a most desirable object to obtain a theatre, strictly appropriated to the Higher Drama. Your exertions cannot but do good.'

From Charles Dickens: 'That such a theatre as described would be but worthy of this nation, and would not stand low upon the list of its instructors, I have no doubt. I wish I could cherish a stronger faith than I have, in the probability of its establishment on a rational footing within fifty years.'

From William Howitt: 'I think yours is a grand plan for a "House for Shakespeare" and what ought to be carried out.'

From Sheridan Knowles: 'I have perused your paper. I admire the argument, and wish it may be turned to account.'

From Charles Kemble: 'I read it with great pleasure; and, at the conclusion heaved a sigh, that so much enthusiasm should be doomed to disappointment.'

From Eliza Cooke: 'I beg to acknowledge the receipt of your most interesting and nobly directed papers, and be sure, I am too ardent a worshipper of our "Immortal Bard" not to thoroughly appreciate your effort. May it tend to awaken a just and elevated sense of our *true* glory in many an English heart, and may all honour be given to *you* for helping the cause.'

Mr. Effingham Wilson's
PROPOSITION FOR A NATIONAL THEATRE
MADE IN 1848

1. That the Committee formed for the purpose of preserving to the nation the house in which our 'poet of all time' had birth, having satisfactorily effected that object,[1] should now dissolve.

2. That, it being generally acknowledged that the human mind receives most quickly and retains most durably, impressions made by dramatic representations, the importance and expediency are suggested of purchasing by national subscription, on the part of and for the people, some theatre wherein the works of Shakespeare, the 'world's greatest moral teacher', may be constantly performed.

3. That the said theatre should be opened at such reasonable charges as shall be within the reach of all.

4. That the most able manager and best working company should be engaged and constantly retained; and that only one five-act drama should be performed in the course of one evening.

5. That the Government for the time being, or any other body of men agreed upon, should hold the said theatre in trust for the nation, appointing a committee for the management of the same.

6. That the said National Theatre should be made to act as a great and true dramatic school, at which alike the poet and the performer,

[1] See page 26

the creator and the embodier (in the highest walks of the dramatic and histrionic arts), should receive their diplomas, living genius and talent being so fostered and sustained.

My idea arose thus: The then 'Shakespeare Committee', having completed the good work of purchasing for the nation Shakespeare's House, my hope was that they might be induced not to stop there, but to continue their endeavours to secure to us 'A house for Shakespeare' as the best and truest, as the only adequate and appropriate monument. As Byron has it—

A shrine for Shakespeare worthy him.

The times were then, however, so thoroughly 'out of joint' that the plan was, necessarily, temporarily abandoned.

> I am, Sir,
> Your obedient servant,
> EFFINGHAM WILLIAM WILSON.

II, Royal Exchange
19th January 1864.

In spite of the interest which had evidently been aroused by Wilson's first proposal and subsequently by Tom Taylor's, no practical steps were then taken. It may have been noted that both Charles Dickens and Kemble, while generally favourable to the Wilson plan, were pessimistic as to its practicability in the then prevailing circumstances.

Such pessimism was the more disappointing in that both public and private benefactions were being generously lavished on other fields of art. The Great Exhibition of 1851 was a striking example of the nation's growing awareness of the social values not only of industry but of culture. And of course this trend had begun much earlier. The British Museum, for instance, may be said to date from 1753, when Parliament granted the sum of £20,000 and authorized a state lottery of £300,000 to purchase and accommodate a collection of books, etc., belonging to Sir Hans Sloane. The Bloomsbury building was started in 1823, and the original collection increased to its present dimensions by gifts and state purchases as well as, so far as the library is concerned, by the operation of the Copyright Act. Similarly the National Gallery is the result of a Parliamentary grant of £60,000 made in 1824 for the purchase of the Angerstein collection of pictures, part of the present building in Trafalgar Square being opened in 1838, and enlarged at varying intervals thereafter at the public expense. The municipal Museum Act of 1845 enabled Town Councils throughout the country to found and maintain museums from the rates, a permission of which wide advantage was taken, with the results we know. The same kind of thing was taking place all over the Continent, not only for art but for the drama also. But here in England the theatre was left severely alone. A business-minded community might understand and even welcome the expenditure of public money on museums and picture galleries, whose contents were lasting commodities, realizable in good hard cash; but this excuse did not apply to transient stage performances which had no value as real property and at best could be regarded as a very doubtful speculation.

Another factor which distracted the public attention from the need of a National Theatre was the growing prosperity of the commercial theatre. It is true that the plays performed in the earlier part of the nineteenth century were mostly poor in quality; but it was an age of great acting—the age of Macready and Phelps, of Charles Kean and Mrs. Kendal, and of the début of Ellen Terry. Moreover, the new licensing Act of 1843 had freed the stage from many disabilities. With the abolition in that year of the two royal patents which hitherto provided Drury Lane and Covent Garden with what was virtually a state endowment, new theatres were springing up everywhere, no longer obliged to ply their trade by subterfuge or artifice. Long runs became more frequent, fortunes were made and lost, adding thus to the zest with which theatrical ventures of all kinds could be undertaken. Finally, the star of Henry Irving was in the ascendant, a portent which was to transform the whole scene of the theatre. His knighthood in 1895 set the seal, as it were, on a professional career which had already achieved for his theatre a national status without any help from Authority as such. In a manner of speaking, the Lyceum *was* a National Theatre; but its position depended on the genius of a single individual who at last was forced to throw in his hand, and to spend the closing years of his life touring the country with waning powers and beset by financial anxiety. His death left nothing but a great tradition, a unique personal memory, and a band of devoted followers who one by one themselves would sooner or later pass into the dark.

Aware as he must have been of the transient nature of the theatre which he had founded, Irving at the height of his career composed a remarkable manifesto in response to a request he had received for his views on the National Theatre idea. The paper was read at the meeting of a Social Science Congress held in October 1878, and I doubt if anything has ever been said or written which in so short a space expounds so perfectly the fundamental case for a National Theatre seen from an artist's point of view.

Sir Henry Irving speaks

The question of the establishment of a National Theatre is surrounded by so many difficulties, and has so many side issues, that the time at present at my disposal does not allow me to go properly into it. The two questions which must from the beginning be held in view are: Is a National Theatre desirable? Is its establishment upon a permanent basis a possibility?

With regard to its desirability, I have little, if any, doubt. In this country, artistic perfection of a high ideal is not always the road to worldly prosperity; and so long as open competition exists there will always be found persons whose aim is monetary success rather than the achievement of good work. In order that the stage may be of educational value, it is necessary that those who follow its art should have an ideal standard somewhat above the average of contemporary taste. This standard should be ever in advance, so that as the taste and education of the public progress, the means for their further advancement should be ready. To effect this some security is necessary. If the purifying and ennobling influence of the art is to be exercised in such a manner as to have a lasting power, it is necessary that the individual be replaced by something in the shape of a corporation, or by the working of some scheme by its nature fixed and permanent.

It would, I think, be at present unadvisable to touch upon the subject of State subsidy with reference to the British stage. The institutions of this country are so absolutely free that it would be dangerous—if not destructive—to a certain form of liberty to meddle with them. *Quid pro quo* is a maxim which holds good of State aids, and a time might come when an unscrupulous use might be made of the power of subsidy. Besides, in this country, the State would never grant monetary aid to individual enterprise under any guarantees whatsoever. As the State could not possibly of itself undertake the establishment and management, the adoption of some corporate form would be necessary with reference to the stage before the subsidy could be raised with any possibility of success.

A 'National Theatre' implies an institution which, in its nature, is not either limited or fleeting. Such a scheme must be thorough, must rest upon a very secure basis, and must conform to the requirements of art, polity, and commerce. It must be something which, in the ordinary course of things, will, without losing any of its purpose or any of its individuality, follow with equal footsteps the changes of the age. In order to do this, it must be large, elastic, and independent. Let us consider these conditions. Firstly, as to magnitude. As the National Theatre must compete with private enterprise, and be with regard to its means of achieving prosperity weighted with a scrupulosity which might not belong to its rivals, it should be so strong as to be able to merge—in its steady average gain—temporary losses, and its body should be sufficiently large to attempt and achieve success in every worthy branch of histrionic art. Secondly, the corporate body should be to a certain extent elastic. The production of talent in a country or an age is not always a fixed quantity; and whilst for the maintenance of a high standard of excellence no one manifestly under the mark of his fellows should be admitted, all those worthy of entrance should be absorbed. Thirdly, the National Theatre should be independent. Once established under proper guarantees, it should be allowed to work out its own ideas in its own way. Art can never suffer by the untrammelled and unshackled freedom of artists—more especially when the idiosyncrasies of individuals, with the consequent possible extravagance, are controlled by the wisdom and calmness of confluent opinion. The difficulties of systematization would be vast, but the advantages would be vast also.

GENESIS OF AN IDEA

The merits of the concentration of purpose of men following kindred pursuits have been tested already, and the benefits both of individuals and bodies are known. Our art alone has yet no local habitation, no official recognition, no political significance. Should the scheme of a National Theatre be carried out, great results might follow—much good to the great body of aspirants to histrionic fame. Provision might, at a small expense to each individual, be made for the widow and the orphan. Old age would be divested of the terrors of want. A restraining influence would be exercised on unscrupulousness. A systematic school of teaching would arise; and the stage would acquire that influence and position which, whatever they may be in the present, are to be in the future great.

So much for the views of a famous actor. It was left to an eminent literary man, writing only a couple of years later, to present another facet of the same problem, based this time less on artistic than on social grounds, and on much the same estimate of the propagandist value of drama as that of the wily churchmen of medieval days. Matthew Arnold, for his part, was primarily concerned to find an antidote to the vulgar materialism of democracy let loose. By nature an ardent lover of the theatre, he was quick to recognize it as the most powerful of weapons for the cultural education of the masses; and if the theatre could make for righteousness as well, it behoved his followers, many of whom had viewed the stage with suspicion, to reconsider their attitude.

So I need make no apology for quoting at some length from the chapter on 'The French Theatre' which appeared in Arnold's *Irish Essays*, published in 1880. Though certainly underrating the chances during the following years of an unorganized dramatic revival, he showed remarkable foresight into the future of a National Theatre, even to anticipating its ultimate place in some kind of publicly supported civic theatre scheme for the whole country. But let me leave his words to speak for themselves:

We in England [he writes] have no modern drama. Our vast society is not homogeneous enough for that. Yet we have remembrance of better things in the past, and the elements of better things in the future,

C

33

a splendid national drama of the Elizabethan Age, and a later drama of 'the town' which has no lack of pieces conspicuous by their stage qualities, their vivacity and their talent, and interesting by their pictures of manners. We have had great actors. We have good actors, not a few at the present moment. But we have been unlucky, as we often are, in the work of organization. In the essay at organization which in the patent theatres, with their exclusive privilege of acting Shakespeare, we formerly had . . . we find such a machinery as might be devised by a man prone to stand in his own way, a man devoid of clear notions of the consequences of things. It was inevitable that the patent theatres should provoke discussion and attack. They were attacked and their privilege fell. Still, to this essay, however imperfect, of a public organization for the English theatre, our stage owes the days of power and greatness which it has enjoyed. The system had its faults and was abandoned; but then instead of devising a better plan, we gladly took refuge in our favourite doctrines of the mischief of State interference, of the blessedness of leaving every man to do as he likes, of the impertinence of presuming to check any man's natural taste for the bathos and pressing him to relish the sublime. We left the English theatre to take its chance. Its present impotence is the result.

Still, that does not prevent the theatre from now exercising upon us a great attraction. For we are at the end of a period, and have to deal with facts and symptoms of a new period on which we are entering; and prominent among these fresh facts and symptoms is the irresistibility of the theatre. We know how the Elizabethan theatre had its cause in an ardent zest for life and living, a bold and large curiosity, a desire for a fuller and richer existence, pervading the nation at large, as they pervaded other nations after the long medieval time of obstruction and restraint. But we know, too, how the great middle class of this nation, alarmed at grave symptoms which showed themselves in the new movement, drew back; made choice for its spirit to live at one point instead of living, or trying to live, at many; entered, as I have so often said, the prison of Puritanism, and had the key turned upon its spirit there for two hundred years. Our middle class forsook the theatre.

I remember how, happening to be at Shrewsbury, twenty years ago, and finding the whole Haymarket Company acting there, I went to the theatre. Never was such a scene of desolation. Scattered at very distant intervals through the boxes were about half-a-dozen chance comers like myself; there were some soldiers and their friends in the pit, and a good many riff-raff in the upper gallery. The real townspeople, the people who carried forward the business life of Shrewsbury, and who filled its churches and chapels on Sundays, were entirely absent. I pitied the excellent Haymarket Company; it must have been like acting to oneself on an iceberg. Here one had a good example—as I thought at the time, and as I have thought ever since—of the complete estrangement of the English middle class from the theatre. . . .

But now I see our community turning to the theatre with eagerness, and finding the English theatre without organization or purpose or dignity, and no English drama at all except a fantastical one. And then I see the French Company from the chief theatre in Paris showing themselves in London—a society of actors admirable in organization, purpose and dignity. What then, finally, *are* we to learn from the marvellous success and attractiveness of the performances at the Gaiety Theatre? What *is* the consequence which it is right and rational for us to draw?

The performances of the French Company show us plainly, I think, what is gained—the theatre being admitted to be an irresistible need for organized Communities—by organizing the theatre. The French Company shows us not only what is gained by organizing the theatre but what is meant by organizing it. The organization in the example before us is simple and rational. We have a society of good actors, with a grant from the State on condition of their giving with frequency the famous and classic stage plays of their nation; and with a commissioner of the State attached to the society and taking part in council with it. But the Society is to all intents and purposes self-governing. And in connection with the Society is the school of dramatic elocution of the *Conservatoire*.

It seems to me that the pleasure we have had in the visit of the French Company is barren unless it leaves us with the impulse to mend the condition of our thetare, and with the lesson how alone it can be rationally attempted. 'Forget'—can we not hear these fine artists in an undertone to us, amidst their graceful compliments of adieu?—forget your clap-trap, and believe that the State, the nation in its collective and corporate character, does well to concern itself about an influence so important to national life and manners as the theatre. Form a company out of the materials ready to hand in your many good actors and actors of promise. Give them a theatre at the West End.

Let them have a grant from your Science and Art Department; let some intelligent and accomplished man like our friend Mr. Piggott, your present Examiner of Plays, be joined to them as Commissioner from the Department, to see that the conditions of the grant are observed. Let the conditions of the grant be that a repertory is agreed upon, taken out of the works of Shakespeare and out of the volumes of *Modern British Drama*, and that pieces from this repertory are played a certain number of times in each season; as to new pieces, let your Company use its discretion. Let a school of dramatic elocution and declamation be instituted in connection with your company. It may surprise you to hear that elocution and declamation are things to be taught and learnt, and do not come by nature; but it is so. Your best and most serious actors [this is added with a smile] would have been better if in their youth they had learnt elocution. These recommendations, you may think, are not very much; but as your divine William says, they are enough; they will serve. Try them. When your institution in the West of London has become a success, plan a second of like kind in the East. The people *will* have a theatre; then make it a good one. Let your two or three chief provincial towns institute, with municipal subsidy and co-operation, theatres such as your institute in the metropolis, with State subsidy and co-operation. So you will restore the English theatre. And then a modern drama of your own will also, probably, spring up amongst you, and you will not have to come to us for pieces like *Pink Dominoes*.'

No, and we hope, too, that the modern English drama, when it comes, will be something different. But let us not say a word to wound the feelings of those who have given us so much pleasure, and who leave us as a parting legacy such excellent advice. For excellent advice it is, and everything we saw these artists say and do upon the Gaiety stage inculcates it for us, whether they exactly formulated it in words or no. And still even now that they are gone, when I pass along the Strand and come opposite the Gaiety Theatre, I see a fugitive vision of delicate features under a shower of hair and a cloud of lace, and hear the voice of Mdlle Sarah Bernhardt saying in its most caressing tones to the Londoners: '*The theatre is irresistible; organize the theatre!*'

Before closing this chapter, we must recur for a moment to our interrupted tale of events at Stratford-on-Avon, for these begin to have an important bearing on our main theme. As already mentioned, Shakespeare's Birthplace had been acquired for the nation in 1847. The tercentenary of the poet's birth in 1863 was celebrated even more gloriously than had been the famous Garrick Jubilee of 1769, and in this later festival the prime mover was Mr. E. F. Flower, citizen of Stratford, first of a long line of Flowers who were to devote conspicuous talents to the same great cause. It was his son, Charles Edward Flower, who set himself to found a permanent Shakespeare Theatre inStratford. In this he was stimulated, perhaps, by a similar movement emanating from London. But while the Londoners talked, Flower acted, and was rewarded for his efforts when on 23rd April 1879 the famous Stratford Memorial Theatre was opened with a performance of *Much Ado About Nothing*, starring Barry Sullivan and Helen Faucit in the two chief parts. By his own efforts Flower had raised the £21,000 required to build the theatre, and his metropolitan rivals were put to shame.

However, the example of Stratford, together with the Irving and Arnold manifestos, offered a challenge which, as never before brought the claims of a metropolitan National Theatre into the limelight. The claims were now seen to be threefold: firstly, for a worthy memorial to Shakespeare in the capital of the British Empire; secondly, as Irving had pleaded, for an 'exemplary theatre' that would provide a permanent machine or factory for the production of plays on the highest artistic level; and thirdly, as in Matthew Arnold's vision, for a central organization able to spread throughout the country an appreciation of great drama as a major factor in popular education. It would be thirty years at least before this threefold impulse could be focused on a single practical scheme. But the demand was recurrent through the eighteen-eighties and nineties. And now in the first years of the new century it was to come to a head.

III

THE RIVALS

The year 1910 comes midway in a wonderfully fruitful period in the history of the English theatre. On Shakespeare's birthday in that year the following plays were being publicly performed in the metropolis. Neither Shaw nor Barrie happen to figure in the list, but it is only an accident that they did not, and the general level of contemporary drama was high, while the number of classical revivals is notable:

The Rivals, by Sheridan (Lyric).

The Fighting Chance (Lyceum).

The Whip, by Cecil Raleigh and Henry Hamilton (Drury Lane).

Hamlet and *Julius Caesar.* London Shakespeare Festival (His Majesty's).

The Importance of Being Earnest, by Oscar Wilde (St. James's).

Dr. Jekyll and Mr. Hyde, adapted from R. L. Stevenson, with special matinées of *Hamlet* (Queens).

Tantalizing Tommy, by Paul Gavault and Michael Morton, together with special matinées of *The Toymaker of Nuremburg,* by Austin Strong (Playhouse).

The Blue Bird, by Maeterlinck (Haymarket).

Dame Nature, by Henry Bataille (Garrick).

A Pot of Caviare and *The House of Temperley,* both by Arthur Conan Doyle (Adelphi).

Trelawney of the Wells, by Arthur Pinero (Duke of York's Repertory season).

The Tenth Man, by W. Somerset Maugham (Globe).

Jimmy Valentine, by Paul Armstrong (Comedy).

THE RIVALS

When Knights Were Bold, by Charles Marlowe (Criterion).
The Scarlet Pimpernel, by Baroness Orczy (New Theatre).
The Naked Truth, by George Paston and W. B. Maxwell (Wyndhams).

At this time the Actor-Manager was still in command at several theatres, and though advanced critics were already beginning to deplore his régime on various counts, to-day it has become the custom to regret him. At least he assured a continuity of purpose in several of London's most important theatres, and scope was given for an artistic policy on the part of many managers who took a real pride in their contributions to drama through the theatres with which they were personally identified.

But this is not the whole story. Alongside the normal stage activities a small but insistent minority began to seek a wider field for experiment both in choice of play and in methods of production. The Stage Society, founded in 1900, became a focus of the new movement, and was followed by other Sunday evening producing societies which did a great work in opening up fresh avenues. There was, for instance, the Elizabethan Stage Society, with William Poel at its head, sworn to the heroic task of upholding the creed that Shakespeare could only be properly understood if acted under conditions similar to those for which his plays had been written. As early as 1881 William Poel had given an ever memorable performance at St. George's Hall of the First Quarto *Hamlet*—the first attempt, perhaps, since Jacobean times to produce Shakespeare in the way he intended. Fourteen years later the Elizabethan Stage Society came into existence, and Poel began to find many sympathizers in his perception of the need for a playhouse in London specially fitted for the 'Elizabethan' performance of Shakespeare's plays. The main features of the Poel productions were the abandonment of the current fashion for pictorial and realistic scenery, the abolition of the proscenium arch, and provision of a stage which protruded into the auditorium so that the action of the play was surrounded on three sides by members of the audience. In spite of public indifference, Shake-spearian scholars and the more intelligent amateurs of the theatre were fascinated by what they saw, and a new impulse was given to the study and appreciation of the plays. This new interest was canalized and promoted by the London Shakespeare League, in-augurated at a meeting on Shakespeare Day, 23rd of April 1902, at Clifford's Inn Hall, with Dr. F. G. Furnivall as its first President, and with the following objects:

(1) To extend the recognition of the interest which London possesses as the scene of the lifework of William Shakespeare.
(2) To organize an Annual Commemoration of the poet in London.
(3) To focus the movement for a Shakespeare Memorial in London.

Many and various would be the activities of the League during the next twenty years. No longer was Stratford-on-Avon to have it all its own way in the matter of Shakespeare commemorations. But little was done in respect of the League's third objective until an unexpected stimulus was given by a letter which appeared in *The Times* of 28th of May 1903, from a Mr. Badger, a wealthy brewer in the North of England, then in the eighty-fourth year of his age, who had been educated at the Stratford Grammar School, and whose life-long ambition, it seems, had been to see a fitting memorial erected in London to the great dramatist. The letter read as follows:

SIR,

Shakespeare's own words are 'An honest tale speeds best, being plainly told', and I shall adopt his dictum in this communication.

Of all the luminaries any country has produced, the brightest light is William Shakespeare, and to my thinking his countrymen have, as yet, failed to properly memorialize his marvellous talent as evidenced by his literary and sublime conceptions.

In 1833 and 1834 I was a schoolboy at Stratford-on-Avon, 'with shining morning face', no doubt, and as a recognition of my good fortune at having been sent there, whereby I acquired a Shakespearian taste, which has been to me a life-long joy, and moreover has, I feel, been an important factor in the success of my career, I am pledged to place at my sole cost, if permitted, a statue to his memory at Stratford-on-Avon, a town well known as 'the birthplace, the home and the grave of the bard.' Having had communications with the municipal authorities there, I am desirous before proceeding with my scheme to lay before the world, through the agency of *The Times*, an alternative one, which is to collect by voluntary contributions, a sufficient amount to cover the cost of erecting in London and at Stratford-on-Avon, a statue worthy of Shakespeare's fame. I have no doubt the requisite sum will be forthcoming if an influential, competent, and Shakespeare-loving committee can be found for the realization of this project, and I shall gladly avail myself of the privilege of contributing £1,000 in aid of the effort suggested.

It is recorded that the noblest statue to Shakespeare's greatness yet raised stands in New York; all honour to our Transatlantic cousins, but I trust that Englishmen and English women will, as Miss Tox says in the novel, 'make an effort' to remedy the incongruity.

Yours, etc.,

RICHARD BADGER.

Anglesea House,
Devonshire Place, Eastbourne.

This appeal seems to have fallen flat, but nothing daunted, Badger went ahead on his own account, and had the bright idea of approaching the London County Council in the hope that they would give a further impetus to his scheme by offering a site for the statue on the South Bank of the river. The Council favoured this idea, and a little more than a year after the publication of his first letter to *The Times*, Mr. Badger found himself in a position to send a further letter to that journal which was published on 12th August 1904.

NATIONAL STATUE TO SHAKESPEARE

SIR,

On 28 May 1903 you did me the favour to insert a letter on the above subject, and my obligation will be greatly increased if you find it convenient to insert the enclosed. The matter has ever since occupied my thought, which has been productive of some success. The latest phase is a communication from the London County Council, expressing full concurrence in the scheme, and offering to provide a site; but to my disappointment, they are unable to take part in the collection of the necessary funds. I may add that as an initiative, I am still prepared to give £500 down towards the expenses of the appeal for funds, and an additional £2,000 in aid of the cost of the statue, provided the result of the appeal is sufficient to raise one commensurate with the vast debt the world owes to Shakespeare's memory. My difficulty now is finding an influential representative committee to make an appeal for funds. If I can calculate on the sympathy of *The Times*, I shall look upon the subject as an assured *fait accompli*.

Yours,

RICHARD BADGER.

This time the writer's challenge did not fall on stony ground. Favourable comments on the scheme were printed in *The Times* and other papers, notably from Beerbohm Tree and Sarah Bernhardt, and I can only hear the echo of one discordant note sounded by Owen Hall of the Prince of Wales's Theatre.

Sir [he wrote to the Editor of the *Daily Telegraph*], I don't think the present generation ought to be asked to subscribe to another statue of Shakespeare. He hasn't amused them much during the last twenty years. If there is to be a new statue to one who has entertained the British public in modern times, surely it ought to be some popular author of musical comedy.

There may have been some common sense in this; but the London Shakespeare League at any rate thought otherwise, and was quick to seize the opportunity. Within a week of the appearance of Badger's letter, the secretary of the League wrote off to him offering to establish such a committee as that for which he pleaded. The offer was accepted, and Professor Israel Gollancz, on behalf of the League's Council, left posthaste for Scarborough to interview Mr. Badger and arrange details.

A document was drawn up and subsequently printed whereby it was agreed that by 'Memorial' was to be understood some such monument as the Albert Memorial, or the Scott Memorial in Edinburgh, and that it was to be erected in a prominent site in

London, granted by the Government or by the London County Council, the latter body having already expressed its willingness to co-operate.

Moreover, in the event of sufficient funds being raised, a Shakespeare Memorial Committee was to be established consisting of eminent men and women of the day, drawn from all departments of public life, and from all parts of the Empire, including also representatives of the English speaking race, notably American, together with certain distinguished foreigners as endorsing the unanimous homage to Shakespeare throughout the world. His Majesty King Edward VII was to be invited to show his interest in the movement, and the Prince of Wales to accept the position of Hon. President. A great Public Meeting was to be held as quickly as possible, at which the scheme was to be launched, and a Provisional Committee was to be appointed of not more than twenty-four members, eight of whom should be members of the London Shakespeare League, together with the Presidents or Directors of the Royal Academy, the British Academy, and other important bodies, and including the Chairman of the London County Council, and the Lord Mayor of London. Of this Committee, Dr. Furnivall was elected Chairman, and Professor Gollancz the Hon. Secretary.

The great Public Meeting was duly held on 28th February 1905 at the Mansion House under the chairmanship of the Lord Mayor, when the following resolution, moved by Dr. Furnivall and seconded by Beerbohm Tree, was carried with acclamation:

> That this meeting approves the proposal for a Shakespeare Memorial in London. It appoints a General Committee for the purpose of organizing the movement and determining the form of the memorial.

It will be noticed that the exact 'form of the memorial' was left undefined. Perhaps the Provisional Committee had become aware that opposition might be encountered to the suggestion of another 'Albert Memorial' as recommended in the original document

43

signed by Mr. Badger. Gollancz, we know, had hopes of 'a Shakespeare temple to serve the purposes of human learning, much in the same way as Burlington House has served those of natural science.' Indeed, a circular embodying this suggestion had been despatched to a number of eminent people, whose opinions and support were invited. But the morning before the Mansion House meeting a letter appeared in *The Times* condemning the scheme, asserting that 'any museum which could be formed in London would be a rubbish heap of trivialities', and signed by J. M. Barrie, Prof. A. C. Bradley, Lord Carlisle, Sir W. S. Gilbert, Edmund Gosse, Maurice Hewlett, the Earl of Lytton, Dr. Gilbert Murray, Lord Onslow, A. W. Pinero, Sir Frederick Pollock, A. B. Walkley, and Prof. Aldis Wright.

Be that as it may, from now onwards the records become somewhat confused, and your historian finds himself lost in a kaleidoscopic maze of committees—General, Special, Advisory, Executive, and I know not what. And behind them all, flitting to and fro, one glimpses the mercurial figure of Israel Gollancz, Professor of English Literature at King's College, Strand, benign, discreet, master of innocent intrigue, Hon. Secretary of all the Memorial committees, with every thread in his hands, and alone capable of unravelling the tangled skein when the right moment came. So it was that within a month or two the General Committee met again, and appointed a new Special Committee which was charged to investigate the various proposals which had been made, and to report progress as occasion arose. The first of these reports is dated 6th July 1905. It was evident that the Special Committee had spared no pains in surveying the ground. Here is a sample of the thorough way they had gone to work:

The six schemes considered by the Special Committe are the following: (1) A Statue; (2) An Architectural Monument; (3 A small Theatre for the furtherence of Dramatic Art and Literature; (4) A National Theatre; (5) A Shakespeare House; (6) a Shakespeare Fund. These six proposals naturally differentiate themselves into two main divisions:

(*a*) primary and (*b*) secondary. To the former class (*a*) belong (1) and (2), i.e. the proposals to erect a Statue or an Architectural Monument, to the latter class (*b*) the suggested memorial buildings enumerated in (3), (4), (5). Proposal (6) may be left for the present.

Concentrating for the most part on proposals (1) and (2), in virtue of Mr. Badger's initiative and generous promise of a contribution, the Committee considered itself bound to include a statue in any scheme to be carried out. On the other hand, it was felt that a statue alone would be inadequate, and doubts were expressed, in view of what the committee described as the infelicitous examples of sculpture already existing in London, as to whether any contemporary artist could do justice to the scheme. But in spite of these doubts the committee concluded that the arts of sculpture and architecture might well be stimulated by the opportunity of providing an architectural memorial which was to include a statue. It was therefore decided to organize a worldwide competition for the best design.

Three alternative sites were suggested:

(1) The new Kingsway and Aldwych. (2) The neighbourhood of Buckingham Palace. (3) The south side of the Thames.

The following paragraph in the report dealing with the question of a site is particularly interesting, as foreshadowing what was in fact to become the site of the National Theatre in the fullness of time.

Each of these sites has much to commend it; but in view of the proposed opening up of the South side of the Thames by the L.C.C. for its new County Hall, it is felt that the South Bank of the river, so full of Shakespearian associations, must be considered a very fitting place for the Memorial. By a happy coincidence, the L.C.C's decision to improve the whole aspect of the other side of the Thames synchronises with the present endeavour. It is hoped that the Council which has already expressed so much interest in the proposed Memorial will welcome this suggestion, and reserve a central and conspicuous position for the site of the Memorial so that it may form an integral part of their scheme.

Turning to the secondary proposals, the committee recommended that the idea that a small theatre for the furtherance of dramatic art and literature, and for the performance of Elizabethan and other plays, be erected on land adjoining might be borne in mind. Such a building, however, would not be of an ambitious character. As to a National Theatre, the Committee was quite emphatic.

The suggestion that the most fitting Memorial in London would be a National Theatre has reached us from many quarters; and indeed one definite offer of a sum of about £13,000 has been made to the Committee, conditionally on its support for this proposal. Without pronouncing on the necessity for a National Theatre the Special Committee has come to the conclusion that it cannot recommend the General Committee to adopt the scheme for a National Theatre as that most likely to be successful. The controversial character of the proposal, and the very large sum of money that would be required for building and endowment, have, among other considerations, weighed with the Committee.

It was also stated that the Municipality of Venice had asked to contribute 1,000 lire in consideration of its 'debt of gratitude to the English nation and its great poet'. Also that Mr. Richard Badger had provided in his will that the sum of £3,500 should be paid by his executors to 'a memorial in London to commemorate the poet Shakespeare' at whatever time they thought such a scheme sufficiently advanced, their decision to be free and final.

Appropriate resolutions were passed by the General Committee to enable the Executive to proceed with the plan for an Architectural Memorial, but so far as the public were concerned the scheme had apparently been put into cold storage, for it was not till nearly three years later that the General Committee were summoned again to a meeting at the Mansion House, this time under the chairmanship of Lord Reay. Then it was that the following Report from the Executive was considered, adopted, and passed for publication in the press:

THE RIVALS

PROPOSED SHAKESPEARE MEMORIAL
REPORT OF THE EXECUTIVE COMMITTEE

*To be presented to the General Committee at a Meeting to be held
at the Mansion House on 5th March 1908*

In accordance with the Resolutions adopted by the General Committee, at the Meeting held at the Mansion House, on 6th July 1905, the Executive Committee, with the co-operation of an Advisory Committee, consisting of Sir E. Poynter, P.R.A., Sir William Richmond, R.A., Sir Aston Webb, R.A., Mr. Belcher, A.R.A., Mr. Brock, R.A., Mr. Sidney Colvin, and Mr. Hugh Chisholm, have had under consideration the main problems affecting the progress of the movement for the proposed Shakespeare Memorial in London, to be erected by the time of the Tercentenary of the poet's death in 1916.

As regards the question of Site, the possible sites under the control of H.M. Government, or other authorities, have been carefully considered. The following suggestions were before the Committee: (1) The Open Space between Constitution Hill and St. George's Hospital (Hyde Park Corner); (2) Lincoln's Inn Fields; (3) The South Bank of the Thames, near the site of the new County Hall; (4) The Green Park, facing Piccadilly; (5) Park Crescent, at the top of Portland Place.

Sites (1) and (5) commended themselves most strongly to the Committee; but on enquiry it was found that there were insuperable difficulties in respect of Site (1). The Office of Woods was then approached, and Sir Aston Webb was invited, officially, on behalf of the Executive and Advisory Committees, to submit to H.M. Commissioners a request in respect of the Site in Park Crescent, with a view to the granting of the Site, conditionally, for the proposed Shakespeare Memorial—the Memorial to be a World's Tribute to Shakespeare, and to be erected in connexion with the Tercentenary of the Poet's death in 1916.

The Crown Paving Commissioners, after considering the proposal, were advised that they could not authorize any such alteration to the Gardens, as proposed, without special legislation, and the Commissioners of Woods demurred to depriving the lessees of the Crown houses adjoining Park Crescent of the use of the Gardens, but they were of opinion that a smaller scheme would not be open to the same objection. Subsequently the Commissioners of Woods, Sir J. Horner

THE RIVALS

and Mr. E. Stafford Howard, were good enough to indicate to the Committee, by means of plans drawn up by their Surveyor, the space which they thought could be spared, without serious objection, as a site for the Memorial; and they expressed their willingness, if the Committee approved, to bring the matter formally before the Crown Estate Paving Commissioners at their meeting on December 2nd last. The Committee were unanimously of opinion that the proposal of the Commissioners of Woods should be accepted with best thanks, and that the Commissioners should be asked to be good enough to allot the site in Park Crescent as shown on the plan submitted. The area proposed to be given for the Monument is at the top of Portland Place, the diameter of the semi-circle being 126 feet—a little greater than the width of Portland Place, which is, from house to house, 120 feet. The Committee consider the site a very fine one, and the termination by the Memorial of such a fine vista as is provided by Portland Place should, if worthily carried out, form a noble addition to the beauties of London, in addition to being a notable Memorial to England's great Poet.

There is at present standing on the site a statue to the Duke of Kent, but His Majesty the King has most graciously assented to the transference of this statue to an adjoining spot of equal prominence. The Executive Committee have already tendered to His Majesty their grateful recognition of His Majesty's gracious readiness to facilitate the project for the Shakespeare Memorial by this generous concession.

The Executive Committee are advised that considerable delay would be inevitable if the proposal made as regards the south bank of the Thames near the County Hall were adopted, and it must be borne in mind that the competition should be proceeded with as soon as possible, as there is by no means too much time at the disposal of artists between now and 1916, for the carrying through of the work.

All countries will, it is hoped, in their enthusiasm for Shakespeare, evince their goodwill towards the movement, and join the British Empire and America in an epoch-making effort to raise the proposed Memorial as a World Tribute to Shakespeare.

It is recommended that whatever sum may be collected over and above that required for the Memorial should be administered by an International Committee as a Shakespeare Fund for the furtherance of Shakespearian aims.

The Executive Committee in making the following recommendations

48

Prof. Sir Israel Gollancz

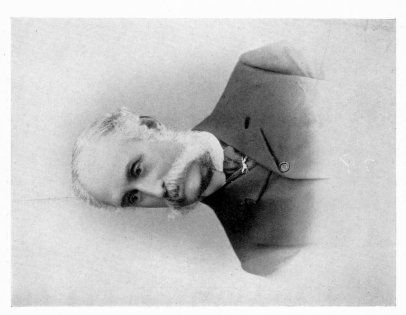

Richard Badger

Lena Ashwell, O.B.E.

William Archer (from the bronze by Derwent Wood, R.A.)

to the General Committee beg leave to emphasize that such modifications as are suggested of the resolutions passed at the last General Meeting are the outcome of long and earnest deliberations, and are brought forward in the hope and belief that on the basis proposed by them, the movement may be so organized that the Shakespeare Memorial may stand for future ages as the monumental record of the great fact in the history of modern civilization, that the peoples of this age, putting aside national, political, religious, and other differences, were at one in their desire to pay homage to Shakespeare, and to attest the World's immeasurable debt to his supreme genius. They are of opinion that the general organization of the movement should be taken in hand as soon as possible, so that the public dedication of the Memorial as the World's Tribute to Shakespeare may be the crowning event of the Shakespeare Tercentenary in 1916.

The Executive Committee therefore make the following recommendations to the General Committee:

1. That the Site in Park Crescent looking down Portland Place as indicated on the plan be gratefully accepted as the Site for the Shakespeare Memorial.

2. That the Competition be open to English-speaking races all over the world.

3. That the form of the Memorial be an architectural Monument including a Statue, and it is suggested that each design be submitted by an Architect and Sculptor in collaboration.

4. That the Competition be in two divisions, the first consisting of Sketched Designs to a small scale, and the second to be limited to six Competitors selected from the preliminary competition, who would each receive an Honorarium, and work out their designs on a larger scale, and more in detail.

5. That the Sketched Designs be submitted not later than 31st July 1908, and the final Designs not later than 28th February 1909.

6. That the Authors of the Designs selected by the Committee of Selection be employed to execute.

7. That an effort be made to raise a sum of £200,000, half the amount to be allocated to the purposes of the Monument; the remaining sum to be administered by an International Committee for the furtherance of Shakespearian aims.

8. That the following be invited to act as the Committee of Selection: His Excellency The American Ambassador; The Rt. Hon.

Viscount Esher; The Rt. Hon. Lord Plymouth; The Rt. Hon·
Lord Reay; Sir E. Poynter, Bart., P.R.A.; Sir Aston Webb,
R.A.; Mr. Belcher, A.R.A.; Mr. Thomas Brock, R.A.; Mr·
Sidney Colvin.

9. That a Committee of Representative Women be formed, and that
the Executive Committee be asked to invite, on behalf of the
General Body, some distinguished lady to form the Committee
and act as Chairman.

10. That the General Committee shall forthwith use their best endeavours to obtain a sum of at least £20,000 as a nucleus of the
Fund, and for the working expenses of the project.

11. That the following (Names to be submitted to the Meeting), and
others to be selected by the Executive Committee, be invited to
join the General Committee. That the Executive Committee be
empowered to add to their number. And further that the Executive Committee be authorized to form such Committees as may
be necessary, and to expend such amounts as may be required for
the Competition, and for the general organization of the movement.

12. That an Executive Committee of 31 persons, incorporating the
members of the Advisory Committee, be now constituted.

THE RIVAL SCHEME

Now, at about the same time that Richard Badger was ponder-
ing his plan for a commemorative statue to Shakespeare, William
Archer, eminent dramatic critic and translator of Ibsen's plays,
had invited a young friend of his, Harley Granville-Barker by
name, to collaborate in investigating the problems involved in the
foundation of a National Theatre. The result of their labours was
issued privately in 1904, under the title of 'A National Theatre:
Scheme and Estimates' with a contributed 'endorsement' signed
by some very important persons indeed:

Having read and carefully considered this scheme for a National
Theatre, we desire to express our belief that such an institution is
urgently needed, and that it could in all probability be successfully
established on the general lines here indicated.

HENRY IRVING	JOHN HARE
SQUIRE BANCROFT	HENRY ARTHUR JONES
J. M. BARRIE	A. W. PINERO

Accompanied by such an encomium, the book could not but be viewed with respect, and though for the time being its circulation was limited to the few, its influence on theatrical opinion was profound. Unblushingly the work of two idealists, the method of approach was severely technical. The bulk of the book consisted of a detailed examination of such fundamental matters as the size and character of the building, its probable cost, the theatre's constitution and government, methods of selecting and maintaining a permanent company of players, the repertory of plays, the system to be adopted in producing the plays, the relation of the theatre to living authors, the Training School, how to wind up the theatre in case of failure, and how to apply the surplus funds in case of success. Nothing seemed to be overlooked. Yet in spite of the meticulous accuracy lavished on the details of the scheme, this was no dry-as-dust compilation. It was written throughout in a spirit of courageous gaiety, and the Preface illustrates so aptly the purpose of the authors and the fine taste which they brought to their investigation that I cannot forbear to quote it in its entirety.

The Archer-Barker Preface

There has hitherto been one enormous obstacle to the establishment of a National Theatre in England. However willing a man or body of men might be to give a new impulse to the art of the theatre, and place England abreast of France and Germany in respect of theatrical organization, he or they could have no definite idea how to set about it. A public park, a picture gallery, or a free library is very easily created, and, once created, it practically 'runs itself'. There are a hundred recognized models for its organization and management. But an Endowed Theatre is, in England, a wholly unfamiliar piece of mechanism, and the management of it an unknown art; while there are many reasons why no foreign institution of the kind could be imitated in detail with any hope of success. There is no clear-cut channel, as it were, in which liberality and public spirit can easily flow in the direction of theatrical reform. It is scarcely an exaggeration to say that you can buy a free library or a picture gallery ready made, and present it as a 'going concern' to whatever community you please. But the man who wished to endow a Theatre would first have to invent it—a laborious task, for which he would probably have no preparation and no facilities.

In the following pages we take this off his hands. We present, for the first time in England, a detailed 'Scheme' with Estimates, for the creation, organization, and management of a National Theatre. We are far from believing that our plan is perfect in all its details. It might even be that every crank and every lever in our design would have to be somewhat modified before the machine could be run smoothly and satisfactorily. But we believe that, in merely outlining the organization, and suggesting the interplay of its parts, we have made an essential step in advance. We have substituted clear and definite for vague and formless ideas.

It is needless to discuss at any length the abstract desirability of the institution which we have outlined. Many of our readers are doubtless convinced on that point; others will, we hope, gradually realize the uses of the institution as they study its details. We present in our Appendix some extracts from the very considerable literature published during recent years, in which the theatrical situation and the theory of theatrical endowment are discussed.

To assert the urgent need for an Endowed Theatre is not necessarily to adopt a wholly pessimistic view of the existing condition of the English drama and stage. On the contrary, the present writers are convinced that dramatic authorship, at any rate, has greatly advanced in recent years, though there is reason to fear that hostile conditions are beginning to check that advance. We also admit that the stage owes much, in many ways, to the actor-manager and the long run. Both of these institutions have their merits; and a National Theatre, while excluding them from its own economy, would in no sense be hostile to them. What is harmful is their present predominance over the whole field of theatrical enterprise. In the interests both of authorship and of acting, a fair proportion of Repertory Theatres ought to co-exist with the actor-managed and long-run theatres; and in order to set the repertory system firmly afoot, a certain measure of endowment is necessary.

It follows from what we have said that we do not regard the National or Central Theatre here outlined as, in itself, a sufficient cure for all that is amiss in our theatrical life. Even if it stood alone, it would do incalculable service; but the most useful of all its functions, perhaps, will be that of supplying an incentive and model to similar enterprises in provincial cities, in the colonies, and in America. The acted drama ought to be, and indeed is, one of the great bonds of union between all the Anglo-Saxon peoples; but at present, unfortunately, it may be said to 'draw the whole English-speaking world together in the bonds of a racial vulgarity'.

In the provinces and beyond the seas, Repertory Theatres would no doubt be designed on many different scales, according to the circumstances and resources of each particular locality. A much less ambitious theatre than that which is here outlined would be adequate to the needs of many provincial towns. We do not, however, profess to give any estimates for minor theatres. Our forecasts and figures refer to a Central Theatre, to be situated in London, and organized on such a scale as to justify it in assuming, without incongruity or grandiloquence, the rank of a National Theatre, worthy of the metropolis of the Empire. At the same time, we hope and believe that our Scheme and Estimates will prove helpful to the organizers of Repertory Theatres on whatever scale. It is easy to 'take in' a garment that is cut too large; difficult, if not impossible, to 'let out' one that is cut too small.

An enterprise on a large scale—short of extravagance or ostentation —would have a far greater chance of succeeding in establishing itself in a permanent and honourable position than an enterprise on a small scale, however ably conducted. It is essential to break way, completely and unequivocally, from the ideals and traditions of the profit-making stage; and it is essential that the new system should have sufficient resources to give it time to establish itself and take hold upon the public. Moreover, the National Theatre must be *its own advertisement* —must impose itself on public notice, not by posters and column advertisements in the newspapers, but by the very fact of its ample, dignified, and liberal existence. It must bulk large in the social and intellectual life of London. There must be no possibility of mistaking it for one of those pioneer theatres which have been so numerous in late years, here and elsewhere, and have in their way done valuable work. It must not even have the air of appealing to a specially literary and cultured class. It must be visibly and unmistakably a popular institution, making a large appeal to the whole community. So manifest does this appear to us that we should strongly deprecate any effort on a small scale, until it shall be absolutely apparent that no effort on the scale here indicated is within the range of practical politics. A struggling enterprise with narrow resources, might prove a mere stumbling block in the path of theatrical progress at large. Its failure would be disastrous, and its partial success only less so.

It will be seen that the Theatre we propose would be a National Theatre in this sense, that it would be from the first conditionally— and, in the event of success, would become absolutely—the property of the nation. It may be asked why, in that case, we do not suggest going direct to the Government (which would mean, of course, to Parliament) for the money required. The reason is simply that we believe that it would be waste of time. It is not to be expected that, at the present stage of affairs, Parliament would vote money for the establishment of a theatre in London or elsewhere. We must look to private liberality to present a Central Theatre to London and to the Empire. That is not only the most probable, but, on the whole, the most desirable event. In the provinces it is otherwise. There one would hope that municipalities would in many cases undertake the urgent duty of bringing wholesome and rational theatrical entertainments within reach of the people. The successful establishment of a Central Theatre in London would most probably be followed by legislation, empowering municipalities to do what is required of them in this respect. At present their powers are ill-defined and inadequate; and the same remark applies to the powers of local bodies within the metropolitan area. A Central Theatre would not by any means supply all the higher theatrical needs even of London alone. But it ought to lead the way in the reform of our theatrical system; and the establishment of it ought to be, and probably will be, effected by the public spirit of individual citizens.

Our estimates, it will be seen, refer exclusively to dramatic, as distinct from operatic, performances. We are by no means hostile to the idea of a subsidized Opera-House; but we hold that the drama claims precedence, inasmuch as England possesses a National drama, but does not as yet possess a National opera. Some of our calculations may possibly be of use to the promoters of an operatic scheme; but the conditions of the two arts are so radically different that it is almost impossible to reason from one to the other. There is no doubt, however, that the success of a National Theatre would greatly simplify the task of those who are agitating for a subsidized Opera-House.

We venture to request the reader to suspend judgement upon details until he has taken a general view of the whole scheme. Many points which may at first seem obscure or questionable will, we hope, become clearer and perhaps more convincing as the project develops. We would also beg him, in criticizing our proposals, to distinguish between essential matters—matters of principle—and merely illustrative details. For example, in our list of a season's repertory, the reader will very likely find several plays which he, personally, does not greatly long to see, at a National Theatre or elsewhere. If he holds that the *class* of play should not be admitted to the Theatre, we will give our best consideration to his criticism; but if his objection is merely to the individual play, we suggest that to urge it would be to waste time. The repertory includes more than one play for which we ourselves cherish no particular enthusiasm. No theatre can live entirely on plays which appeal equally to everyone. In any season's repertory of the Théâtre Français or the Burgtheater—the reader would certainly find many plays which seemed to him tedious or otherwise objectionable. If the repertory we have outlined exactly represented either our own personal taste or the reader's, the presumption would be that it was badly chosen. Helpful criticism, then, will confine itself to the discussion of our principles of selection, and will regard the particular plays set down merely as the representatives of their respective classes in dramatic literature. If our scheme were to be realized to-morrow, it is more than probable that half the plays of our suggested repertory would be struck out and others substituted for them; though there is not much probability that the changes would bring the repertory into closer accord with the personal taste of any individual reader.

There never was, and there never will be, an ideal theatre. The theatre is too complex and too delicate a machine, depending on the harmonious co-operation of too many talents and influences, ever to reach perfection for more than a passing moment. The very greatest theatres at their greatest periods have been severely criticized, not, as a rule, without reason. The reader, we are sure, will not let his craving for what is ideally desirable render him careless of what is practically desirable as an improvement upon existing conditions. And he will not fail to bear in mind, we trust, that it is no magical recipe we are offering, no instant and miraculous cure for all the shortcomings of our theatrical life, but merely a plan for an institution which, being based on sound artistic principles, may develop far beyond immediate probabilities or possibilities, and may give a healthy impulse to theatrical progress throughout the English-speaking world.

As we have seen, the volume from which this preface has been quoted was first printed as a sort of Blue Book for private distribution by the authors among their friends and others whose criticisms might be helpful or likely to provide a nucleus of instructed support. Sir Arthur Pinero, Sir Edmund Gosse, and Sir James Barrie gave ungrudging service—Pinero especially, as shown by numerous letters relating to interviews and luncheons arranged by him to enlarge the circle of Archer's contacts. Apart from these, the following letters from Thomas Hardy and George Meredith are of historical interest:

Max Gate, Dorchester,
1st November 1904

MY DEAR ARCHER,

I have read the Blue Book so far as is necessary for understanding the general principles of the Scheme; and I can say, as you wish, that it seems to be a desirable one in its main points.

On details I will express no opinion, except to remark cursorily that the bodies proposed for nomination to the Board of Trustees, etc., do not seem divergent enough in character, and may produce a net result of Philistinism. Indeed it is in this direction that the *crux* will be found to lie: Where are you to get in England people with ideas detached enough to form, or nominate, the working committee. 'Quis custodiet ipsos custodes?'

But this *may* be got over: and I must say that it is most praiseworthy devotion in you to theatrical art to labour so sincerely in its cause.

To my mind a humorous feature in the movement has been the earnestness in supporting it of those living English dramatists who, by writing bad plays, are piling up vast fortunes through the absence of such a theatre. They are like smugglers who should earnestly entreat the Government to establish a more efficient system of coastguarding.

Believe me,
Yours sincerely,
THOMAS HARDY

Box Hill, Dorking,
27th November 1904

DEAR MR. ARCHER,

The need for a National Theatre has long been felt, both by dramatists and that portion of the public which looks to the dignity of the art of acting in England. For this reason, the scheme to establish such a theatre as is proposed will be welcomed by all who hope to see our stage representative of the best that the services of the country can produce besides offering a school for actors and something of a guide to popular taste. He whose means and good will prompt him to support the enterprise may be assured that his generosity will count for patriotism and clothe him in a lasting name.

(If you find any excess in the above, strike it out. I am not in perfect condition for writing even a scrap.)

Warmly yours,

GEORGE MEREDITH

Granville Barker was also very active, losing no opportunity to help in distributing the book, as witnessed by the following letter to Mr. Winston Churchill.

DEAR WINSTON CHURCHILL,

Your improvement on the occasion on Sunday last was unexpected but most welcome to at least two of your hearers. I could hardly refrain from bestowing all my cheers on your remarks about State Patronage of the Theatre, and Archer informed me that he was sorely tempted to abandon his arrangements for his own speech and devote it to seconding your remarks. You will understand this if you glance at the 'Blue Book' I am sending you. You won't have time to more than glance at it nor perhaps is there any need. But if you will keep it by you, then when the subject of Repertory Theatre, State aided or otherwise, comes to the front next (it is bound to do so sooner or later, and I hope sooner), you might like to be posted in some of the technicalities of the subject. And we should like you to be posted in them.

I am, Yours very faithfully,

H. GRANVILLE BARKER

The surprising event which evoked this letter can have been none other than the banquet given in honour of Ellen Terry at the Hotel Cecil, on Sunday, 17th June 1906. An all-star benefit matinée had also taken place at Drury Lane a few weeks earlier, and at the banquet, the speech of the Chairman, Mr. Winston Churchill (then Secretary of State for the Colonies), was reported by *The Times* as follows:

The great demonstration of admiration for Miss Terry which had been so general of late, showed, Mr. Churchill thought, that the British were sincere lovers of the drama, and were genuinely grateful to all who raised its tone and its quality in our country. He thought that they ought to be very grateful, because we did not do much in England for the dramatic art. We left it to shift for itself. We were content to let it be governed and guided, to ebb and flow hither and thither, merely by chance and caprice, and to regulate it, so far as the nation was concerned, only by commercial considerations. He could not help thinking that was a great pity. We did not as in Germany or France, endeavour to sustain the drama by national influence and by national agencies; and although he knew that this was a subject on which opinions were widely divided, he considered it was a pity, and even a folly that we did not make some national effort to aid and assist dramatic representation. [*Cheers.*] He was not going to decry the great principle of self-interest. It was a very flexible principle, and it had this advantage, that, as a motive power, it was almost universal. But, after all, it was self-sacrifice and not self-interest which was the parent of the arts. [*Hear, hear.*] He was one of those who held that it was the duty of the State to be the generous but discriminating parent of the arts and the sciences; and if we could only divert national attention from the often senseless process of territorial expansion, and the ugly apparatus of war, to those more graceful and gentler flights of fancy and of ambition which were associated with the theatre and the drama, we should more securely vindicate our claim to be a civilized people. [*Laughter and cheers.*] Let them think how money could always be easily obtained for any purpose involving the destruction of life and property; let them think with what excitement and interest this people witnessed the construction or launching of a Dreadnought. What a pity it was that some measure of that interest could not be turned in the direction of the launching, say, of a National Theatre? [*Cheers.*] He looked forward to some time when that reproach upon us would be removed. He confessed to having the idea that a great national theatre with branches in the large provincial cities, and with connections, or similar sister bodies in the Colonies throughout the Empire, would have a great effect on the solidarity of the English-speaking people all over the world. In the Shakespearian drama we had links of gold, if we would only use them, which were strong enough to resist the shocks and changes of time. We suffered because we did not attempt more thoroughly to organize this great branch of human effort. Why was it that we did not suffer more? It was because we had been particularly fortunate in this, as in many other spheres of human activity. The drama in England was sustained and supported by a comparatively small number of gifted individuals, individuals of grace and power and distinction, who in their own persons elevated and sustained the dramatic art in this country. We owed, he thought, a great deal to Mr. Beerbohm Tree [*cheers*] and to others who were gathered about this board that night, but perhaps most of all we owed this great advantage to the guest of the evening. [*Loud cheers.*] It was her interpretations of the great characters of Shakespeare which, more than anything else, would constitute the memorable achievement of her life. He thought it no exaggeration to say that the happy conjunction of her gay and charming genius with the mysterious and sinister grace of Henry Irving [*cheers*] kept Shakespeare upon the English stage during the 70's and 80's of the last century. And if that evening they were gathered together to do Miss Ellen Terry honour, it was not only because they were anxious to show themselves grateful for the pleasure and instruction they had so often derived from seeing so many characters of history and romance vivified and illuminated by her delightful personality, but it was also because they knew that by her personal gifts and power she had elevated and sustained the quality and distinction of the theatrical art in England during long years when that duty was somewhat discreditably neglected by the State.

I have failed to discover if Granville Barker's letter evoked any response from the Great Man. But his surprising affirmation of support was sure enough, and must have come as an unique encouragement to every friend of the National Theatre. The Blue Book itself was issued to the general public, with a few revisions, in 1907, and did more than anything else to enlarge the circle of National Theatre devotees, and to provide them with powder and shot for the assault.

On a small scale, from 1904 to 1907, Granville Barker himself, together with J. E. Vedrenne, had adventured with a series of Repertory seasons at the Royal Court Theatre in Sloane Square. During this historic three-year period, thirty-two different plays by seventeen different dramatists were produced with varying success but with unfailing distinction. Bernard Shaw topped the list with seven hundred performances of eleven plays. Among other authors, and I only mention them as typical, were Euripides, Galsworthy, Ibsen, Schnitzler, Laurence Housman, Masefield and Maeterlinck. And among actors, how many reputations were made or consolidated! Nothing like it had been dreamt of in London before. No wonder that the little playhouse was thronged by the theatrical intelligentsia, as well as by a growing number of the general public. Yet private enterprise did not suffice to carry the economic strain. As had been foreseen in the Archer-Barker book, a National Theatre standard proved to be unmaintainable without National Theatre finance and National Theatre organization. Beginning on a small scale meant only the Beginning of the End. For all that, Granville Barker emerged from the Court Theatre experiment morally fortified, and with heightened reputation soon took his place as the acknowledged leader of the forward movement in the theatre of his day. From now onwards he spoke with unchallengeable authority in any theatrical debate, and though a further experiment in repertory with Charles Frohman at the Duke of York's must be accounted a failure, his name was soon to acquire new lustre from his productions of *Androcles and the Lion*, *The Winter's Tale*, and *A Midsummer Night's Dream* at the St. James's and the Savoy.

Encouraged, doubtless, by the Court and Savoy Theatre experiments, Lord Howard de Walden, whose wealth was legendary and who was already known for generous co-operation with Gordon Craig, was moved at this time to interest himself in a project of his friend Herbert Trench, who at the Haymarket Theatre from 1909 to 1911, directed a series of plays exceptional in standard and equally unusual in the scenic quality of their presentation. William Archer, also a friend of Trench, began to nourish hopes that through him some closer contact might be made with Lord Howard de Walden, who had hitherto shown himself somewhat lukewarm to the claims of a National Theatre. The most modest and retiring of men, Lord Howard was, in fact, a staunch individualist, not easily carried away by visions of State-aided institutions. If nothing came of Archer's attempt to win his support, it was the occasion of some very frank correspondence between himself and Trench, which throws such an intimate sidelight on the personal situation that now that the men concerned are dead, I am fortunate to be able to print it here.

My dear Trench [writes Archer on 15th December 1907],

Under a calm exterior, I concealed the wildest excitement the other night, when you spoke of the possibility of something being done in the National Theatre business. I could not well talk of it then; but I now write to say that *if* anything effectual is to be done, there is not a moment to be lost. Granville Barker is quite clearly *the* indispensable man to such an undertaking; and he, despairing of anything here, is in active negotiation with the governing body of the New York millionaire's theatre, who are offering him a fabulous salary to start their concern. Now, if we let him go to America, we practically lose him altogether. What he really wants to do (and I think he is right) is to write plays. His idea in going to America is to work like a slave for three or at the outside four years, come back with some £20,000 in his pocket, and then devote himself to dramatic authorship. As the theatre won't start for at least a year, this would mean that he would not be free of it until he was 35 or 36; and at that time of life he certainly won't want to devote another three or four years to starting an English theatre, and all the time leaving his plays unwritten. I tell you all this without consulting Barker, and trust to your discretion not to speak of these private affairs of his except to people who *ought* to know. On the other hand, I don't think America in itself has any particular attraction for him, and I think he would—at any rate, he ought to—sacrifice his prospect of 'making his pile' in order to set afoot an English Theatre. If we let him go, we 'sin our mercies', as the Scotch say, or in other words, abuse the gifts of Providence.

When Barker and I three years ago tried to get some one to realize the scheme set forth in our Blue Book (of which I enclose a copy) we were handicapped by the fact that we could not point to a desirable and available manager. Many is the hour I have spent talking over with Pinero, Barrie and others this question of the Director, and we never got any forrader. Of course, I knew all the time that Barker was the man; but he was little more than a boy, and practically unknown. Now it is different; now he has *donné ses preuves*, and circumstances have at the same time shown that even he, with his genius as a producer, and his tremendous power of work, cannot make an artistic theatre without endowment otherwise than a *most* precarious undertaking. Now is the time, then, for the advent of a Saviour or Saviours, who shall say, 'This movement shall not go altogether to waste, or be switched off to America.'

What we want is a solid start—I mean, the promise of a substantial sum on condition that such & such another sum is raised. I know of several people who, I believe, would then come forward. I have not the smallest authority for using his name, but I have reason to think that the Duke of Westminster is not disinclined to help. But we want a solid nucleus for the snowball.

Really, really the time is ripe, and will soon be over-ripe. We have all the materials for a dramatic literature, but we lack the right machinery for developing it to reasonable advantage. Let us make up our minds not to die, on any pretext whatever, until we have seen an English theatre worthy of the name; and then, as the poet says:

> *Never, Sir Herbert, have you seen*
> *A sight the half as fine*
> *As when it heaves up from the West*
> *On our horizon line.*

Only the West mustn't be America!

To which Trench replied on the following day:

Mansfield Place,
Richmond Hill,
16 December 1907

MY DEAR ARCHER,

Many thanks for your long and most interesting letter. I hope I did not give you the impression that matters were clearer to me than they are. I shall be very happy to do what I can in the way of *suggestions*. I think it seemed to Lord Howard de Walden, and to one or two other friends, who, I know, have the project of founding a theatre themselves, that many of the problems dealt with at the Savoy were not fitted for *stage* treatment, although they certainly needed public discussion.

I share to the full your admiration for Barker; and wish we could retain his services. It seems to me if he goes to America he may acquire that hardness in business affairs and that insensitiveness to the finer shades of things, which is precisely what we do not want to happen.

One difficulty is this: my friends do not exactly like the 'tone' of some of the pieces which have been done at the Court. You understand, they have no objection to freedom of thought, either in the morals of the plays produced or adventurous innovation in the theatrical management at the head of the Savoy movement. But they are, perhaps, a trifle *hard*, a trifle callous; and I am sure for my part I do not wonder. The struggles they have had to make would be enough to indurate a sucking babe or an antelope. Still, what these persons say (mind, *I* do not share their position) is that the men guiding the Savoy movement are rather too 'intellectualist'. They therefore do not command a public much greater in extent than the ladies who go to the 'Upper Circle' in the ordinary theatres.

I think it is a great pity if this difficulty cannot be overcome. Possibly we could have lunch together one day and talk it over?

I know many of the facts described in your letter, as I have followed your articles very closely and so was aware of the position. The question really resolves itself into this—is Granville Barker a man who could arouse co-operative *enthusiasm*, as apart from intellectual admiration?

Yours very sincerely,
HERBERT TRENCH

Granville Barker did not depart to America after all. The Millionaire's theatre was to prove a frightful fiasco, and he found more congenial work in England to everyone's content, giving the lie direct to Herbert Trench's fears that he was a man incapable of 'arousing co-operative enthusiasm apart from intellectual admiration'.

IV

HEAD-ON-CRASH

To the possible outcome of all this theatre ferment the Shakespeare memorialists turned a blind eye—or seemed to. Long ago they had decided to ignore the suggestion that a live theatre might be a more appropriate tribute to a living dramatist—as Shakespeare was and always would be—than a dead monument. The Committee, not unnaturally after so much spade work, did not care to risk the loss of the unanimity already achieved by espousing an alternative proposal; for they were aware that despite the clamour of the *avant garde*, the National Theatre idea was not universally accepted even among theatre people themselves. They believed, too, that private generosity would not by itself avail to provide the large amount of capital needed to found the theatre, neither were they more hopeful than Barker and Archer had been that an appeal to the Government would fill the void. Yet again, the fear of State control—in return for State-support—was rampant, and a nationalized theatre smacked of socialism, or at any rate of something out of tune with what would now be called the 'British Way of Life'. Better, so they thought, to play for safety, and do nothing which might embarrass the project for which they had already achieved so large a measure of academic and social support, which moreover had secured the favour of the King himself. With such a backing, the position of the memorialists appeared to be impregnable, and they must have been perturbed, not to say scarified, by the storm of hostile criticism which suddenly broke when their Mansion House report,

64

Harley Granville-Barker, D.Litt.

The Hon. Mrs. Alfred Lyttelton, G.B.E.

already quoted, was published to the world on 5th March 1908. Sir John Hare was first in the field with a letter to *The Times* dated 10th March 1908:

SIR,

I read that a scheme is on foot to raise a Memorial to the memory of Shakespeare. Every Englishman must rejoice that it is in contemplation to give expression to their reverence for the greatest poet and dramatist the world has ever known, and of the countryman of whom they must be for ever proud, by erecting an enduring tribute to his memory. The surprise is that centuries have passed without this expression of national pride and reverence having taken definite form. But I think it behoves us to inquire if the form suggested for this memorial is the right one, or likely to be the most enduring. Shakespeare has, it seems to me, raised the most indestructible monument to his genius by the works he has left us, and it requires no blocks of stone or marble to keep his memory green. But I venture to think that the opportunity has offered itself to associate the name of our national poet, who has enriched the literature of the world and brought imperishable glory to the stage of his native land, with the founding of a national theatre. Such an institution would at once remove the existing stigma of our stage, rescue it from the chaos in which it finds itself, raise the position of the drama in this country to the same dignity it obtains in France, Germany, and Austria, and be a noble and lasting tribute to the memory of one whose genius shed lustre on and whose life's work was devoted to it.

Yours truly,

JOHN HARE

Those were the days of bulky newspapers, and several besides *The Times* were glad to open their columns to the spate of correspondence which ensued. The *Daily News*, inspired by Mr. Scott-James, was particularly favourable, while Sir Robert Donald, the Editor of the *Daily Chronicle*, and his henchman, Mr. S. R. Littlewood, went all out—even to the extent of publishing a special pamphlet stating the case for a National Theatre in a spirit of open partisanship, and paving the way for a great demonstration which was being planned in favour of the Theatre and in protest against the Memorial. It is from this pamphlet that we cull the following extracts:

'What needs my Shakespeare?' Those famous opening words of Milton's immortal lines have been quoted often enough during the centuries. Never, probably, have they been bandied to and fro for such varied purposes—for offence and defence, for satire, for expostulation, or for the sanctioning of mere indifference—as has been the case during these last months of controversy over the vexed question of the Shakespeare Tercentenary Memorial.

Happily, the warfare of ideas to which the project of a Shakespeare statue in Portland Place gave rise has not been fruitless. Out of it has arisen a great, and widespread, and creative movement for the replacing of that scheme with the obviously more appropriate institution of a National Memorial Theatre, to be founded in the honour and to the memory of our—and the world's—supreme dramatist.

A Storm of Disapproval

Out of the first fifty-four letters published in the *Daily Chronicle* forty-four expressed antagonism to the Portland Place statue project, and thirty-one of these pleaded the cause of a National Theatre.

Even several members of the Portland Place Committee admitted the half-heartedness with which they had given their consent, and confessed their entire preference for a National Theatre scheme, if such were promulgated. Correspondence on the subject also appeared in *The Times*, the *Daily Telegraph*, and the *Daily News*.

Offer of the Lyceum

At this juncture, through the medium of the *Daily Chronicle*, the lessees of the Lyceum Theatre, Mr. H. W. Smith and Mr. Edward Carpenter, came forward with a public-spirited offer to lend their historic house for a great meeting, at which the plea for a National Theatre as a Shakespeare Memorial might be adequately urged. The offer was responded to with alacrity. In a few days a Provisional Committee of over 160 distinguished advocates of the need for re-discussion had been formed. Under the chairmanship of Mr. T. P. O'Connor, M.P., a crowded meeting of this committee was held at the Hotel Metropole, at which stirring speeches on behalf of the National Theatre were made by Mr. A. W. Pinero, Mr. H. A. Jones, Mr. J. Comyns Carr, the Hon. Mrs. Alfred Lyttelton, Mr. Bernard Shaw, Mr. George Radford, M.P., Mr. Laurence Gomme, Dr. F. S. Boas, and others.

HEAD-ON CRASH
Lyceum Resolutions

It was unanimously decided at this meeting that the following resolutions should be put before the Lyceum Demonstration:

That this meeting is in favour of the establishment of a National Theatre as a memorial to Shakespeare.

That this meeting be appointed as a general committee, with power to add to their number, to draft a scheme for a National Theatre.

That the committee thus appointed should invite the co-operation of provincial cities, and organize meetings for the formation of a National Theatre Society and for the collection of subscriptions.

That a deputation be appointed to wait on the Prime Minister and the London County Council with a view to seeking their support of the scheme for a National Theatre.

An executive committee was thereupon elected to carry out the final arrangements for this great Demonstration, which it has been decided shall be held on Tuesday, May 19, at 3 p.m., the Right Hon. the Earl of Lytton having kindly consented to take the chair. Among the principal speakers will be Sir John Hare, the Right Hon. Alfred Lyttelton, K.C., M.P., and Mr. Bernard Shaw.

A Last Word

Since the announcement of the date of the Demonstration, many varying schemes have been put forward—some for the immediate erection of a central building; some for the institution first of a National Theatre company, or companies; some for the leasing of a theatre to be conducted by various managers in turn.

The purpose of the Demonstration being not to divide but to unite, and to show forth clearly and simply the public wish for a National Theatre, it is earnestly to be hoped that minor differences will not be allowed to interfere with the main point at issue.

There followed a most impressive list of over three hundred prominent people representing every sphere of influence which had hitherto been associated with the building scheme, and including many eminent recruits. These were to constitute the new Shakespeare Memorial National Theatre Committee.

HEAD-ON CRASH
Pros and Cons

A selection from the arguments hitherto used in the controversy for and against the establishment of a National Theatre

[The 'Cons' are printed in Roman type, the 'Pros' in italics]

That Shakespeare's plays are themselves his best monument.

That Shakespeare's plays do not really exist, in the fullest sense, until rightly produced and acted under appropriate conditions.

That officialism is the death of Art.

That the granting of free powers to a capable director would eliminate officialism, where artistic questions are considered, in a National Theatre.

That the Shakespeare Tercentenary [1916] is not necessarily a time for the foundation of a National Theatre.

That the Shakespeare Tercentenary is a special opportunity for stimulating the growth of an institution which would anyhow have come into being during the next few years, especially as the production of Shakespeare is the matter in which the need of a National Theatre is most clearly felt.

That the proposal to erect a statue in Portland Place is now irrevocable.

That nothing material has yet been done towards the erection of such a statue; that the bequest made by the principal contributor contains no provision which binds the executors to the project of a statue, and that such a statue might quite appropriately be set up in the vestibule of a National Theatre.

That the public do not want a National Theatre, and will not subscribe the necessary funds.

That a great change has come over the public attitude in this matter during the last few years; that this meeting is a test of the public's wishes; that if the public do not want a theatre, a theatre will not be built; that the public have readily subscribed greater sums to less popular causes.

That a National Theatre would enter into unfair competition with private enterprise.

That there is no reason why private enterprise should not continue to perform its present functions, these being entirely different from those of a National Theatre, which are now left unperformed.

That the provinces would have no reason for interest in a National Theatre.

That the National Theatre Company would play in the provinces as

well as in London, and that eventually municipal theatres would be founded in the great provincial centres, in touch with the central institution.

That the religious character of the English nation would rebel against a serious recognition of the theatre.

That among the most enthusiastic regular playgoers are now to be found leaders of religious thought in all denominations, amongst whom are to be included several members of the National Theatre Committee. Also that the theatre will never be reformed by ignoring it.

That a building of ambitious architectural design might prove a 'white elephant' and be turned to baser uses.

That such a building will not be erected until the need for it has been thoroughly tested, and shown to be overwhelming.

That the English stage has got on very well hitherto.

That the most distinguished and successful managers have increasingly expressed their sense of the impossibility of doing their best work under the prevailing circumstances on merely commercial lines.

That Shakespeare himself was the product of an unsubsidized stage.

That this argument would only hold good if the social, political, educational, and theatrical conditions under which Shakespeare's plays were performed were the same now as then.

That if managers do not find it profitable to do the best work under present conditions, such work will not be done without great financial loss in a National Theatre.

That this is a question of organizing and concentrating the limited public who have as yet been trained to appreciate the best work; and that in a repertory theatre, supported by a national organization, it will be possible to present for a limited number of performances, without financial loss, plays which could not profitably be performed under a system of long runs.

That the National Theatre would become a playground for faddists.

That this could not happen in a theatre which had been established on a popular foundation, and whose basis would be the popular will.

That good actors would not work for the salaries that a National Theatre could afford to pay.

That the present nominally inflated weekly fees for actors do not represent a permanent salary, and correspond to a far more modest guaranteed income, for which many good actors would willingly exchange their present conditions. Also that the National Theatre would gradually train its own actors.

That the French people are no longer satisfied with the Comédie Française.

That in a recent debate in the French Senate irrefutable testimony was given as to the hold the Comédie Française has on the French people.

That several great artists have left the Comédie Française, and entered upon successful management.

That they owed their success largely to its training and to the opportunity it afforded: that artists of exceptional individuality are no longer well placed in a company whose excellence depends upon general merit, and that outside the National Theatre the field would remain open.

That it is against the traditions of this country to support artistic enterprise from public funds.

That the National Gallery, and other public galleries, receive public support.

That the public grant of a site would not be sufficient to make the enterprise self-supporting, and that there is no precedent for granting one.

That the theatre would probably be self-supporting even without the grant of a site; but that the Royal Academy, which has never paid anything for its site makes a precedent in this respect, and has been self-supporting ever since the first few years of its existence.

Some Opinions

The following are extracts from a few of the opinions of representative men that have been published in the *Daily Chronicle* and other papers:

MR. ALFRED AUSTIN (Poet Laureate):

'THE PROPOSED STATUE TO SHAKESPEARE'

Why should we lodge in marble or in bronze
Spirits more vast than earth or sea or sky?
Wiser the silent worshipper that cons
Their page for wisdom that will never die.
Unto the favourite of the passing hour
Erect the statue and parade the bust
Whereon decisive Time will slowly shower
Oblivion's refuse and disdainful dust.
The Monarchs of the Mind, self-sceptred Kings,
Need no memento to transmit their name:
Throned on their thoughts and high imaginings,
They are the Lords, not sycophants of Fame.
Raise pedestals to perishable stuff:
Gods for themselves are monuments enough.

HEAD-ON CRASH

A National Theatre, if attainable, would command the approval of every author, of every actor who respects his profession, and of every cultivated person in the Empire.

MR. WILLIAM ARCHER: It is absurd to raise an inert and lifeless monument to Shakespeare while he lacks the living monument of a National Theatre, where his works would be worthily presented. . . . I think we are lowering ourselves and Shakespeare by rattling our collecting boxes at the street corners of Europe.

MR. GEORGE ALEXANDER: Let us have a National Theatre by all means, if half a million of money can be obtained, and the theatre managed on artistic and practical lines by the right people.

MR. OSCAR BROWNING: I am strongly in favour of the establishing of a National Theatre.

SIR F. C. BURNAND: A National Theatre, subsidized by the State, the building as central as the National Gallery, with rooms for various essential studies: than this there can be no worthier Shakespeare memorial.

MR. ROBERT BRIDGES: I think the statue rubbish, and an endowed theatre desirable.

PROF. CHURTON COLLINS: I am strongly opposed to such a monstrously ridiculous superfluity as a monument to Shakespeare, and am amazed that anyone should contribute one farthing to such an inanity. Let us have a National Theatre devoted to his plays of classical excellence.

HERR LUDWIG FULDA (the famous German dramatist): The most beautiful monument which the British nation could erect to their greatest genius and themselves would be to present Shakespeare's dramas to the people, especially to the youth, in a theatre worthy of Shakespeare's name, excellently acted, and at the cheapest possible price.

MR. JOHN GALSWORTHY: I wish to support those who ask that the sum be devoted to the building and endowment of a National Shakespeare Theatre. If ever there was in this island a free, impersonal spirit, who, in essence, was at one with the changes and growth of life, it was the spirit of this same Shakespeare. He is the symbol of our dramatic art; only by doing service to that dramatic art can we fittingly commemorate his greatness.

REV. STEWART HEADLAM: I strongly support the proposal for a National Theatre. The statue scheme, to my mind, carries an impression of someone wanting a baronetcy or a knighthood. I hope something will be done this time. There has been too much talking for too many years.

MR. ROBERT HICHENS: I am strongly in favour of a National Theatre, and think it would be a far more fitting Shakespeare memorial than a statue.

MR. RIDER HAGGARD: I do not approve of a statue as a memorial to Shakespeare.

SIR JOHN HARE: I am heart and soul with those who hold that our admiration, our affection, and our desire to do Shakespeare honour may still find some useful and appropriate manner of proving their sincerity. And what better direction could that feeling take than in striving to secure for England and the English people a really National Theatre—a theatre in which the best interests of players, dramatists, and the public itself would be carefully studied and safeguarded? The question is vital and far-reaching; it goes down to the very root of our national existence. It is a matter which concerns every thinking man.

MR. THOMAS HARDY: I do not consider Portland Place a fitting site for the Shakespeare Memorial. It suggests the Prince Regent rather than Shakespeare.

MR. HENRY ARTHUR JONES: The only monument to Shakespeare must be a National Theatre, where his countrymen can have the privilege of seeing as many of his plays performed in the course of a year as if they were living in a second-rate German town. I believe that in the end the enthusiasm of the English people will be roused in favour of a National Theatre, and against the erection of a mere architectural irrelevance and incongruity.

MR. A. W. PINERO: The notion of offering a tribute to Shakespeare by dumping down a heap of statuary in the Marylebone Road is ridiculous. The scheme for a National Theatre is better, because a National Theatre is needed, whether as a memorial to Shakespeare or Smith.

MR. BERNARD SHAW: From all the risks of jobbery, bathos, and vulgarity that attend the monumental scheme, the National Theatre scheme is free. In such a theatre the living genius of successive generations of

English actors can keep the sacred fire alive. They, and not the eminent firm of monumental masons who would get the Portland Place job, are the rightful custodians and commemorators of Shakespeare's genius. Let us give up our hopeless attempts to do the thing in the wrong way, and do it the right way, as Sir John Hare and all the real lovers of the theatre demand, by refusing to give a farthing for any other memorial than a National Theatre. There are a dozen ways of raising a harvest from the Shakespearian seed if we really wish to honour his art instead of making his reputation the means of 'working' a commission for a sculpture, a job for a contractor, an introduction to the King for a committee, and a knighthood for a chairman.

MR. ARTHUR SYMONS: The erection of a statue to Shakespeare in London would undoubtedly be a public desecration of the memory of one whose work is already his sufficient monument. A National Theatre would be a due homage to the dead, and, if endowed, a permanent benefit to the living.

LORD RONALD SUTHERLAND-GOWER: To select a wholly unworthy site for a memorial, merely to be able to make the opening coincide with the 300th anniversary, is simply ludicrous. I see that all the theatrical managers and actors wish for a National Theatre for the memorial. That is not to be wondered at.

MISS ELLEN TERRY: Surely a subsidized theatre is the only fitting memorial for Shakespeare.

MR. J. E. VEDRENNE: The erection of a statue is quite inadequate, and this seems the proper opportunity to try to establish a National Theatre.

ARCHDEACON WILBERFORCE: I am fully in sympathy with the National Theatre scheme.

MR. A. B. WALKLEY: The Portland Place statue project would merely lead to the creation of another public nuisance.

MR. ISRAEL ZANGWILL: Nothing is worthy of Shakespeare except a National Theatre.

WILLIAM ARCHER

> *'What needs my Shakespeare?' Nothing! What need we?—*
> *A playhouse worthy his supremacy.*
> *Oh bathos!—to the Voice of all our race*
> *We raise dumb carven stones in Portland Place!*

No wonder that the well-timed attack of the National Theatre-ites spread consternation throughout the ranks of the memorialists. Some, like Beerbohm Tree, had already acknowledged their conversion to the ideas of the Theatre group, and if it came to a pitched battle it was evident to the most die-hard supporters of the statue that they risked a heavy defeat. Prompt action alone could save them, and Tree was called in to open discussions with the enemy. As a result of his tactful intervention, a private meeting was arranged between the leading antagonists, followed by an exchange of letters between Lords Plymouth and Lytton, a correspondence which was only concluded on the morning of the great Lyceum demonstration on May 18th. We will leave the reporter of *The Times* to describe what happened at this meeting:

A largely attended meeting was held yesterday afternoon at the Lyceum Theatre in support of the movement to establish a National Theatre as a memorial to Shakespeare. Lord Lytton presided, and among those present on the platform were Lady Lytton, Mr. Pinero, Mr. Alfred Lyttelton, K.C., M.P., Sir Squire Bancroft, Mr. H. Beerbohm Tree, Mr. Jerome K. Jerome, Mr. Comyns Carr, Sir John and Lady Hare, Mr. Rider Haggard, Mr. Bourchier, Miss Violet Vanbrugh, Mr. E. S. Willard, Mr. Robert Barr, Mr. H. O. Arnold Foster, M.P., Mr. T. P. O'Connor, M.P., and many other representatives of politics, society, and the Drama.

The Chairman said that for nearly thirty-two years a movement had been on foot to commemorate the 300th anniversary of the death of Shakespeare. In all the proceedings taken hitherto it had been assumed that we could best show our admiration for the genius and fame of Shakespeare by some sculptured or architectural work of art. That meeting had been called by those who disagreed with the proposal for a statue in Portland Place, and who desired that the monument should take the form of a national theatre—a permanent home for the British Drama. The meeting had been called, however, not to divide but to unite all who desired to join in honouring the name of Shakespeare. [*Cheers.*] It was with the greatest pleasure that those responsible for promoting the meeting had received a few days ago an invitation from the other Shakespeare Memorial Committee with a view to the possible combination of their forces. He thanked those gentlemen for the conciliatory attitude they showed. Referring to the opinion of a few persons who objected to the theatre as an institution at all, he said he did not feel called upon to answer that objection, as he did not think the theatre needed any defence from himself or anyone else. [*Cheers.*] The fact, again, that difficulties existed was no reason for not going on with so desirable a project. . . . He had every hope that the result of that meeting might be a conference which would unite the forces of those desiring to do honour to Shakespeare, and send them forward upon common ground, and he was strengthened in that hope by a letter which he had just received from Lord Plymouth, the Chairman of the organization to which he had already referred. It was Lord Plymouth who had previously invited them to meet him and his friends at the House of Lords, and as a result of that meeting Lord Plymouth had promised to send him a message. The letter ran as follows:

54 Mount Street, W.

19 May 1908.

My dear Lord Lytton,

In accordance with the arrangement at the Conference held last Wednesday between the executive of the Shakespeare Memorial Committee and yourself and other leading supporters of the national theatre movement who were good enough to accept our invitation, I have the pleasure of sending you this letter to be read at the Lyceum Theatre demonstration, as promised by you.

We had a meeting of our general Committee at the Mansion House yesterday, at which the following resolution was passed: 'That the executive of the Shakespeare Memorial Committee be authorized to arrange for a conference between representatives appointed by them and an equal number appointed by the National Theatre Committee, with a view to attempting to arrive at an agreement as to the form which a Shakespeare memorial should take, and to report to the General Committee.

It has seemed to the Shakespeare Memorial Committee, for various practical considerations, that an architectural monument, as a permanent symbol of the world-wide homage to Shakespeare, should be put forward without delay, lest time be lost, and the work be not complete by 1916.

I would, however, carefully point out that the furtherance of serious drama has all along been one of the objects which the Committee have kept in view; indeed, in accordance with the report of the special committee, we had hoped to have obtained a site for the monument, on which a memorial

75

theatre might also be erected for the furtherance of dramatic art and literature.

A sub-committee has been appointed consisting of the following nine members—namely, Lord Esher, Lord Plymouth, Mr. Butcher, Mr. Hugh Chisholm, Mr. Sidney Colvin, Mr. W. L. Courtney, Mr. Beerbohm Tree, Mr. Sidney Low, and Dr. Gollancz—to meet a committee of like number appointed by the supporters of the National Theatre movement, as suggested by you on Wednesday last. Thursday, May 28th is suggested for the conference. I mention these matters at once in case this information may serve the convenience of your committee.

I feel confident that I am giving expression to the fervent hope of many members both of the Shakespeare Memorial Committee and those who are supporting the national theatre movement, as well as the deep-seated feeling of Englishmen generally, that nothing in the nature of strife may mar our efforts to signalize the unanimity in paying homage to the memory of Shakespeare.

I am, dear Lord Lytton,
Yours sincerely,
PLYMOUTH
(Chairman of the Executive Committee,
Shakespeare Memorial Committee.)

Mr. Alfred Lyttelton then moved the first resolution: 'That this demonstration is in favour of the establishment of a national theatre as a memorial to Shakespeare.' He said that the first and almost the last appearance that he had made upon a stage was in a play of Racine in which he had to impersonate 'the crowd'. [*Laughter.*] He was taught to come up to the footlights and say, with great embarrassment: 'Moi, je suis l'assemblée.' [*Laughter.*] He was in that part that day, a member representing the crowd, and he could assure them that he was not the least ashamed of his client, that the instincts of the multitude were perfectly sane and right on the question, not necessarily of an official, but of a national theatre, and he was confirmed in his belief when he thought that there were, so far as he could conceive, not two sides to the question at all. If there were another, Mr. Bernard Shaw would of course be upon it. [*Laughter.*] Now they had the happiness and strength of his support, and he supposed Mr. Shaw was suffering the auguish of for once being in agreement with several human beings. [*Laughter and cheers.*] The principle that it was unwise to leave any art wholly at the mercy of the commercial motive was already conceded in this country—without going to the many and great examples in foreign countries—in the National Gallery, the British Museum, the great public buildings. Let them think of the Royal College of Music. Let them think even of the Parks which were at this moment the peculiar glory of the summer. Nature herself was exalted by the actions and looks of beautiful persons who attuned themselves to glorious fiction. Think how Mrs. Siddons and Miss O'Neill, those great ladies, moved some of the most austere and virtuous to almost a passion of admiration. Yet we exposed this beautiful and splendid art to the ruinous risks of competition and extended no hand to it, isolating it among all the others of the arts in this respect. It was his good fortune years ago to be an almost constant attendant at the Théâtre Français, in the great days of Gort, of Delannay, of Febvre, of Bartet, of Sarah Bernhardt, and many other great artists. He learned there that a National Theatre like that taught clearness and precision of speech, and after all, what was the use of Shakespeare unless we could make him intelligible even to those who sat some way off? [*Laughter and cheers.*] Lastly, he saw in the Théâtre Français that dignified and leisured retreat for those who had done great service to their art—dignified and leisured, but not in the least lost to the nation—which enabled men who were in the profession of the actor, as well as others who ministered to it, to give the best of their time and the best of their youth to the highest and noblest interests of their art. [*Cheers.*]

Sir John Hare, in seconding the resolution, said that they had three distinct courses of congratulation, the first being that they were met to discuss the great question of a National Theatre seriously; the second that the meeting should take place in the theatre and upon the stage to be for ever famous in theatrical annals by its association with the great actor who for twenty years controlled its destinies, and whose sympathies were so entirely with the objects they were there to advocate; and the third that their meeting should take place under the presidency of Lord Lytton, for the name of Lytton must always be revered by lovers of the drama. [*Cheers.*] The idea of a National Theatre in this country, at first ridiculed and sneered at in certain quarters, was actually taking firm root, and commending itself to the minds of that large majority who were jealous of our artistic reputation; who recognized the immense power which the stage could exercise as a refining and educational influence on the great public who support it. Nearly forty years ago Matthew Arnold wrote a plea for a National Theatre, concluding with the famous words: 'The people will have the theatre; then make it a good one. . . . The theatre is irresistible; organize the theatre.' [*Cheers.*] Sir John Hare also quoted from the speech of the Bishop of Ripon, in replying for the guests at the Royal Academy Banquet of 1905: 'We one and all feel honoured to take our place at this table of the great and worthy fraternity of those who are united in their devotion to art. But a feeling of shame strikes across our gratitude, for we represent the great and worthy callings of the world outside your Academy; and we are keenly alive to the fact that we represent that majority of the nation which, though possessed of vast wealth and wide dominions, does so little for literature, the drama, and for art.' Such were the opinions of two large-hearted, intellectual and unprejudiced men. Now it seemed to him that the words of Matthew Arnold were as true to-day as when he wrote them. The state of our theatre was still chaotic and ineffective. Commercial interests paralysed the aspirations and ambitions of the most conscientious of our managers. The Théâtre Français through centuries had maintained its superiority, and preserved all that was best in past and contemporary dramatic literature; it was removed from all sordid financial considerations and from pandering to the vulgar taste, and it placed its actors on an academic footing which dignified and exalted their calling. [*Cheers.*]

Mr. Edmund Gosse supported the resolution, which was carried with one dissentient.

Mr. Pinero moved 'that the honorary committee for this demonstration is hereby appointed a committee with power to add to its number and is instructed to draft a scheme for a national theatre.' In the course of his speech he said that about the middle of her late Majesty's reign a new English drama came into being, initiated by the late Thomas William Robertson, and by Mr. [now Sir] W. S. Gilbert. [*Cheers.*] That movement had constantly increased in strength. Since the accession of his present Majesty much new blood had been infused into our dramatic literature. He hailed the appearance of a new school of vigorous young authors, and he believed that there was every reason to hope that the growth of a drama such as we had not seen in England for three hundred years might be regarded in history as one of the most memorable features of the reign of King Edward VII. [*Cheers.*]

Mr. T. P. O'Connor seconded the resolution, which was carried.

Mr. Comyns Carr proposed the third resolution: 'That the Committee hereby appointed invite co-operation of the provincial cities, and organize meetings for the formation of a National Theatre Society and the collection of subscriptions.'

Mr. Justice Madden, Vice-Chancellor of Dublin University, in seconding the resolution, asked them to authorize him to go back to Ireland with the expression of a hope that they would help in the movement. He could assure them that it would secure practical support and sympathy throughout the whole of Ireland. [*Cheers.*] The resolution was carried.

Mr. W. P. Steadman, M.P., moved that the Committee appoint a deputation to wait on the Prime Minister and the L.C.C. with a view to seeking their support for the purpose of a National Theatre.

Mr. Bernard Shaw seconded the resolution, but though called very earnestly by the audience to make a speech, declined to do so, owing to the lateness of the hour. 'If the subject was not exhausted,' he said, 'those who constituted the meeting *were.*' [*Laughter.*]

The resolution was carried, and the meeting ended with a vote of thanks to the Chairman.

Next morning the meeting had a good 'press', for its tone had been exemplary, and the knowledge that statesmanship and good sense had prevailed over bitter rivalry between two equally well-intentioned parties was universally acclaimed. No time was lost in implementing the proposal that both committees should get together, and a joint meeting of representatives of both sides was held ten days later at the House of Lords. 'The two general committees as they stand at present', so it was resolved, 'should be amalgamated, and an executive committee elected by the joint committee thus formed.' On July 23rd, the promised meeting of the two general committees took place at the Mansion House, the Lord Mayor presiding, when it was decided that '(1) the new Shakespeare Memorial National Theatre General Committee should consist of the members of the two previous committees, and that (2) an Executive Committee should be elected consisting of 21 members, an Hon. Secretary, and a Secretary, with power to add to their numbers.' The following members of this Executive Committee were there and then elected: The Lord Mayor

(Chairman), the Earl of Plymouth, Viscount Esher,[1] Sir John
Hare, Dr. Furnivall, William Archer, H. Granville Barker, S. H.
Butcher, M.P., J. Comyns Carr, Sidney Colvin, W. L. Courtney,
Robert Donald, C. L. Gomme, Edmund Gosse, Sidney Lee,
H. W. Massingham, the Hon. Mrs. Alfred Lyttelton, A. W.
Pinero, George Bernard Shaw, Beerbohm Tree, Johnston Forbes-
Robertson, Israel Gollancz (Hon. Secretary), and Philip Carr
(Secretary).

The first task facing the Committee was to draw up a prospectus stating in so many words the objects of the enterprise, and
at the same time to serve as a bait for donations. So the text for
an 'illustrated handbook' was prepared in time for presentation
to a meeting of the General Committee called at the Mansion
House on 28th March 1909. But this prospectus, it was felt, was
not enough, if the Appeal was to be launched in a manner which
would strike the popular imagination. Some concrete proof that
the appeal was likely to succeed was more important than a
spate of definitions, and of promises, however alluring. If
only some announcement could be made that would bring
reality into what still appeared to most people as little more
substantial than a dream! To Mrs. Alfred Lyttelton must be given
the credit for securing just what, at the moment, was so badly
needed. It was she who contrived to win the interest of her friend,
Mrs. Carl Meyer, and through her the support of Carl Meyer
himself—a wealthy and generous-minded man, later to be
honoured for his munificence by the bestowal of a baronetcy. For
much to everyone's delight, and to the astonishment of not a few,
Mrs. Lyttelton was able to inform the March meeting that there
was now at their disposal the sum of £70,000 for the inauguration
of the Appeal.

This magnificent donation, for the time being anonymous,
immediately established the S.M.N.T. Committee as a body to
be reckoned with, and a Deed of Trust was drawn which, together

---

[1] Father of the present Viscount.

with the Handbook, would form the charter, as it were, under which all further operations of the Committee would be conducted. So that the reader may be able to follow the various controversies and legal difficulties which were to occur later in connection with the disposal of the Fund, he is invited to peruse these two documents with some attention.

DECLARATION OF TRUST

KNOW ALL MEN by these presents that We the Right Hon. Sir Victor Alexander George Robert Bulwer Lytton Earl of Lytton, The Right Honourable Sir John Lubbock Baron Avebury P.C., and the Right Honourable Alfred Lyttelton, P.C., M.P., hereby undertake and declare that we will hold the sum of Seventy thousand pounds which has been given or subscribed for the purpose of the Memorial hereinafter referred to and is now standing to the credit of a Joint Account which has been opened in our names at the London and Westminster Bank at No. 1 St. James Square S.W. and all or any investments which may for the time being represent the same or any part or parts thereof and the income thereof respectively. And all other moneys which may hereafter be subscribed and paid to us upon the same account *IN TRUST* for the Committee which has been formed for the purpose of a scheme to provide a Shakespeare Memorial and to be paid to such persons or Corporation and generally to be disposed of in such manner as the said Committee (which is known as the Shakespeare Memorial Committee) or the Executive or other Committee duly authorized for such purpose shall from time to time by resolution or resolutions duly passed at and recorded in the Minutes of any Meeting or Meetings of such Committee direct and appoint *IN WITNESS* whereof we have hereunto set our hands and seals this twentieth day of May One thousand Nine hundred and Nine.

Let us now consider the original prospectus, or 'Handbook', as it was called, omitting only the illustrations and some passages in the historical section that concern events already described more fully in foregoing pages.

HEAD-ON CRASH
THE PROPOSED SHAKESPEARE MEMORIAL NATIONAL THEATRE
AN ILLUSTRATED HANDBOOK 1909

The creation of a Shakespeare Memorial National Theatre, too long delayed, is at least within sight; and all who revere in Shakespeare the supreme intellectual glory of our race are invited to co-operate in furthering the movement.

A Shakespeare National Theatre is an institution which Britain may fairly be said to owe to herself, and to the memory of her greatest son —an institution which can be founded and established in perpetuity, for a sum which, in relation to the wealth, the patriotism, and the public spirit of Britain and of the Empire, may almost be called trifling.

The following pages contain a brief account of the history of the movement, and of the objects, and proposed constitution of the theatre.

History

The scheme is the outcome of two separate movements which, differing at first in their purpose and supporters, have finally united for the remedying of a great want and the achievement of a great end— the movement for a Shakespeare Memorial, and the movement for a National Theatre.

The demand for a National Theatre goes back at least as far as the year 1879, when Matthew Arnold, in brilliant and convincing words, called attention to the need for theatrical organization, which has grown not less strong, not less urgent, since he wrote.[1]

'The theatre is irresistible. Organize the Theatre.' Matthew Arnold's fine words are not forgotten. He unquestionably had in mind a theatre owned and supported, like so many foreign theatres, either by the State or by the Sovereign. But a little examination of the conditions, both historic and actual, showed that there was no practical probability of inducing the Imperial Government to set about the creation of a theatre. Nor was this necessarily implied in the idea of a National Theatre. In order to merit that name, it was sufficient that a theatre should be owned by the nation, and placed, by some form of endowment, above the necessity of constant and immediate profit-making. It mattered not at all from what funds the theatre was erected, and the

---

[1] See page 33 passim.

endowment supplied. The Wallace Collection is none the less 'national' for having been presented to the nation by private munificence.

The supporters of a National Theatre, then, instead of importuning the Government to take action, studied the means by which private, but public-spirited generosity could best set about the creation of the desired institution, and its transference to national ownership.

It so happened that an elaborate and detailed scheme of this nature, endorsed by Sir Henry Irving, Sir Squire Bancroft, Mr. J. M. Barrie, Mrs. D'Oyly Carte, Sir John Hare, Mr. Henry Arthur Jones, and Sir Arthur Pinero, was published just about the time when the Shakespeare Memorial proposals were under discussion, and gave a stimulus to the National Theatre movement. What more natural than that the two radically similar ideas, each of which may be said to have included the essential part of the other, should unite to initiate a great national effort towards their realization?

In the event, a complete amalgamation of the two movements was arranged, proper guarantees being given that, both in the designation and constitution of the National Theatre, its functions as a Shakespeare Memorial should be unmistakably emphasized.

Objects

The Objects of the Shakespeare National Theatre, as formulated by the Executive Committee, fall under six heads:

(1) to keep the plays of Shakespeare in its repertory;
(2) to revive whatever else is vital in English classical drama;
(3) to prevent recent plays of great merit from falling into oblivion;
(4) to produce new plays and to further the development of the modern drama;
(5) to produce translations of representative works of foreign drama, ancient and modern;
(6) to stimulate the art of acting through the varied opportunities which it will offer to the members of the company.

(1) To keep the plays of Shakespeare in its repertory

Foreign visitors are amazed to find in London no permanent home of Shakespearian drama. They may often pass weeks, and even months, among us with no opportunity of seeing a single play of Shakespeare. Individual artists have given us many admirable Shakespearean productions: it is scarcely necessary in this connection to mention the names of Macready, Phelps, Charles Kean, Sir Henry Irving, Mr. Forbes-Robertson, Sir Herbert Tree, Mr. F. R. Benson. But under the long-run system it is impossible for any one manager to produce more than a limited selection from the splendid list of masterpieces; nor in the nature of things can an enterprise depending entirely on the talent of one man possess the dignity and stability of a great public institution. In the Shakespeare National Theatre, all the poet's plays, with very few exceptions, would be frequently passed in review. No actable play would ever be left unacted (as is now frequently the case) for twenty or thirty years at a stretch. The statutes bind the management to give (on an average) at least one Shakespearian performance a week. The art of Shakespearian production would be thoroughly studied. Traditions would be handed down from generation to generation; while in each generation individual genius would break through them and renovate them. Shakespeare, in short, would receive in his own country an assiduous homage which he now only receives in Germany.

(2) *To revive whatever else is vital in English classical drama*

Apart from Shakespeare, only three classical plays—*She Stoops to Conquer*, *The Rivals*, and *The School for Scandal*—can be said to live on the modern stage; and these are revived at only long intervals. It would be the business of the Shakespeare National Theatre by careful selection and experiment, to discover what other plays of the 16th, 17th, 18th, and 19th centuries have in them dramatic vitality as distinct from mere literary interest, and to give them a prominent place in its repertory.

(3) *To prevent recent plays of great merit from falling into oblivion*

Under the present long-run system, very few plays survive their first spell of popularity. The majority are, as it were, exhausted, squeezed dry, by their hundred or two hundred consecutive performances, and are thereafter dead to the London stage. Many plays of this class ought to be, and no doubt would be, restored to life by the Shakespeare National Theatre.

(4) *To produce new plays and to further the development of the modern drama*

It is a mistake to suppose that the Shakespeare National Theatre would be in any sense hostile to the long-run theatres, or would compete with them to their detriment. There are, and always will be, numerous plays which contain great 'star parts', and are otherwise suited for the huge and instant popularity implied in the long run. But there are also plays, and these often of the highest order, in which the importance of the various parts is more evenly balanced, and which, though appealing to a very considerable public, are unlikely to secure the immediate and enormous vogue necessary for a long run. Under the existing order of things, the outlet for such plays is very limited. The Shakespeare National Theatre, by relieving authors of the necessity of making a long run their one aim and ideal, will undoubtedly remove one of the chief impediments to the fertility and virility of English drama.

(5) *To produce translations of representative works of foreign drama, ancient and modern*

Though it is only at times of extreme decadence that any theatre can live mainly (as did the early- and mid-Victorian theatre) upon adaptations from foreign languages, it is highly desirable that the intelligent public of one country should become acquainted with whatever is most notable in the drama of other countries. The Shakespeare National Theatre, then, will welcome translations of great foreign plays, both classical and contemporary. Recent experience has shown that the masterpieces of Greek art, vividly and beautifully translated, can still appeal to modern audiences. There is little doubt that this movement, too, will be sedulously promoted.

(6) *To stimulate the art of acting*

One of the great evils of the long-run system in London, combined with the touring system in the provinces, is that it gives no opportunity to young actors for varied experience in their art. Repeating the same part night after night for months at a stretch, they fall into fixed mannerisms, and cannot acquire the flexibility which proceeds only from constant practice in a wide range of characters. In the Shakespeare National Theatre every member of the Company will have the most varied opportunities, and the younger members will be stimulated by the knowledge that, even if in one play they have but a small part, the next production, or the next again, may bring them a chance of making their mark. They will not feel themselves chained for weeks and months to one trivial character in which they cannot possibly attract any notice. Moreover, though honest work will be required of all actors, none will be so constantly employed as to be cut off from social life and from all opportunity for study and development on any other than merely professional lines.

It is highly probable that an Academy of Dramatic Art will be affiliated to the Shakespeare National Theatre, and that its students will be enabled to acquire the habit of the stage by appearing as super-numeraries and even in small speaking parts, in one way or other; at all events, a school of acting will certainly be attached to the theatre.

Architecture

All possible considerations, whether sentimental or practical, combine to render it necessary that the Shakespeare National Theatre should be a building wholly different in character and aspect from any existing theatre.

(*a*) As a Memorial to Shakespeare, it must be at once conspicuous and dignified, standing entirely detached from all other buildings, on a commanding site. It ought to be one of the great public edifices of the Metropolis, bearing unmistakable testimony to the nation's reverence for its greatest poet, and respect for the art to which his life and genius were devoted.

(*b*) As a Repertory Theatre, conducted under the principle of a constant alternation of plays, it must possess scenic accommodation and appliances which are unnecessary in long-run theatres, and with which they are not furnished. While it would be a fatal mistake to make the auditorium too large, the staircases, corridors and foyers must be ample and dignified. Moreover, the space between the seats ought to be so liberal that the ladies of the audience can, if they wish, pass out into fresher air during the intervals, or can retain their places without discomfort from the passing to and fro of their neighbours. It is essential, in short, to the success of the Theatre that it should be agreeable as a popular place of resort, irrespective of the particular entertainment on the stage; and to this end a far more spacious building is required than any existing playhouse.

It is a great reproach to England that it contains no theatre that can for a moment compare with the palaces devoted to drama in almost every foreign capital, and in many towns of minor importance. Views of some representative foreign theatres are included in this Handbook.

In some of them opera as well as drama is performed; but no theatre is included which is entirely devoted to music.

Methods

Under this heading it is unnecessary to say more than that the theatre is to be, in the full and exact sense of the term, a Repertory Theatre. The statutes define a Repertory Theatre as one 'able to present, and bound to present, at least two different plays of full length at evening performances in each week, and at least three different plays at evening performances and matinées taken together'. This is a very liberal definition, which would permit one play to be acted all the week from Monday to Friday inclusive, if only a second play were presented at the Saturday matinée and a third on the Saturday evening. In all probability, however, this would be a very infrequent arrangement. As a rule no play would be given more than four times in a week (say at three evening performances and one matinée), while the remaining three evenings and matinée might be devoted to three or even four plays. There is no fixed limit to the number of times a particular play may be performed in a season; but practically it would probably be found impolitic to give any play more than a hundred performances (say four performances a week for 25 weeks). The statutes provide that at least one English classical play shall be given in each week, and that not less than 25 plays of full length shall be performed in each season.

Endeavours will be made to arrange for visits of the Shakespeare National Theatre Company to provincial cities. But it is by no means the aim of the institution to render local effort in the cause of dramatic art superfluous. On the contrary, the Shakespeare National Theatre ought to serve as a model for repertory theatres in all the great centres of population, and as an incentive to their establishment. Not otherwise can it completely fulfil its function in promoting popular culture and enlightenment.

Government

In order that the whole nation and the Empire at large may share in the ultimate control of the Theatre, it has been decided that the Governing Body shall be a large and widely-representative one. Here it may suffice to say that the Governors are to be appointed by the Crown, the Universities of Oxford and Cambridge, by the Universities of the capital cities of the three kingdoms, by the University of Wales, by the Royal Academy, the British Academy, the Workers' Educational Association, the London County Council, the Corporation of London, and the Municipalities of five great cities of England, two of Scotland, and two of Ireland. Moreover, there will be certain ex-officio Governors, to wit, the High Commissioners of Canada, Australia, and of any other federated Colonies, the President of the Board of Education, the Chairman of the President of the Academy of Dramatic Art, and, last not least, the Ambassador of the United States, that great English-speaking nation which justly claims its share in the heritage of Shakespeare's renown. It is further provided that these Governors shall co-opt others in proportion of one to every three of their number, and that one at least of these co-opted Governors shall be a woman. Though it cannot be prescribed by statute, there is every reason to hope that some of the nominated members would also be women.

Such a body of Governors could not, of course, meet very frequently, nor would it be possible for them to supervise the daily routine of management. They are therefore directed to appoint from among their number a Standing Committee of not more than seven, of whom at least one shall be a woman. This Committee, in its turn, is to nominate the Managing Staff of the Theatre, to consist of a Director, a Treasurer, and a Literary Manager, who shall be responsible to the Standing Committee (and in the last resort to the Governors) for the conduct of the Theatre.

It is not pretended that this is a perfect system, which will work with mechanical precision. Much must depend on the tact of the Standing Committee and on the ability and loyalty of the Director and his assistants. But it is believed that the constitution, as outlined, will obviate all the dangers of the Theatre falling into the hands of any one party or clique, and will at the same time prove sufficiently elastic to allow the development of a thoroughly efficient system of management.

The General Appeal

Some people may be inclined to think that, as the Shakespeare National Theatre must be situated in London, London alone will reap the benefit of it, and ought to bear the whole cost. This is not so. London will doubtless bear her full share of the cost—she has already given substantial earnest of her readiness to do so. But it is untrue—it is very far from the truth—that London will benefit exclusively or unfairly by the existence in her midst of the Shakespeare National Theatre. It is not true for these reasons:

The common reverence for the great spiritual heirloom of our race is one of the deep-seated emotions which secure the unity of the English-speaking world. All, therefore, to whom that unity is precious ought to join in a corporate and conspicuous homage to Shakespeare.

All portions of the British Empire must desire, and take pride in the architectural dignity and beauty of its Metropolis. The Shakespeare National Theatre will fill a manifest gap in the architectural equipment of London, placing her in this respect, on a level with the other great capitals of Europe.

The drama, as an instrument of culture and enlightenment, suffers from the comparative disesteem into which, owing to the misfortune of historic circumstances, it has fallen in our islands. A public and conspicuous testimony to the dignity of theatrical art will inaugurate a new era in its history, and help to render it doubly and trebly a force for good.

It is admitted on every hand that the theatrical life, not of London alone, but of the whole country, suffers from the exclusive dominance of the long-run and touring system. The whole country, then, will gain by the establishment of an institution specially designed to counteract the chief evils of this system.

Both in the ordinary course of its work, and in the School of Acting which must be attached to it, the Shakespeare National Theatre will train a new generation of actors, to the great benefit of the whole theatrical life of the country.

As every London theatre of to-day is largely supported by playgoers from the country, there is no reason to doubt that this would also be the case with the Shakespeare Memorial National Theatre; which means, of course, that thousands of non-Londoners would directly participate in the benefits of the institution.

While the country would come to the Theatre, the Theatre would also go, as before stated, to the country, thus enabling the classes which visit London infrequently, or not at all, to see whatever is best in Shakespearian acting and modern drama.

But the final and most substantial benefit the Shakespeare National Theatre would confer would lie in its pervasive influence on theatrical enterprise throughout the three kingdoms and the Empire. There would soon come a time when no great city would be without a worthy repertory theatre of its own (perhaps affiliated to the central institution and working in concert). For the establishment of theatres the Shakespeare National Theatre would supply a model and an incentive. Every city, in contributing its proportional share to the central enterprise, will thus further its own theatrical interests, without sensibly diminishing the resources available for local effort.

On these grounds the Executive Committee feels that it may rely with confidence on ungrudging support from all classes and localities. While it is hoped that men of great wealth will contribute large sums in aid of the movement, it is earnestly desired that a considerable portion of the money should be raised in comparatively small subscriptions, so as to render the institution as wide a tribute as possible to the genius of Shakespeare and the dignity of his art.

For the purposes of appeal the following four funds have been instituted:

Fund A.	Site	Sum required about £100,000
Fund B.	Building and Equipment	Sum required about £150,000
Fund C.	Endowment	Sum required about £250,000
Fund D.	To be allocated to Funds A, B or C at the discretion of the Committee	From any balance obtainable

Though this prospectus contained a certain amount of sheer window-dressing, and though some of it was couched in a rhetorical style that to-day is out-moded, the gist of it has stood the test of time, and may still be taken as a fair statement of the fundamental aims of the national theatre movement. In the final constitution of the theatre many modifications will no doubt be made, largely in the direction of simplification; and of course financial liabilities have grown beyond belief. Only the cost of the site has been much reduced from the Handbook figure of £100,000—this being the result of the favourable exchange of the South Kensington site, purchased in 1938 for £75,000, for that provided by the London County Council on the South Bank.

But we anticipate unduly. Let us rather end this chapter on a note of rejoicing at that happy union which common sense had achieved between hostile forces. Hereafter the voyage will be no plain sailing. Tempest, contrary winds, rocks where sirens sing will all conspire to deflect the good ship from her course. But the harbour-bar has been crossed under fair auspices and with a favouring breeze.

> *Now is there mirth in heaven*
> *When earthly things made even*
> *Atone together.*

V

TOGETHER WE STAND

In spite of the satisfaction felt by supporters of the National Theatre at the happy outcome of the afflictions recorded in the last chapter, it must not be supposed that the project was to remain for long free from attack from outside. The bogey of State-control raised its head again and again, though as yet there had been no sign of an approach to the Government for State aid. And then, as already mentioned, the theatrical profession was still by no means unanimous in its approval. Significant in this respect was a circular which, though undated, must have been going the rounds at some time subsequent to the issue of the 1909 Handbook.

It is proposed to invite the public to subscribe £500,000 for the establishment and endowment of a Shakespeare Memorial National Theatre.

We, the undersigned, feel that we ought to make some protest against the scheme as at present put forward without, we fear, mature or sufficiently practical consideration. In the general appreciation of such a scheme, it must always be remembered that, in the words of Sir Charles Wyndham's letter to the *Daily Telegraph* of 26th March 1908, 'A National Theatre, if it is to be in fact what is indicated by the name, would be a type of institution alien to the spirit of our nation and of our age, which has always believed in, and relied on, individual effort and personal competition as a healthier stimulus than the motherly or grand-motherly fostering of a State nurse.'

This scheme is the outcome of two separate proposals, one to erect a memorial to Shakespeare, the other to found a National Theatre—with the result that a number of distinguished persons favouring a memorial to Shakespeare, but in no way connected with, or having

TOGETHER WE STAND

any practical knowledge of, the theatre, have been placed in a position which must be as puzzling to them, as it is unconvincing to us.

The greatest possible care must be taken that such a scheme, if put before the public, should be one possessing a very real possibility of success. We do not see promise of this in the present scheme. We feel it our duty, from our own experience, to call attention to the possible dangers which should be strictly guarded against, before public money is asked for towards so important an enterprise.

We consider, firstly, that the sum of £500,000 is insufficient for such an establishment of a National Theatre as will make for lasting success. Among other considerations, we would call attention to the warning of Sir Charles Wyndham, in a recent interview, that no National Theatre which does not provide pensions for its players, can hope to retain the services of actors of the first rank. It is only by the prospect of such a pension that the Continental theatres can reserve to themselves the services of those leading actors, who are not tempted by personal ambition to embark on management on their own account. The history of the Théâtre Français pension has proved that the spirit of com-mercialism must inevitably operate. Nevertheless, the co-operation of the best actors of the day is an absolute requisite to the success of a National Theatre. Has the enormous cost of such a necessity been practically estimated? There are, we think, indications that this im-portant consideration has been hardly realized by the promoters of the present scheme. To found a National Theatre on a permanent basis, making due provision for a pension fund, we believe that a sum, con-siderably in excess of £500,000, or even £1,000,000, would be neces-sary and that even then, there would be considerable uncertainty as to the permanent establishment of such a pension fund.

We consider secondly that the scheme for the administration of the Shakespeare National Theatre, as set out in the report of the Executive Committee of March 1909, is cumbrous and unpractical to the last degree. The system by a which a theatre is to be managed by such a multiplicity of authorities, as a body of Governors, highly academic in character, a Standing Committee, a Director, a Treasurer, and Literary Manager, can, we think, lead only to confusion and must prove ultimately to be unworkable. No theatre can be run efficiently on such lines as these.

Whilst we recognize the good intention of those responsible for the present scheme, we hold that its success is greatly endangered by

93

idealism, and by lack of that practical foresight which can only create a National Theatre in any sense material, moral, intellectual, or social, belonging to the people.

In conclusion, we hold very strongly that no precaution can be too great to ensure such a scheme as this against possible failure, which would not only be grievously disappointing to the subscribers to the scheme, but most damaging to the dignity of dramatic art in this country.

This letter has been approved by the following members of our profession:

Sir Squire Bancroft	Mr. Lewis Waller
Sir Charles Wyndham	Mr. Arthur Bourchier
Mr. W. H. Kendal	Mr. Weedon Grossmith
Mr. Edward Terry	Mr. H. B. Irving
Mr. Charles Hawtrey	Mr. Seymour Hicks
Mr. Cyril Maude	Mr. Herbert Sleath
Mr. Fred Terry	

Efforts seem to have been made to get further signatures; e.g., on 4th December 1909 Arthur Bourchier was writing to Sir Arthur Pinero:

MY DEAR PINERO,

While feeling very strongly that some sort of protest ought to be made against the present National Theatre scheme, for reasons set out in the enclosed letter, the endorsers of it are aware of the inclusion of your name on the Executive Committee of the scheme. While anxious to dissociate themselves from it in the public eye, they are very loth to do so without your concurrence. I therefore enclose you a copy of the proposed letter in the hope that you may be induced to sign it.

Yours very truly,

ARTHUR BOURCHIER

But Pinero stuck by his guns, and this particular antagonism seen petered out. As for the S.M.N.T. committee, they paid little attention to it; or to subsequent criticisms which were made from time to time. This may seem a high-handed attitude, but in cases of this kind it is often better to note objections, and if need be profit by them, but to refuse to enter into a barren controversy which only exacerbates the cleavage. The Committee, indeed, was much too busy following up the favourable impression that had been created by the Mansion House meeting to be led away into side issues. An appeal office was rented in Whitehall, and for the next two years the Secretary, Mr. Philip Carr (at that time dramatic critic of the *Daily News*, and later the London theatre correspondent of the *Manchester Guardian*), was very active in arranging, with a band of willing helpers, a series of 'events' which served to carry the idea of a National Theatre to the world of society, and to many of the general public who till then had never so much as heard of it. The Lord Mayor's Show of 1910 had Shakespeare and the Elizabethan stage for its chief motif; a Shakespeare Pageant was held at Knowle, both organized by Mr. Carr, while that famous leader of Edwardian fashion, Mrs. George Cornwallis West, promoted a glittering Shakespeare Ball at the Royal Albert Hall, which was the high-light of a London season. This lady was also the moving spirit of the Shakespeare Exhibition at Earl's Court in 1911. Here a replica of the old Globe Theatre was erected, where Shakespearian plays were acted under the direction of Patrick Kirwin. The present writer well remembers the excitement of sitting on a wooden bench in one of the shallow galleries, fascinated not only by the play itself but by the orange-girls and brawling hangers-on who lounged about the pit of the theatre, doing comic turns from time to time, all in contemporary costume. Hopes were entertained that the Play-house would be re-erected somewhere else at the close of the Exhibition as a permanent reminder of the great days, and as a fulfilment of the ideals of William Poel. But, alas, it was only a gimcrack affair of lath and plaster, nor had the response of the Earl's Court public been too encouraging. They preferred the side-shows and the illuminated carnivals, and the attractions of the Welcome Club.

More permanent in its effect on the popular mind, and truly the most startlingly original plea for a National Theatre ever made, was the one-act play written by Mr. Bernard Shaw at the instigation of Mrs. Alfred Lyttelton, and presented for the first time at the Haymarket Theatre on the afternoon of Thursday, 24th November 1910, under the title of *The Dark Lady of the Sonnets*. Repeated every so often on every kind of stage, both professional and amateur, and later to be broadcast, this brilliant *piéce d'occasion* obtruded on the notice of the general public the basic claims of a National Theatre as nothing else could.

Most of my readers will recall the ingenious story of the play, which tells of the consequences of a midnight tryst on the terrace of the Royal Palace at Whitehall between Shakespeare and the Dark Lady, here identified with Mary Fitton. Before the Dark Lady arrives, Shakespeare becomes aware of a heavily cloaked female, walking in her sleep like another Lady Macbeth and uttering strange words. Mistaking her in the darkness for his beloved, the poet approaches her amorously, nor does the lady shun his advances; but when it comes to an attempted embrace, she scornfully rebuffs him. Entering at that moment to keep her tryst, the real Mary Fitton is outraged by her lover's apparent infidelity. After fisticuffs all round, Shakespeare ignominiously topples over, while the cloaked lady reveals herself as no less a personage than the Virgin Queen. Consternation all round. But discomforted as he is, Shakespeare recovers his balance, and soon regains the initiative. With disarming effrontery he overwhelms the Queen with flattery, and turns the subject, as it were, by an eloquent plea for a 'boon of state'.

ELIZABETH. You have an overweening conceit of yourself, sir, that displeases your Queen.

SHAKESPEARE. Oh, madam, can I go about with the modest cough of a minor poet, belittling my inspiration and making the mightiest wonder of your reign a thing of nought? I have said that 'not marble nor the gilded monuments of princes shall outlive' the words with which I make the world glorious or foolish at my will. Besides, I would have you think me great enough to grant me a boon.

ELIZABETH. I hope it is a boon that may be asked of a virgin Queen without offence, sir. I mistrust your forwardness; and I bid you remember that I do not suffer persons of your degree (if I may say so without offence to your father the alderman) to presume too far.

SHAKESPEARE. Oh, madam, I shall not forget myself again; though by my life, could I make you a serving wench, neither a queen nor a virgin should you be for so much longer as a flash of lightning might take to cross the river to the Bankside. But since you are a queen and will none of me, nor of Philip of Spain, nor of any other mortal man, I must e'en contain myself as best I may, and ask you only for a boon of State.

ELIZABETH. A boon of State already! You are becoming a courtier like the rest of them. You lack advancement.

SHAKESPEARE. 'Lack advancement.' By your Majesty's leave: a queenly phrase. [*He is about to write it down.*]

ELIZABETH. [*striking the tablets from his hand*] Your tables begin to anger me, sir. I am not here to write your plays for you.

SHAKESPEARE. You are here to inspire them, madam. For this, among the rest, were you ordained. But the boon I crave is that you do endow a great playhouse, or, if I may make bold to coin a scholarly name for it, a National Theatre, for the better instruction and gracing of your Majesty's subjects.

ELIZABETH. Why, sir, are there not theatres enow on the Bankside and in Blackfriars?

SHAKESPEARE. Madam: these are the adventures of needy and desperate men that must, to save themselves from perishing of want, give the sillier sort of people what they best like; and what they best like, God knows, is not their own betterment and instruction, as we well see by the example of the churches, which must needs compel men to frequent them, though they be open to all without charge. Only when there is a matter of a murder, or a plot, or a pretty youth in petticoats, or some naughty tale of wantonness, will your subjects pay the great cost of good players and their finery, with a little profit to boot. To prove this I will tell you that I have written two noble and excellent plays setting forth the advancement of women of high nature and fruitful industry even as yourMajesty is: the one a skilful physician, the other a sister devoted to good works. I have also stole from a book of idle wanton tales two of the most damnable foolishnesses in the world, in the one of which a woman goeth in man's attire and maketh impudent love to her swain, who pleaseth the groundlings by over-throwing a wrestler; whilst, in the other, one of the same kidney sheweth her wit by saying endless naughtinesses to a gentleman as lewd as herself. I have writ these to save my friends from penury, yet shewing my scorn for such follies and for them that praise them by calling the one As You Like It, meaing that it is not as *I* like it, and the other Much Ado About Nothing, as it truly is. And now these two filthy pieces drive their nobler fellows from the stage, where indeed I cannot have my lady physician presented at all, she being too honest a woman for the taste of the town. Wherefore I humbly beg your Majesty to give order that a theatre be endowed out of the public revenue for the playing of those pieces of mine which no merchant will touch, seeing that his gain is so much greater with the worse than with the better. Thereby you shall also encourage other men to undertake the writing of plays who do now despise it and leave it wholly to those whose counsels will work little good to your realm. For this writing of plays is a great matter, forming as it does the minds and affections of men in such sort that whatsoever they see done in show on the stage, they will presently be doing in earnest in the world, which is but a larger stage. Of late, as you know, the Church taught the people by means of plays; but the people flocked only to such as were full of superstitious miracles and bloody martyrdoms; and so the Church, which also was just then brought into straits by the policy of your royal father, did abandon and discountenance the art of playing; and thus it fell into the hands of poor players and greedy merchants that had their pockets to look to and not the greatness of this your kingdom. Therefore now must your Majesty take up that good work that your Church hath abandoned, and restore the art of playing to its former use and dignity.

ELIZABETH. Master Shakespeare: I will speak of this matter to the Lord Treasurer.

SHAKESPEARE. Then am I undone, madam; for there was never yet a Lord Treasurer that could find a penny for anything over and above the necessary expenses of your government, save for a war or a salary for his own nephew.

ELIZABETH. Master Shakespeare: you speak sooth; yet cannot I in any wise mend it. I dare not offend my unruly Puritans by making so lewd a place as the playhouse a public charge; and there be a thousand things to be done in this London of mine before your poetry can have its penny from the general purse. I tell thee, Master Will, it will be three hundred years and more before my subjects learn that man cannot live by bread alone, but by every word that cometh from the mouth of those whom God inspires. By that time you and I will be dust beneath the feet of the horses, if indeed there be any horses then, and men be still riding instead of flying. Now it may be that by then your works will be dust also.

SHAKESPEARE. They will stand, madam: fear not for that.

ELIZABETH. It may prove so. But of this I am certain (for I know my countrymen) that until every other country in the Christian world, even to barbarian Muscovy and the hamlets of the boorish Germans, have its playhouse at the public charge, England will never adventure. And she will adventure then only because it is her desire to be ever in the fashion, and to do humbly and dutifully whatso she seeth everybody else doing. In the meantime you must content yourself as best you can by the playing of those two pieces which you give out as the most damnable ever writ, but which your countrymen, I warn you, will swear are the best you have ever done. But this I will say, that if I could speak across the ages to our descendants, I should heartily recommend them to fulfil your wish; for the Scottish minstrel hath well said that he that maketh the songs of a nation is mightier than he that maketh its laws; and the same may well be true of plays and interludes. [*The clock chimes the first quarter. The warder returns on his round.*] And now, sir, we are upon the hour when it better beseems a virgin queen to be abed than to converse alone with the naughtiest of her subjects. Ho there! Who keeps ward on the queen's lodgings to-night?

THE WARDER. I do, an't please your majesty.

ELIZABETH. See that you keep it better in future. You have let pass a most dangerous gallant even to the very door of our royal chamber. Lead him forth; and bring me word when he is safely locked out; for I shall scarce dare disrobe until the palace gates are between us.

SHAKESPEARE [*kissing her hand*]. My body goes through the gate into the darkness, madam; but my thoughts follow you.

ELIZABETH. How! to my bed!

SHAKESPEARE. No, madam, to your prayers, in which I beg you to remember my theatre.

ELIZABETH. That is my prayer to posterity. Forget not your own to God; and so good night, Master Will.

SHAKESPEARE. Good night, great Elizabeth. God save the Queen!

ELIZABETH. Amen.

Exeunt severally: she to her chamber: he, in custody of the warder, to the gate nearest Blackfriars.

Inspired maybe by these challenging sentiments, or rendered desperate by the comparative failure of their appeal for funds, the Committee was now tempted to reconsider its early policy of abstaining from any direct appeal to the Government. Hitherto they had taken the line that the time for that would come, if ever, when there was greater evidence that the public really wanted a National Theatre and had shown themselves ready to back their desire by widespread and substantial contributions. But now the need was urgent, if even so much as the foundation stone of the theatre was to be laid in time for the Tercentenary. The Committee therefore decided to test the opinion of the House of Commons on the general principle of State Aid; and this debate actually took place on a private member's bill on St. George's Day, the 23rd April 1913. It was opened by Mr. H. J. MacKinder, who moved the Resolution '*That in the opinion of this House there shall be established a National Theatre, to be vested in trustees and assisted by the State, for the performance of the plays of Shakespeare and other dramas of recognized merit.*'

This is a fair Spring afternoon [he continued], and for the purpose in view we could hardly have a fairer, because, as the newspapers have been pointing out, it is the traditional anniversary of the birth and death of Shakespeare. We who have taken some interest in this momentous undertaking are thinking more of this day three years hence than we are of to-day. This day three years hence there will be celebrated a festival throughout a large part of the civilized world—the tercentenary of the death of Shakespeare, which festival, if we play our part in it, as I hope we shall do, may be utilized for the purpose of peace in the world. Along with everyone else I have long been aware that the name of Shakespeare is great, not only in English literature but in German. But I confess until I came to think over what I shall say this evening, and to review the facts as they stand at the moment, I had no idea of the depth and breadth of the influence of Shakespeare, and therefore of our country, in the literature in which the German youth is brought up. I hold in my hands advance sheets of the *Shakespeare Jahrbuch*, and in this volume shortly to be published, there will appear statistics which, from more than one point of view, are worth recording. To take the first typical example, I find that *Hamlet* was performed in the year 1912, 148 times by no fewer than 52 theatrical companies, an average of about three times for each company; *The Merchant of Venice* 141 times by 57 companies; *A Midsummer Night's Dream* 124 times by 38 companies; *Othello* 119 times by 59 companies, and so on. The total may be summarized thus: There were 178 separate theatrical companies who performed 21 of Shakespeare's plays on 1,156 occasions. That is in a single year; and having looked through the list, I can vouch for it that these numbers are not made up by taking into account the performances of amateur companies, but that in the vast majority of cases we are dealing either with municipal or State theatres.

There are two or three things remarkable in that list. In the first place, of course, there is the enormous influence of our poet in Germany, and the reality of the homage which will be paid to this nation —the nation of Shakespeare—three years hence, and also for the purpose of this evening there is the very pertinent fact that these performances were not long runs, but were performances in repertory theatres to the number of approximately 180. I venture to think that we have nothing in this land of Shakespeare to show which is comparable in the least degree to the facts indicated by these figures.

The speaker then went on to point the moral, to quote the, by now, inevitable words of Matthew Arnold, and to give a brief résumé of the history and present position of the S.M.N.T. movement: More recently, he said, the L.C.C. had again been approached for a site, and among those who signed the appeal was even, I believe, the present Chancellor of the Exchequer and the present First Lord of the Admiralty. The idea was that the site of the present offices of the L.C.C. in Spring Gardens should be devoted to the purpose, when on completion of its new building on the far side of the river, the County Council should migrate from its present offices. The County Council were quite willing that this should be the destiny of the site. The land belongs to the Crown, and I believe there are somewhat complicated conditions in connection with it, and owing to the difficulties involved, I understand that the Crown could not see its way to extend the duration of the lease. It was felt that to place a great national monument on anything short of a freehold site would be a mistake.

There has been some criticism with regard to the delay which has occurred. That delay has been in a large measure advised, because it has been felt that it would be foolish to make any approach until conditions were such as to make probable the success of the approach. It was felt that above all two things were necessary: on the one hand that a site should be in existence which could be pointed out to the donor; and on the other hand—a feeling that had strengthened of late —that there should be some support, recognition and sympathy from the Government of the country.

We have at the present time, admittedly, increased the leisure of vast masses of people. Moreover, you have at the present time, as all will admit, an increasing monotony of employment. Machinery, mechanical operations, division of labour have brought that about. The result is that men are having less and less interest in the daily work by which they earn their bread, and they are driven to look for intellectual interest outside. I believe the immense vogue of football, and in our long evenings of drama, is a natural and healthy result of that condition of things. Provided that the leisure is well used, I am not at all sure that it is not in the long run a matter making for higher civilization that we should be able to earn the necessary living by less consumption of the higher powers of the mind, and that we should be able to devote to the higher things which we have had handed down to us from the Greeks, an increased portion of time not only of the few but of the great mass. There is just another point in regard to the general position to which I would like to refer. It is that, admittedly, the character of our education is changing. If I may put it shortly, there is a revolt against the excessive use of books. There is a demand for more concrete life in the teaching which we give, whether to children, adolescents, or adults. In science, long ago, students turned to the laboratory, and away from the mere book. So it should be in literature. After all, a composition was originally intended to be *delivered*, even poetry, certainly the drama. What we want is education through our Shakespeare, and that we are seeking through our national theatre, and not mere amusement as a spectacle.

An Amendment is to be moved by the Hon. Member for Clare [Mr. Lynch]. I am not in the least antagonistic to the idea which I believe is contained in that Amendment. The only thing I have to say is that it seems to me that for the esoteric drama, for the drama which must necessarily be in advance of its time, there should be some appropriate stage, but it can hardly be a national stage. For this reason, although I sympathise with the Hon. Member's aims, I believe that his Amendment does not in the least traverse the case which we put forward for a National Theatre. Our idea is that a theatre of this kind should be popular and educational, that you should allow schools opportunities for attending *en masse*, and to form the whole audience on occasion.

From the imperial point of view I believe that it is necessary for another reason, and that is that our language is in danger of breaking into dialects. We live at great distances from each other, in Australia, in South Africa, in America, and here in this land. If we wish to retain a language which shall be, when spoken, and not merely when written, a national one, then we must have a standard for that language, and where better than in a National and Imperial Theatre, in a central position which might be visited, and would be visited, by the vast mass of Americans or Provincials, or of men from the Dominions who visit this country.

I do not believe that a National Theatre would have any evil influence on dramatic enterprise of a private character. This would be a school for Drama. There would be no great salaries for stars of the first order. The experience of the Théâtre Français is that when an artist has obtained a certain celebrity, a certain power in his or her art—has obtained, so to speak, a certain monopoly value—as often as not, as the great Sarah Bernhardt did, he or she will migrate, and become a star or central celebrity for a rival theatre.

This is a case in which, like so many others, if you cast your bread upon the waters you will find it again. Why do we trust not to the small private donor, not to the mass of small subscriptions, but to State aid? I hope I need not argue the question that endowment is necessary if you are to have anything in the way of such a theatre as I have been describing. The effort has been made again and again in this country to run a great repertory theatre, but notwithstanding the enterprise, notwithstanding the losses incurred and accepted by those who initiated it, we cannot agree that we have anything at the present time approaching the theatre at which we aim, or even the theatre which has been realized in France and in Germany. The sum of £500,000 has been put as the coast of such a theatre—£250,000 to bring in the £10,000 a year subsidy which has been found necessary in the case both of the Théâtre Français, and of the Court Theatre in Berlin; £100,000 as the cost of the site, and £50,000 for the equipment. I imagine that the site and the building may quite probably cost more. I am quite certain that the equipment would cost more.

Therefore we believe that as in other countries, there must be some sharing between the private donor and the State, and we ask that the State should do something in the way of an annual subvention to meet what I believe would be, if the subvention were once promised under certain conditions, the magnificent generosity which would be called out, not only in this country, but in the Dominions and probably in foreign countries, in connection with the tercentenary three years hence. We make grants for Universities, and those grants are met by the fees from students. Why should we not make a grant for what we regard as a school for literature which shall be met by payments for entrance in order to see presented great works? That you place the State in competition with private enterprise is nothing new. You already build some of your battleships in Government dockyards. You even exchange your instructors between the national dockyards and private dockyards. And so it might be with your actors.

In conclusion, I believe that a small grant made by the State would have the effect, in not a long term of years, of stimulating drama throughout the country by, in the first place, cultivating the public, in the second place by training actors, and in the third place by holding up a high standard. I believe that these are functions in which the State may legitimately take the lead, and with that object I have brought forward the Motion which I now beg to move.

MR. NEILSON, in seconding the resolution, said that now the matter had been brought to the floor of the House of Commons, he sincerely hoped that if the Government were going to give it their blessing, they would do so, because it was a great big scheme that would inspire enthusiasm all over the land. I can imagine a National Drama House, he continued, not tucked away in a corner of some place in the crowded centre, but where there is plenty of air and space round it, such as you see at Wiesbaden. I should like the house itself to be an architectural monument, not only to Shakespeare, but in some form to nationalistic architecture here. I should like the stage to be of such a nature that people all over the country would be interested in it, not only in the mechanism of the stage itself, but in the productions which, having such a stage, could be put before the public. There is no doubt that the stage of Buda-Pesth is spoken of in many little country towns. The people discuss it and its mechanism, and when they come to Buda-Pesth they like to go to the national opera house to see the Asphale system in operation. This system is one of hydraulics.

TOGETHER WE STAND

The stage is raised by hydraulics 20 feet above and 20 feet below the level of the auditorium; it is in many sections, and can be thrown into any position in which they wish to mount the drama.

I believe that the lighting of a theatre can call forth enthusiasm in people. There, the whole of the lights on the stage can be worked from a machine no larger than a typewriter, and the man working the machine can be in full view of the stage all the time without being seen by the audience. Scenery can inspire enthusiasm. I believe that when a new drama is read in the perfectly organized system in Germany, Austria, or Hungary, every person that is interested in the production and the performance of that play is called to the first reading—the man who makes the shoes, the man that makes the wigs, the man that makes the armour; not only the actors and actresses, but the man who is attending to the lighting, the man who paints the scenes—everybody is there to begin with. That can only be done when you have a National House. In the equipment of such a theatre, I do not suppose that we should for some time reach the stage that exists in Germany, where there are 21 plays of Shakespeare in the season. An attempt could be made to do ten, if you had a national theatre on a small scale. Even then, before the production on the first night, you would need special rehearsal, special valet rooms, special staging rooms. All that has to be done apart from the stage itself. You would have to have special painting rooms so that the work could be expedited by the scenic artists. What I mean by just giving the house these one or two details is to show the necessity of looking forward to a National Drama House on a big scale; on such a scale, indeed, that we should be proud of it.

Besides Shakespeare, there are other plays that I want to see done. Marlowe, Beaumont and Fletcher, *The Blot on the Escutcheon*, a great play, Synge. Beside that, I do not want to see *Becket* fall into oblivion and never be heard of again. Those managers are passing away to-day who, like Sir Henry Irving, brought poetry into his house, and gave the poets of his day as fine a production as he did for Shakespeare. I feel deeply on this question; my heart has been in it for a long time, and I sincerely hope that those who to-night lay their case before the Government will not hesitate to ask for a lot. Let us do things as befits this great Empire which we mouth so much about. Do not let us have our House compared to some House in Germany like Stuttgart or Wiesbaden. Let it be a British House of which the United Kingdom can be proud, and in the words of the Mover of the Amendment, let it be a House that will speak to Canada, South Africa, and the Antipodes.

MR. LYNCH. We have listened to two interesting and eloquent speeches, but I am inclined to think that the manner in which this object is sought to be carried out will be greatly detrimental to the best interests of the drama in this country. The same project has been tried out in other countries—France, Italy, Spain, and elsewhere—and I believe only in France has it been an undoubted success, and there it has been a success for many reasons which do not pertain to this country. You can hold up to us no greater warning that this Berlin system, and this desire to Prussianize our institutions. The Schauspielhaus is one of the innumerable ways of glorifying that stupendous Prussian system. Who are the Berlin dramatists? Where is their great national drama? Where is their great inspiring work? Why, their best plays are all adaptations from the French, and when they do adapt plays from French authors they invariably choose second-rate writers. The attempt to establish a National Theatre in Spain almost killed the national genius of Spain in this respect, which afterwards found such extraordinary expression in the works of Lope de Vega and Cervantes. I join issue with what has been said in regard to Shakespeare, for this reason, that if such a national theatre had been in existence in Shakespeare's time, I doubt if he would have had a chance of being represented. All through his wonderfully interesting sonnets one finds a complaint about the low esteem in which he was held by the great patrons of his own time. I have seen great representations of Shakespeare's plays, and if I were to make a confession I would say perhaps that at no other plays have I been so unutterably bored. The fault was not with Shakespeare, but it was due to the travesty of Shakespeare which is generally given.

My objection, however, has a deeper base. Certainly I approach Shakespeare's name with veneration, and I am inclined to agree with Byron:

> *I beg his British Godship's humble pardon,*
> *If in my extremity of rhyme's distress*
> *I touch a single leaf where he is warden.*

But after all, I owe allegiance to something greater than Shakespeare, something more real and actual, and that is my aspiration for the free development of literature. I doubt whether Shakespeare is a great model for the literature of the time to come. All through Shakespeare there is in the construction of his plays the fairy-tale model. Shakespeare was not a man greatly alert to the more modern influences even of his own time, and so far from being the great eponym and governor of English literature for time to come, he was rather the closure and apotheosis of the feudal system, which he did so much to glorify. Therefore I think that Shakespeare is a bad model for a great National Theatre for the years to come. Then, proceeding from Shakespeare, what representatives have we, and how could a National Theatre foster them? There is something in organization alien to what is the very spirit and essence of literature; and taking the example of our Universities, I would ask: can any man point out any great writer in the English language who has been a real and veritable product of our Universities? [Hon. Members: 'Tennyson'.] Well, yes, I have a prejudice against Tennyson perhaps on that very account, but I am quite content to give you a present of Tennyson. I had drafted an Amendment to the Motion, but I do not propose to move it so as to keep the debate within the limits of the Motion, because I am doubtful still whether I am wholly opposed to the spirit of the Motion. I believe if this National Theatre could be removed from a certain type of Trustee, it might possess many valuable points—the dry-as-dust trustee, the Trustee educated too much in book-keeping, the Trustee attaching too much importance to the University, or the Trustee holding up Tennyson as a great national poet. If he were a trustee of flesh and blood, or a trustee endowed with some of the spirit of Robert Burns, if that were possible, if he were a trustee who could look upon all our institutions with a candid eye and touch them fearlessly with a little rod of light, then the National Theatre might be saved. What I fear is that this subject so pompously introduced—I mean, with such pomp and circumstance—will be somewhat too pompously managed, and will not encourage what is really vivid and true in the literature of to-day; and literature is moribund unless it takes its interest and stimulus from actual life, life more complex, more various, more instinct with quick, vivid feeling than that of Shakespeare's day. I fear that genius such as we want to encourage will not be discovered and encouraged by this project, but will rather be frowned upon, and a man will have his dramatic genius crushed out by another dead weight added to the *vis inertiae* of our society. If it were possible to appoint a trustee such as I have indicated, who would make it his business actively to search for genius and encourage it, then we might have a theatre which would give a soul to the nation, which would lead its aspirations, and point its destiny.

SIR WILLIAM ANSON. I hope the Government will give very serious attention to this Motion. It is very easy to describe this thing as a great measure of social regeneration. On the other hand, it is easy to minimize it and regard it as a dilettante proposal. I venture to put before the Under-Secretary the suggestion that this really is a practical measure for the improvement of the drama, and for the creation of a high standard of the drama and the performance of it. The Hon. Member who has just spoken seems to consider that the result of any such proposal would be to crush out all new merit, and that even Shakespeare, who had great difficulties of his own, in spite of which he managed to get his plays acted, with the result that they survived, would have found greater difficulty nowadays. But I take it that it would be the business of those responsible to seek out signs of dramatic merit wherever it presented itself, and to take care that it had its opportunity under the best possible conditions. The primary desire of those who support this scheme is to secure that we should get continuous representation of our great national dramatist Shakespeare. But not only Shakespeare, for the scheme is designed, if I understand the promoters rightly, to afford the opportunity for the revival of other good plays which have lost their popularity for the time being.

Nobody can say at this moment that a dramatic standard is presented to the public. We have the melodrama, a most entertaining performance; we have the musical comedy, which begins with some semblance of a plot and ends in a romp; and we have a type of drama, which I have been to see once or twice, admirably acted, in which a number of dreary-looking persons in a very ill-furnished room say unpleasant things to one another during three acts, at the end of which time everyone is unhappy and nothing else has happened. I confess that this style of drama seems to be somewhat attractive at the present time and there is some hope on the part of those who have had the misfortune to witness it that some more cheerful performance, in which human action is presented in a more favourable light and with more vivid results, may be presented in this theatre.

MR. ELLIS GRIFFITH. I have no right to speak in the literary tone of the Gentlemen who have hitherto addressed the House. I must speak from the lower level, but perhaps one which will be easily understood. The real meaning of the Resolution is this, shall there be or shall there not be a recognition of the theatre by the State as a matter of vital national concern? The appeal for which the Hon. Gentleman, amongst others, is responsible, is £100,000 for a site, £150,000 for the building and equipment, and another £250,000 for endowment purposes. These are big figures, and although there has been at any rate one very beneficent contribution, all the subscriptions up to now amount to about £100,000. That is to say, a fifth of the capital required has been voluntarily subscribed. As I understand it, the position put by those who support the Resolution is that State recognition and endowment of drama is justified in the same sense as the State recognition and endowment of music, painting, and sculpture in the Universities, and other institutions of a similar character. As I understand it, they put their case a little higher than that, and in this I think they are right, because the drama is more intimately connected with the everyday life of the citizens of this country than either music or painting or sculpture could possibly be. It has been said that if you had this national theatre there would be a revival of the most characteristic English drama that cannot possibly be produced now because the people do not want it. As I understand it, the national theatre is to produce plays to which, if they were produced by private enterprise, no one would go.

MR. MACKINDER. Let me point out the difference. You would not get people to go to a long run, and many of the best things you cannot, as a commercial speculation, produce on short runs.

MR. ELLIS GRIFFITH. I think in the long run it comes to the same thing. I quite recognize the hon. Member's point. In order that private enterprise may succeed, you must have a certain duration of a play, and although it might last for a week, which would exhaust the people of culture for which the hon. Member acts, still you cannot in private enterprise produce only for people of culture. That is the difficulty. I also wish to remaind him that they must recognize one thing: they are in a minority. Under these circumstances, if the Government is asked to support a theatre which is to produce plays which, if produced by private enterprise, would not be successful, it requires a little caution—I put it no higher than that—when we propose to spend public money upon this kind of work. It is quite true that a small country like Denmark has, I think, £20,000 a year for its national theatre; but, on the other hand, there is a precedent in New York

which has not been mentioned to-night. In 1904 a new theatre was
built under the auspices of some millionaires. They only gave money,
I understand, and not advice; therefore all their influence was for good.
The new theatre was opened and a play was produced there, and it
went on for two seasons with a varied programme, and there were
often enormous losses—enormous to the ordinary man, not to
millionaires, but the enterprise was abandoned and the theatre was
given over to public spectacles. The reason was, of course, that the
general public had not been educated and were not prepared for this
cultural representation, which was given in the new theatre. The hon.
Gentleman rather admits that the public of this country are not educated up to that level any more than himself. It would, I think, be
rather a serious risk to run to produce these plays for the General Public.
Money and equipment and all that are not enough, because you must
have at the back of a movement of this kind an interested, educated,
and enthusiastic public opinion.

It is perfectly well known that the Members of this Government are
not so well acquainted with theatrical affairs as to be able to speak
with authority on the subject raised in the debate. Speaking for myself,
I would say that there are cases in which the House can give guidance
to the Government, and this is one of them. I am rather inclined to
accept what was said by the Mover of the Motion, when he stated that
the duty of the Government was not to initiate but to crown a project
of this kind. The time for crowning has not come. The hon. Member
admitted that only £100,000 out of £500,000 had been subscribed
voluntarily. I think the hon. Member, on consideration, would agree
that until at any rate, by far the greater part of the £500,000 has been
subscribed voluntarily, the time for crowning has not arrived. That
is the view which I take. When the project is matured, when the site
about which negotiations have been going on is obtained, when the
building is erected, when the theatre is equipped, and when it has a
reasonable endowment, I think that then the time for crowning the
movement will very nearly have been reached. I think that then
the time will have come for asking the Government to take into consideration the view it should take in regard to this Motion. But I must
say this: If and when a contribution is made by the State to a project
of this kind, the contribution when made should be in the form not of
a capital grant but of an annual subsidy, I think that this is the form
which would commend itself to all sections of the House. We look to

the House for guidance, and I now ask the House to take whatever view it pleases, and let us know the result.

SIR FRANK BANBURY opposed the Motion mainly on economic grounds. I am very fond of the theatre, he admitted, when the Government give me an opportunity to attend it, which is not often; but I think we should reach the limit of extravagance and foolishness if, with an expenditure of £195,000,000 a year, instead of thinking how we can retrench, we spend more money in this direction. For nearly two thousand years—and very much longer before that—this country has been in existence without a National Theatre. Would it not be advisable to go on for a little longer in the state in which we have been for so many years?

MR. PONSONBY. I want to say a very few words in favour of this Motion. Education, as I understand it, is chiefly valuable for teaching people how to employ their leisure. An enormous number of people now go to the theatre. I have had experience of the State-endowed theatre in France, Germany, and Denmark, and in all these cases I must say it has a most beneficial influence. I sympathize with the Member who spoke from the Nationalist benches when he expressed the fear that the State Theatre might be utilized for merely archaeological purposes —for unearthing the old classics, and not encouraging modern plays. I should be the last to encourage any scheme that was directed to this end. I think it is of the utmost importance that modern drama should be supported, and it is only by a State-endowed theatre that you can adequately support it. We have lately seen attempts made in London to support the best modern dramatists. These attempts have generally failed. A repertory theatre was started not long ago. The result of that repertory theatre was that there was a conflict between art and commerce. Unless the play paid it could not be put on a long enough time for the public really to enjoy it.

SIR F. BANBURY. Perhaps the public did not want it.

MR. PONSONBY. It does not always follow that because the public do not go to a play for a few weeks, that in the long run they will not come round and appreciate that particular play. If there is sufficient money to give the play a long enough trial the public will come round and appreciate it. We have seen a very good instance in the attempt at a repertory theatre by Mr. Granville Barker. We know that he has produced plays which in the ordinary commercial run would never have seen the light, and has educated the public; but I should say he often found considerable difficulty in making both ends meet, because he always had to find plays that may be beyond the public taste, or plays which in some way or other do not draw large audiences. The result is that efforts of that sort are continually failing, and I feel sure that without State support you cannot encourage modern dramatists, and therefore you cannot educate the public taste properly. The day is past, I think, when the arts are merely looked upon as trivial and frivolous adjuncts to our ordinary life. The arts have come to be part and parcel of our ordinary lives, and nobody's education is complete without the arts. It is time in this country that we should have a Minister of Fine Arts, who should be responsible for pictorial art, for music, and for the drama.

SIR F. BANBURY. May I ask the hon. Member where the money for all this is to come from?

MR. PONSONBY. The money for the endowment of the arts of this country could be easily produced.

SIR F. BANBURY. Where from?

MR. PONSONBY. From the Treasury. It is perfectly ridiculous to say that a country spending £195,000,000 on various subjects cannot spare £200,000 to endow what I consider one of the most important branches of our public life, namely, the encouragement of our arts, and I shall support this Motion most cordially.

MR. BOOTH raised the question of the propriety of bringing forward such a motion as the present one which totally ignored Scotland and Ireland. Whom do you wish to attract to this theatre? he continued. Is it the poor? I have heard no suggestion that the money is to be used to bring the priceless gems of literature within the reach of the poor. As far as I can make out, the idea is rather to pamper the intellectuals who can well afford to pay for their own theatres. The expenses of the theatre largely arise from the scenery that is used. What has been the characteristic of recent productions of Shakespeare? Simply gorgeous scenery and expensive panoramas passing before our eyes. The hon. Member says he wants to change that, but he will not change it by a State-subsidized theatre. That would encourage it. He would change it by cheap production, cheap because there is an absence of expensive machinery. The Chinese can give us a lesson in this. I do not know whether hon. Members have been to the National Theatre in China. I have been privileged to attend a dramatic representation in China by one who has been called the Henry Irving of China . . .

MR. MACKINDER rose in his place, and claimed 'That the question be now put', but Mr. Speaker withheld his assent and declined to put that question.

MR. BOOTH. That actor had not any elaborate scenery. In fact, children were playing and people were drinking cups of tea within a few feet of where the actors played. If there is anything in the dramatic force and the intense power of an actor with a message, he is able to give that message without the adventitious aid of expensive scenery. If the object is to get back to good literature and to our great dramatists, it is not to be done by expensive machinery and employing an army of scene shifters. It is suggested that only the plays of Shakespeare and melodramas of recognized merit should be performed in this National Theatre, and I want to ask: what are the dramas of recognized merit?

MR. MACKINDER rose in his place to move, 'That the Question be now put.'

Question put.

The House divided: Ayes (among whom were Stanley Baldwin, J. R. Clynes and William Crookes), 162. Noes, 32.

Whereupon MR. SPEAKER declared that the Question was not decided in the affirmative, because it was not supported by the majority prescribed by Standing Order No. 27.

The next event which demands our attention followed an opportunity which occurred in the autumn of 1913 to acquire a site which in some respects seemed highly suitable for the building of the Theatre. True, it was some way from 'the magic circle of the West End', but it was situated in the very heart of the educational quarter in Bloomsbury, immediately behind the British Museum at the corner of Gower Street and Keppel Street, and within a stone's throw of the Royal Academy of Dramatic Art, with the easy implication that the Academy might become in some way attached to the Theatre as a training school. Over an acre of land was available at the moderate cost of £50,000 for the freehold. All things considered it appeared a good 'buy', and the Committee, taking its courage in both hands, acquired the site. Incidentally they believed that this concrete evidence of progress might facilitate the further collection of funds. And so it might, had not all such hopes been dashed first by the imminence and then by the outbreak of the world war.

In August 1914 the S.M.N.T. committee suspended operations, and it was not until 1916 that they bethought them of the vacant site and of the possibility of turning it to patriotic account by lending it to the Y.M.C.A. for the erection of a Shakespeare Hut for the entertainment and social service of the troops.

But even before the end of the war, the purpose of the National Theatre was not quite forgotten, and on 23rd July 1918, at the instance of Sir Israel Gollancz, a conference was held between members of the Executive and other representatives at which it was resolved that, without in any way abandoning the main scheme, the time had come when as an immediate and practical step, it was desirable to organize a special company of players, well trained and of recognized status, to act Shakespeare and other first-rate plays throughout the United Kingdom and in various parts of the Empire. It was further resolved that when the period of the loan of the Bloomsbury site came to an end, the Y.M.C.A. should be permitted to take out a new lease at a rental of £3,000 per annum—the income thus accruing to go towards the expenses of the proposed touring company. In the eyes of the public this was a popular decision, and one which was to bear good fruit. For all that, it was the entry on to a primrose path which was to lead the Committee into all sorts of difficulties, and bid fair to end in the failure of the entire National Theatre scheme as originally conceived.

VI
TRIALS AND ERRORS

For the moment all went merrily enough. In 1919 Sir Frank Benson resigned his leadership of the Shakespeare Company which had for so many years been responsible for the spring and summer seasons at the Stratford Memorial Theatre, and the Governors of that theatre were themselves looking around for a successor. Their choice fell upon Mr. W. Bridges Adams, a young producer who had already won his spurs in London, Liverpool, and elsewhere. The funds of the theatre, however, were much depleted, and it was not surprising that the S.M.N.T. committee in its then mood should have been willing to consider a co-operation with Stratford in founding a new Shakespeare company to fill the gap resulting from Benson's retirement, and incidentally to keep the National Theatre idea in being.

As regards finance [so it was stated in the annual S.M.N.T. report for 1919], during the war about £2,300 has been actually saved in income, and with the help from other sources, the Executive Committee felt justified in guaranteeing the sum of £3,000 towards the formation of a Company under Mr. Bridges Adams, the Company to be charged with the Shakespeare Summer Festival at Stratford-on-Avon. Well nigh on all sides there has been commendation of this effort which was to be in the nature of propaganda work for the National Theatre movement; and certainly so far as public attention being directed towards the movement is concerned, no one can deny that the 'New Shakespeare Company' as it is called, has been successful.

It will be admitted that an integral part of the Shakespeare National

Theatre scheme is the training of a Company, and if under present conditions the Executive Committee have deemed it expedient to start with this living element without abandoning the hope in due course of an adequate Memorial, they are not, it would seem, departing in any way from the object near to the heart of all those concerned.

We deem that by means of a well-trained Company we are paving the way for the realization of the National Theatre Scheme, which can only be attained through the ready enthusiasm of people far and wide, an enthusiasm supported by the necessary practical contribution towards a large sum of money which now more than ever will be required.

Accordingly, the Executive Committee has resolved to secure the continued services of Mr. Bridges Adams and those associated with him for a further period in the first instance till August next year, and they have decided to devote the income accruing from the Y.M.C.A. for one year's rent of the site, towards what they deem to be a most important step forward in the direction of the National Theatre Scheme. They trust that in their efforts to do their best for the Movement they have interpreted aright the wishes of the General Committee and the general body of subscribers.

So, on the 2nd August 1919 the New Shakespeare Company started on its career at the Stratford-on-Avon Summer Festival and produced *The Merry Wives of Windsor, Julius Caesar, The Tempest, A Midsummer Night's Dream*, and *Romeo and Juliet*, with an unqualified success. In December Mr. Bridges Adams revived the Stratford production of *The Merry Wives* with a fresh company for the Christmas season at the Gaiety Theatre, Manchester, by arrangement with Miss Horniman. A profit was made on the actual performances.

The Executive Committee then resolved to make a further guarantee as from October 1919 to August 1920, it being understood that the Shakespeare Joint Committee were arranging for the New Shakespeare Company to carry through the Birthday Festival at Stratford-on-Avon. The Festival opened, accordingly, at Stratford on 19th April 1920, with six new productions: *The Merchant of Venice, Much Ado, The Taming of the Shrew,*

Richard II, Cymbeline, and *Hamlet.* The success was once more a record. At the conclusion of the Festival, the Company proceeded on tour, visiting Malvern, Cardiff, Manchester, and Cheltenham, playing to an excellent average gross weekly return, with only one setback, due to special local circumstances.

The Executive Committee felt justified in making a further guarantee to the Shakespeare Joint Committee in respect of this year's Summer Festival at Stratford-on-Avon, which opened on July 19th with a total repertory of ten plays, including four new productions, *As You Like It, Twelfth Night, King Henry the Fifth,* and *Macbeth.* Records were again broken both for attendances and for the length of the season, six weeks.

In all these productions the policy of the Shakespeare Joint Committee had been consistently carried out by the Director:

(1) The plays were given with quick action, unobtrusive mounting, without mutilations or transpositions, and, as far as possible, without cuts; (2) The star system had been altogether abandoned. Leading parts were shared among the company, the only person starred was 'Shakespeare' himself.

The success of the New Shakespeare Company, under Mr. Bridges Adams's able direction, seemed to warrant the Executive Committee in offering yet a further guarantee to the Shakespeare Joint Committee—£3,000 as from September 1920 to September 1921, with special reference to the coming Stratford Birthday Festival, and this period began with a six weeks' season of matinée performances of *Henry V* at the Strand Theatre, London, during October and November, which performances attracted much favourable attention, and fully demonstrated the desirability, if not the absolute necessity of a London House for the Shakespeare Company, if the aims of those responsible for the movement were to be adequately carried out.

We are now approaching a critical phase in this early post-war period, when the Bloomsbury site was to become untenable, with momentous consequences to the whole movement.

During the present year the Executive Committee, in accordance with the policy approved by the General Committee, has continued to grant to the Shakespeare Joint Committee subsidies derived from the income of the Shakespeare Memorial Fund, for the purpose of the New Shakespeare Company.

The Shakespeare Joint Committee reports that nine Shakespearian Plays and one Old Comedy were produced during the year, viz., *Antony and Cleopatra*, *The Merry Wives of Windsor*, *Macbeth*, *As You Like It*, *A Midsummer Night's Dream*, *King Richard III*, *The Winter's Tale*, *King Henry IV* (Part II), *The Merchant of Venice*, and *The School for Scandal*. The Company undertook the Birthday Festival at the Memorial Theatre, Stratford-on-Avon, lasting four weeks, also the Summer Festival at the same theatre, lasting seven weeks, and a short Provincial Tour of six weeks, visiting Malvern, Cheltenham, Bath, Cardiff, Worcester, and Redditch, making a total of 17 playing weeks for the year. During the Birthday Festival roughly 20,000 people visited the Theatre; during the Summer Festival 28,000. It is estimated that 5,000 persons were present weekly at the Birthday performances and some 4,000 at the Summer Festival. Since August 1919 the New Shakespeare Company has produced 19 plays of Shakespeare.

Sale of the Bloomsbury Site

So far, the financial help granted by the Shakespeare Memorial Committee to the Shakespeare Joint Committee for the new Shakespeare Company has been mainly derived from the annual rent of £3,000 paid by the Y.M.C.A. for the site in Gower Street. In view of the fact that the London County Council has given notice that the licence for the huts on the site must be terminated on 16th February 1922, the Y.M.C.A. has found it necessary to cancel its agreement with us from that date. In view of the circumstances produced by the War, e.g., the increased cost of building and the general scarcity of money, the Committee concluded that it would be impracticable to attempt to erect a theatre on the site upon the scale that had been originally intended. Accordingly, the Executive feels it incumbent to offer the site for sale so as to realize the capital invested therein in 1914 before the War, when it was acquired for the Shakespeare Memorial National Theatre. It was then hoped that the scheme would be carried through on the occasion of the Shakespeare Tercentenary in 1916. The War frustrated these hopes; and present economic conditions make it impossible to find the financial support needed for the adequate building and endowment of the proposed Theatre.

The Executive hopes at no distant date to submit to the General Body its proposals in respect of future policy. The present capital remains intact.

Report dated 23rd November 1922

The Executive Committee, in accordance with the proposal approved by the General Committee, has during the past year confined its subsidy to the Shakespeare Joint Committee, for the New Shakespeare Company, to the year ending June 1st last, though it was found convenient to continue till September 2nd last the representation of the Shakespeare Memorial Committee on the Shakespeare Joint Committee, no further financial responsibility being incurred.

The Shakespeare Joint Committee has already reported that the New Shakespeare Company's Season at the Stratford-on-Avon Birthday Festival was very successful, and that financially the Festival was a record one, the receipts being over £400 better than last year. A short season in Norway, from June 20th to 22nd, on an independent guarantee, proved a great success. The visit of the New Shakespeare Company to Christiania was on the invitation of the Norsk-Engelsk Forening (Norwegian-English Society). The efforts of Mr. Bridges Adams and his Company called forth high commendation from the chief Norwegian critics. The National Theatre, where the performances took place, was crowded on each occasion. At the first performance the Company was honoured by the presence of the King and Queen and leading representatives of the Court, diplomacy, literature, and art. This success was followed up by an equally successful Summer Season at Stratford-on-Avon on a guarantee provided locally.

In accordance with the Statement of the Executive, the site in Gower Street was offered for sale, and in April last was disposed of to the representatives of the Rockefeller Trustees for the sum of £52,000, the conveyance to be completed on 8th January 1923. The School of Hygiene, ultimately to be a constituent institution of the University of London, will in due course be erected on the site.

In view of the resolutions passed at the General Meeting, held on March 23rd last, the Executive has reconsidered the question of future policy, and recommends as follows:

(i) That while re-affirming the proposal to build and endow a National Theatre as the Shakespeare Memorial in London, this Committee resolves (pending the accomplishment of that project) to assist financially out of income approved objects likely to promote the national recognition of Shakespeare; (ii) That the Executive pursue the Scheme for the foundation of a Shakespeare Memorial National Theatre on the scale originally proposed.

As an application of recommendation (i) and as the outcome of the Executive's consideration of resolutions submitted at previous General Meetings, the following proposals are submitted for confirmation by the General Committee:

That whilst the Old Vic. pursues its present policy of making the production of Shakespeare's plays in a practically complete form the characteristic feature of their activity, an Annual Grant of £1,000 for at least three years, be made to the Old Vic.

That a representative of the Shakespeare Memorial Committee not a Governor of the Old Vic., be added to the Executive of the Old Vic., an annual report being made to the General Committee.

In connection with the recommendation (ii), the Executive proposes as follows:

That a Company to be called provisionally the Shakespeare National Theatre Company be forthwith established, and that for this purpose a sum not exceeding £5,000 per annum for three years be provided from the Shakespeare Memorial Fund, such expenditure to be controlled by a special Committee to be appointed by the Executive.

Facilis descensus Averni, and looking back, one can see how readily the entire fund might have been dissipated, of course with the best intentions, in support of enterprises which however worthy in themselves were yet quite alien from the purpose for which the fund had been originally subscribed. It is vain to argue that already valuable propaganda for the National Theatre had resulted from the support of Mr. Bridges Adams's company, or that financial profit might accrue from further performances which could be added to the central fund. Experience teaches that propaganda unaccompanied by deeds is soon forgotten and that financial loss from theatrical performances is just as likely as financial profit. To do the Committee justice I cannot find that this particular bait of profit was ever dangled before their eyes. Yet the worst might well have happened were it not that in the course of completing the sale of the Bloomsbury site the question arose as to whether the Shakespeare Memorial Theatre was in fact a 'Charity', and its finances therefore under the jurisdiction of the Charity Commissioners. In such an event, the Committee were advised that no sale of their freehold property could be effected without the consent of the Commissioners.

Having duly considered the various documents, the Commissioners reported that although, on the whole, they were of opinion that the scheme was 'philanthropic' but not 'charitable' within the meaning of the act, the position was by no means plain. An application was therefore made to the Court to determine the point and to obtain official sanction to the sale of the land. Evidence of the facts was given in an Affidavit by Sir Israel Gollancz, who affirmed the intention of the Committee to carry out the original scheme when that became practicable. All the various handbooks, reports and other documents were brought in as evidence of the committee's plans. As a result the Court decided that the Shakespeare Memorial Trust was indeed a valid 'charity' and that its objects had not failed by reason of the failure hitherto to achieve its primary object. Nevertheless the completion of the sale of the Bloomsbury site was authorized, subject to the consent of the Charity Commissioners. This consent was duly given and the sale completed.

This was not, however, an end to the legal difficulties, for the Charity Commissioners now contended that the funds of the Committee could only be used in connection with the foundation and management of a National Theatre and in no other way, nor in particular, to assist in financing other theatrical concerns. Against this, the Committee contended that the Court had not in any way defined the objects of the Memorial Scheme, and that the Trustees had a wide discretion in the use of the funds. Agreement, however, could not be reached, and in 1925, in order to avoid a further application to the Court, the result of which seemed so doubtful, an undertaking was given to the Treasury Solicitor in the following terms, and signed by two of the Trustees.

We, the undersigned, hereby agree that the acquisition of a Theatre is essential for the carrying out of the objects of the Charity known as 'the Shakespeare Memorial Trust' and undertake that the funds and income of such Charity will not be applied to any of the six objects for which a Shakespeare Memorial Theatre was to be established as set out in the Appendix to the handbook entitled 'the proposed Shakespeare Memorial National Theatre' unless and until a Theatre has been acquired Provided always that this undertaking shall not prevent payment out of the income of the Charity funds of the proper costs and expenses incidental to the administration and management of the Charity.

For and on behalf of the Executive Committee
of the Shakespeare Memorial Trust,
FRANK C. MEYER
J. FORBES-ROBERTSON

Henceforth it would not be possible to continue financial assistance to the Stratford Company, nor yet to the Old Vic; and the funds of the Committee could be used only for such purposes as would be likely to lead directly to the achievement of the main object. I do not know in what spirit the Committee accepted this decision. Some no doubt were disappointed; others may well have breathed a sigh of relief, for at last they knew where they stood in respect to further attempts from inside or out to raid their funds. Unfortunately these attempts were recurrent, and the inevitable refusals of the Committee brought the National Theatre into bad odour in some quarters. The would-be marauders would not take 'no' for an answer, accusing the S.M.N.T. of a dog-in-the-manger attitude, or attributing to malevolence what was in fact a legal obligation. It is true that some members of the Committee were sometimes liable to sympathize with one or other of the requests which came from some worthy cause in which they were personally interested, and if only it could have been agreed that the original purpose of the Trust had failed, the Court might have been persuaded to permit expenditure on the ground that the object in view was cognate or *cy près* to the original scheme. But the Committee as a whole could never consent to acknowledge defeat, and this refusal became the ultimate preservative of the Fund.

Before finally disposing of this subject, I should like to quote from a memorandum prepared by Sir Israel Gollancz dated 13th August 1924, for his interpretation of the controversy is a comment on the whole affair which deserves a permanent record.

... The Gower Street site for the Theatre was secured early in 1914. Then came the War; and of necessity the project had to be put aside. The only possible use was made of the site, for the purposes of a great 'Shakespeare Hut'—a congeries of Y.M.C.A. Huts for H.M. Overseas Forces. It is not necessary to deal with the history of the movement from this date, unless it be to emphasize that the money later granted to the Shakespeare Joint Committee for the New Shakespeare Company was the outcome of an arrangement between the Committee and the Y.M.C.A., whose expenditure on the Huts had been about £20,000, to use the annual rent thereafter to be paid by them for the site, after the War, pending a purchaser thereof, for the organization of a Company of Players. This must be regarded as exceptional, and due to War conditions. Without the Y.M.C.A. Huts the site would have been of no monetary value for merely temporary use.

The Company in question would, it was hoped, pave the way for the National Theatre Company—an essential element in the foundation of a National Theatre. There was, however, no idea that the Committee was thereby providing a 'Memorial' to Shakespeare. The subsidizing of the 'New Shakespeare Company' must, I think, be placed in an entirely different category from the proposed grants to the Old Vic and the Stratford-on-Avon Memorial Theatre—as 'approved objects likely to promote the national recognition of Shakespeare'. These grants, to my mind, and in my repeatedly expressed opinion, demanded legal sanction, which could hardly be granted, unless the National Theatre project were declared to be no longer practical, and it were decided to revert to the erection of a Shakespeare Monumental Memorial, the surplus of the Fund to be used generally to advance Shakespearian aims.

Accordingly I agree with the Charity Commissioners that the only object of the Charity at present is the provision and endowment of a National Theatre to serve as the Shakespeare Memorial in London, in accordance with resolutions passed on 28th May 1908, 21st July 1908, 23rd March 1909, and the re-affirmation by the General Committee at the Annual General Meeting, 23rd November 1922, of the proposal to build and endow a National Theatre as the Shakespeare Memorial National Theatre on the scale originally proposed.

As regards the Trust Deed, it should be noted that, in accordance with the opinion of Counsel, Sir Francis Palmer, it was merely a provisional arrangement. He advised 'that in the first instance Trustees should be appointed and that steps should be taken for ultimately obtaining a Royal Charter', by which no doubt was meant a Royal Charter for the Shakespeare Memorial National Theatre.

The late Sir Carl Meyer, the donor of by far the greater part of the present fund, Chairman of the Finance Committee, and Trustee, was anxious as far as possible to act in accordance with the wishes of the Committee, and did not in any way attempt to assert any special position in view of his donation. As Messrs. Bircham (Solicitors to the Trust) have referred to his express approval of certain expenditures of the Fund, it is right that I should quote from his last letter, dated 22nd November 1922, addressed to the Annual General Meeting: 'Whilst sympathizing with the desire to make a start and do something towards carrying out the original idea of the National Theatre, I am afraid I should be compelled to vote against the proposal of the Executive "that a sum not exceeding £5,000 per annum for three years be provided from the Shakespeare Memorial Fund" on financial grounds, as I do not consider it prudent to diminish the capital of the Trust by some £15,000, leaving only a very limited capital and income to draw on, should the larger scheme materialize at a later date.' It should be noted that Sir Carl Meyer's objection was on financial grounds, for the vague Trust Deed seems to give power to the Committee to dispose of the funds in such manner as they shall direct. A clearly defined scheme should elucidate the Deed of Trust.

TRIALS AND ERRORS

The advent of the first Labour Government in 1924 suggested that a new attempt should be made to introduce the National Theatre project to our rulers, and Granville Barker (henceforth to be known as Harley Granville-Barker), set the ball rolling by a letter to *The Times*. It was followed by a correspondence which raised many interesting points, and certainly deserves to be recorded.

To the Editor of *The Times*

SIR,

The Labour Party's election manifesto spoke for the abolition of the entertainment tax. What the Chancellor of the Exchequer may be able to do this year is, of course, another matter. The interests of the theatrical industry, however, are competently represented in the House of Commons, and we may be sure that no chance of urging them will be missed.

But will not some member of this Parliament constitute himself the champion of the theatre as an art and an aid to education? He could call Mr. Snowden's attention to the fact that ten per cent of the proceeds of the tax in 1922 would just have sufficed—by present calculations—to build and endow the Shakespeare National Theatre. (Nor is the million pounds wanted cash down; a hundred thousand a year would probably do.) He could suggest to Mr. Trevelyan that the study of drama now carried on in schools and teachers' colleges throughout the country as a means (among others) to the betterment of our English speech needs just this as a keystone. Perhaps it is against the canons of good finance to hypothecate a particular tax to a particular purpose. But if the last year of this one is in sight, might not the irregularity be forgiven, and would not the still vexed theatre managers at least pay with a better grace if they knew that a little of the money was to go to the accrediting of their own calling?

The relations of public authority to art are up for discussion at the moment in various directions. We are celebrating the centenary of the National Gallery. There is the matter of the County Hall and its cartoons. The principals of our two chief colleges of music have effectively protested against a visit from the Vienna State Opera Company, in the supposed interests of British opera. As to this, the public that likes good music for its own sake can hardly be expected to rejoice in the loss, and British opera, struggling for its very existence, may well exclaim: If we are to compete with Vienna, give us Vienna's chances, building, subsidy, recognition.

And as for the drama; we have a British Empire Exhibition this year, but when a worthy theatre was projected there the project was turned down as too costly. (It will be interesting to discover hereafter for what better regarded enterprises money has been quite easily found.) London will be as full as ever this summer, no doubt, of excellent entertainment. But the cry will certainly be raised: Where, upon such an occasion, is our Shakespeare and the rest of our classic drama? We must send our visitors, I suppose, to the Old Vic. But the wisest friends of this gallant little institution will not, I think, claim that it does much more than bear witness to our melancholy lack of a theatre, properly, adequately endowed and able to set a standard to the English-speaking world in the presentation and cultivation of the by no means negligible part of that world's common inheritance, the English Drama. And to suppose that private enterprise can ever supply the lack is absurd; it merely shows a quite inadequate conception of what a National Theatre should be.

This, one may be told, is no time to demand even the smallest public expenditure. One can only answer that the true believer in a cause must plead it in season and out; and if it is a good cause even the unlikeliest moment may turn in its favour. Matthew Arnold started to plead this 45 years ago; it has had and has many able advocates, and the prejudice against it, which is largely composed of inertia and indifference, will certainly go down sooner or later. May it be sooner!

Faithfully yours,

March 2nd.   HARLEY GRANVILLE-BARKER

SIR,

The question of a National Theatre in connexion with our National dramatic art has been brought up again in Mr. Granville-Barker's letter in your paper to-day. But although much has been said in the past as to how much money might be provided, nothing has been said clearly and concisely as to what this money has been and is still being asked for.

Mr. Granville-Barker mentions the National Gallery, the County Hall and its cartoons, the British National Opera Company, and the Old Vic; he mentions Vienna and what it has done for its national art and music, and what Wembley has not done for the British drama; but, with all this, he has not given the public or its Government a clear idea, in a few well-chosen words, for what purpose they are asked to subscribe a million pounds. I, among others, wish to see a National Theatre, but have at the same time a very definite idea as to what it should and must inevitably be, and I think it is only fair to the public to state clearly what we advocates of this cause have to offer. The public have a right to know, and will only give when they know definitely what they will receive. Such a theatre can never be more or less than a National Gallery of past and perhaps a little present dramatic art, held up as the standard, up to date, of our achievements and aspirations in that direction. Like the National Gallery in Trafalgar Square, it will have the same comforting, inspiring, and motherly influence, and will, therefore, never be more than educative—a background or springing-off ground from which the adventure of further dramatic art may happily begin.

Would it not be as well, if this is the case, to tell the public clearly of it? For they would be more than disappointed if they were hoodwinked into paying for what they might expect to be 'the very latest', when they will at best get soberly arrayed before them the latest dramatic effort that has passed a national committee's censorship. The theatre of adventure has nothing to do with, and never will be controlled by, any national committee, but a theatre that constitutes a school of drama may be a great national port of art, that I for one believe is well worth national expenditure. Is this the Theatre for which Mr. Granville-Barker and others are asking?

Faithfully yours,

NORMAN WILKINSON

March 3rd.

SIR,

Mr. Granville-Barker's letter in *The Times* of to-day will once more focus public attention on a matter of concern to a larger number of people than is generally recognized. Since it has become clear that private enterprise is itself incapable of bringing the National Theatre scheme to fruition, the idea of an effort to invoke the support of the Government should win wide acceptance. But much ground remains to be cleared before the Government could be fairly asked to offer a subsidy in any form. What, for instance, do we precisely mean by the words 'National Theatre'? And even granting the million pounds or so, on what basis should such a theatre be run, and with what chances of success?

It would seem desirable that a committee of inquiry should be instituted similar in scope to that which, under the chairmanship of Sir Henry Newbolt, has recently issued so valuable and effective a report on the teaching of English. If no Government Department felt competent to set up such a committee, the Prime Minister might well be approached with the suggestion that he himself should initiate the inquiry. This could be done by the stroke of a pen and at little or no expense to the country.

Yours faithfully,

GEOFFREY WHITWORTH,

Hon. Sec., British Drama League

March 3rd.

SIR,

Mr. Granville-Barker complains that the idea of a 'worthy theatre' at the British Empire Exhibition was turned down as too costly. He wonders for what better regarded enterprises money has been found. He has apparently forgotten that he is himself one of the jury in an architectural competition organized by the British Drama League with a view to producing a design (to be shown at the Exhibition) that shall be worthy of a national theatre. Perhaps he has forgotten that the same League is organizing an exhibit of the art of the theatre in two galleries which the Exhibition has provided for this purpose in the Palace of Arts.

The experience of Munich in building a theatre within the exhibition grounds of that city did not encourage the idea of repeating the experiment at Wembley. When I was at the Munich Exhibition in 1922 the theatre was closed.

Yours faithfully,

LAWRENCE WEAVER,

Director, United Kingdom Exhibits,

British Empire Exhibition (1924)

SIR,

Will you spare me space for a few more words upon a National Theatre? My cry has aroused the accustomed echoes, but new ones. And the question still is: What do Brown, Jones, and Robinson think about the matter? And the answer still is, I fear, that they do not feel called upon to feel seriously about it at all. Remind them that Shakespeare still lacks his due memorial, and they appear politely shocked; that England lacks such a theatre as most other countries of a like social development possess—well, the more England she! But their unspoken answer to one's pleading—the more positive because it stays unspoken—is 'does it really matter?' And this, I suggest, points to the fundamental difference which underlies all these disputes about opera, County Hall panels, London's architecture and its bridges, funds for the National Gallery, a National Theatre, and the rest. And this is why, in my first letter, I raised the larger issue. Art is an amusement. Better, of course, to have a healthy drama, pretty pictures to look at, streets that are not too sordid. But if you don't it really doesn't matter. Is not this the dominant opinion in England to-day? (There are, besides, the neo-puritans, conscious and unconscious, who definitely dislike art and fear it.) Another and more articulate opinion holds art, and the love of art, to be a necessity of civilized life, a factor, indeed, in the nation's vitality; not therefore a thing to be imposed upon it, but educable, as is any other faculty of expression or appreciation.

How the articulate opinion may concern the inarticulate is the question, and, where a national theatre is concerned, the only question of present importance. For, in its very nature, the thing is either of national importance or none; it either matters a great deal or it does not matter at all. Therefore, appeals for a guinea or a shilling, or to millionaires to deflect some of their super-tax to this worthy object, are yet unprofitable and tend rather to aggravate than help. Let dominant public opinion be converted and there will be small difficulty about money. We have to be thrifty in these days; but, after all, it is capital for an enterprise that is asked for, not a million pounds to be thrown into the sea. By all means, then, as Mr. Geoffrey Whitworth proposes, let Parliament pronounce upon the matter and let a Committee advise them, if the Prime Minister thinks well to appoint one—not, I suggest, a Committee of 'experts' whose minds are already set, nor of Brown, Jones, and Robinson, but of men whose tradition and training fit them to judge the question as a part of the larger cultural issue. Can the theatre of to-day play a worthy part in that issue? If it is fairly appraised and its history for the last 300 years is considered, I think its friends need have no doubt but that it can.

As to the architectural competition and the theatrical section at

Wembley, had I forgotten them it would have shown gross ingratitude to Sir Lawrence Weaver, without whose kindly enthusiasm and help drama would not, I expect, have been represented in the Exhibition at all. There were, of course, good arguments for and against building a theatre there, but the best was just the lack of any settled organization which could furnish it with a fit supply of plays. In Munich this difficulty did not exist. Moreover, the theatre was, if I remember right, experimental in design and stage mechanism and only meant for 'festivals'; it was appropriate to an exhibition. Our architectural competition is an act of faith in the future. The rest of what we show in the Exhibition will be mainly a show of the past, and it is right it should have its place. But it will be sad evidence, too, of the comparative ease with which one can obtain support for an art once it is comfortably dead and ready to be embalmed in a museum. (At least it can do no harm there, thinks Jones, neo-puritan.) But the drama is, in the very simplest sense, a living art. And the thought of a pious pilgrim from New Zealand, searching for his Shakespeare and finding a first folio in a glass case, with a portrait of David Garrick hanging above it, is food for the ironist.

Faithfully yours,

HARLEY GRANVILLE-BARKER

Sir Israel Gollancz also took part in the correspondence, which was finalized in a somewhat evasive leading article printed in *The Times* of March 25th, and headed 'Smith's Theatre'.

In a letter on the idea of a national theatre, which we published on Saturday, Mr. Barker laid the blame for the scheme's stagnation on the shoulders of Brown, Jones, and Robinson. They do not, he said, 'feel called to think about it seriously at all'; their unspoken answer to his pleading is, he believes, 'Does it really matter!' 'Jones, the neo-puritan', he singles out for particular censure, for Jones 'definitely dislikes art and fears it and will support it only when "it is comfortably dead and ready to be embalmed in a museum".' This may all be true; the Philistine trio may be as apathetic, as stubborn, and as blind as Mr. Barker supposes, and their conversion may be, as he suggests, the chief problem of the national theatre's advocates. But he has largely forgotten Smith. Smith, who represents a large section of the public, is neither an apathetic Philistine nor, in Mr. Barker's sense, a neo-puritan. He is fully aware and does not need to be told that art 'does matter'; he likes playgoing and has a taste for good plays; but he is not at present an active supporter of any existing scheme for a national theatre. In short, far from being ignorant or indifferent, he is a reasoned sceptic, and he it is whom enthusiasm must first convert. He in his turn will then persuade Robinson, Jones, and Brown, who, though willing to listen in a club or train to their old friend Smith, are a little afraid and resentful of Mr. Barker's Olympian scorn.

What is the basis of Smith's scepticism? His doubts, many and various though they are, may be divided into three main groups—financial, artistic, and administrative. First, he has a strong objection to a million pounds' worth of avoidable expenditure. 'Avoidable' is the word he uses—not 'unnecessary' or 'valueless'. He does not think of a national theatre as a waste. He shares Mr. Barker's ideals, but, unlike Mr. Barker, he measures their value, not by the absolute rule of an enthusiast, but by the comparative rule of a citizen who needs to be convinced that no need is more pressing and that the necessary sum cannot be better spent. After his financial come his artistic doubts. They arise from his mistrust of the academic influence on art. He is afraid that a national theatre might become a monument rather than a living playhouse, and might accumulate a stiffly devotional tradition which, by investing greatness with ritualistic pomposity, would dull the drama's past and prejudice its future. These doubts are not lessened by the prominent connexion of Shakespeare's name with the national theatre scheme. When Brown, Jones, and Robinson are reminded in Mr. Barker's phrase 'that Shakespeare lacks his due memorial', they may 'appear politely shocked', but Smith makes no such pretence. He is, indeed, inclined to think that Shakespeare is by no means a neglected dramatist. Lastly, Smith has his doubts about administration. He is confronted by a number of conflicting enthusiasts, each, in fact, pleading a different cause under a common title. He finds that even producing societies with many merits but with no sort of claim to be regarded as nationally representative, are eager to take over the administration of the whole scheme. And he is, in consequence, desperately afraid that, if the money were subscribed, its control might be given over to old ladies and gentlemen whom he abhors as cranks. To-day the project appears to be in confusion, and Smith, a supporter of its principle, cannot see how the issue can be made plain until it has been reported on by a committee having the authority of Government appointment. When the theatre's scope and purpose have thus been authoritatively stated and its constitution has been outlined, when the cranks have been check-mated, and the whole matter has become a national and not a sectional question, Smith will be prepared to discuss it. Until then his difficulty will remain.

Spurred on, perhaps, by this correspondence, the Executive Committee determined in May 1924 to request the new Prime Minister, Mr. Ramsay MacDonald, to receive a deputation embracing every organization connected with the theatre and the most prominent national figures of the day. This deputation was empowered to ask for the allocation of a site, at the same time intimating that the Committee was in a position to place a theatre on the site forthwith. A reply came saying that the Prime Minister was anxious to receive the proposed deputation, but that at the moment he feared that it was impossible for him to make any definite arrangements. He would, however, bear the request in mind, and communicate with the Committee again at the conclusion of the Inter-Allied Conference then about to take place in London, when the pressure on his time would be relaxed to some extent. This response was regarded as most encouraging, but the fall of the Labour Government supervened, and all hopes were dashed.

However, the question of a deputation was again before the Committee early in the following January, when a letter on similar lines was sent to the new Prime Minister, Mr. Stanley Baldwin. Here surely was another favourable opportunity, for Mr. Baldwin, like his predecessor, was known to be a man of culture and friendly to the arts. At a meeting of the Executive held on 12th February 1925, it was reported that the Prime Minister had referred the matter to the first Commissioner of Works, who had already received a deputation which, on account of the short notice given, consisted only of the Chairman, Mr. W. L. Courtney, Mr. Alfred Sutro, and the Secretary, Sir Israel Gollancz. Mr. Sutro reported that in answer to a question from Lord Peel, he had stated that the Committee would be able to start building operations at once, since in addition to the £70,000 donated by the late Sir Carl Meyer, Lady Meyer had generously promised a further sum of £30,000 should a suitable site be offered by the Government. Sir Israel Gollancz reported that he had emphasized the aspect of a National Theatre as a Shakespeare Memorial in the Metropolis of the Empire, and Mr. W. L. Courtney added that in his opinion, the deputation to Lord Peel must be regarded as having taken the place of the larger deputation which in the first instance the Prime Minister had been asked to receive On the whole, it was apparent that those who had called on Lord Peel had been favourably impressed by the cordiality with which they had been received, and it was decided to send a letter to his Lordship thanking him for receiving the deputation, and intimating that after consultation with experts the Committee found that approximately three-quarters of an acre would be needed, and that further details would be furnished if desired:

Nothing more happened till the end of April, when the following reply came to hand:

H.M. Office of Works,
Storey's Gate,
Westminster, S.W.
27th April, 1925

My dear Mr. Courtney,

With further reference to your letter of the 17th March and the deputation which came to see me regarding a site for the proposed Shakespeare Memorial National Theatre, the Government have given most careful consideration to your suggestion, but I much regret to inform you that they find themselves unable to place a site at your disposal.

Yours sincerely,

Peel

So that was that, and once again the S.M.N.T. Committee was thrown back on its own resources with no immediate prospect of advance. But as a body they showed some resilience, for after hearing the disappointing news from Storey's Gate they at once settled down to a discussion as to the suitability of a site which might be available in Chandos Street, St. Martin's Lane. Mrs. Lyttelton also called attention to the garden between the Belgrave Hotel and Grosvenor Gardens, the property of the Duke of Westminster, and the Hon Secretary undertook to obtain particulars. At the next meeting, Sir Israel submitted the particulars which had been asked for, together with a plan. Having agreed that the Westminster site would be adequate and suitable, the Committee asked Mrs Lyttelton to be good enough to approach the Duke. At the same time the leasehold site in Chandos Street was to be further investigated. Mr Acton Bond, who was specially keen on this latter proposal, had asked Sir Frank Meyer, now Trustee of the fund, if he thought that some bank could be induced to advance money for the building of the theatre, on the security of the site. He reported that Sir Frank was of the opinion that it would be useless to approach a bank with such a suggestion. It might be worthwhile to consider whether a big insurance company with funds to invest would lend on mortgage up to about 60 per cent of the value of the building—but here also the fact that the site was leasehold, not freehold, would prove a stumbling block.

At this same meeting a letter was laid on the table from the Hon. Secretary of the British Drama League, an organization of which we shall hear more later, enclosing a copy of a unanimous resolution passed at the League's Annual Meeting held in London on 3rd July 1925, with its President, Lord Howard de Walden, in the chair:

Resolution proposed by Mr. Holford Knight, seconded by Mr. Sharman of the Liverpool Playgoers, with an amendment proposed by Miss Gertrude Kingston and accepted by Mr. Holford Knight: '*That this meeting deplores the delay in the foundation of a National Theatre, but reaffirms the belief of the British Drama League that no Theatre can rightly be called "National" unless building, equipment and endowment are adequate to the presenting of British Drama, both old and new, at its best.*'

134

No one could cavil at these sentiments, least of all the S.M.N.T. Committee. But they were now too entangled with worries of their own to pay much attention to prods from outside. Having lately turned down a request from Sir Reginald Rowe that they should purchase Sadler's Wells Theatre for the benefit of the Old Vic, they were busily engaged with Mrs. Lyttelton's efforts to persuade the Duke of Westminster to present them with a site, as already recorded. Here at last the prospects seemed brighter. The site in question was that triangular garden near Victoria Station where the Foch memorial now stands. It had actually been offered by the Duke, subject to the consent of certain leaseholders of premises overlooking the garden who held rights of entry during the period of their tenancies. This consent was withheld. And there were other difficulties. It transpired, for instance, that the Duke himself was unable to grant a lease for a longer period than his own life-time. Nevertheless, so ready was he to fulfil his promise, that he empowered his representatives to make every effort, either by applying to the Court or by means of a private Bill, to allow him to grant a lease of ninety-nine years, and if possible longer.

It is true that the site itself was not all that could be desired. Its shape was inappropriate for the building of a theatre, and as an alternative the Duke now offered a larger and more convenient site at Horseferry Road. Here at least there would be plenty of room for storage of scenery, costumes, and a museum. But the Duke was away in foreign parts, and to the relief of many, I suspect, the idea came to nothing. Critical opinion was perfectly expressed in the following letter from Mr. Bernard Shaw, dated 3rd November 1925.

MY DEAR GOLLANCZ,

It is quite impossible for me to take any part in asking people privately to give thirty thousand pounds to the S.M.N.T. They would immediately ask me why I did not give it myself. In fact Lady Meyer has already asked me that. On the only occasion in my life when I asked a rich man to put money into a theatre I offered to find half of the required sum myself, and I did so. The poor (comparatively) can make these appeals without fear of reprisals; but I, though far from being the multi-millionaire I am imagined, cannot afford to do it.

Besides, I happen to want thirty thousand pounds very badly for rebuilding the Royal Academy of Dramatic Art, at present housed in two ordinary old Gower Street houses with only a remnant of a lease to run; and if I could lay hands on that sum I would spend it on that rather than on the projected Horseferry Theatre.

I do not like looking a gift horse in the mouth, especially when it is the only site we seem likely to get; but let us not deceive ourselves as to its eligibility. Whatever it may develop into in twenty years or so, it is at present a site on which no sane theatrical expert would dream of putting a theatre larger than the Margaret Morris theatre in Chelsea. Instead of having a crowded thoroughfare on all four sides, it stands at the crossing of two lonely roads and a condemned bridge. At the busiest hour of the day there are never more than ten people within sight of it; and at night it moves painters and composers to produce nocturnes. In the eighteenth century it would have proved an ideal site for a gibbet. Its sole advantage from our point of view is that it is conveniently near Mrs. Lyttelton's.

I wonder would it be possible to swap the site with the Government for some of their Whitehall sites?

Ever since I realized the horror of the thing I have been haunted by a vision of Columbia Market, that ghastly Gothic temple that Lady Burdett Coutts stuck in the East End. Have you ever seen it? A hundred-thousand pound theatre in Horseferry Road would be a companion Folly to it.

What on earth are we to do? Parliament Square is what we want. Or the Horse Guards Parade—as a gesture of disarmament.

G. B. S.

As for the Grosvenor Gardens site, that having proved so difficult for reasons already explained, further negotiations with the Duke of Westminster petered out, and for some months the S.M.N.T. Committee relapsed into inactivity. But in June 1927 Sir Israel summoned it once more, the business before it being a proposal from Lady Beecham for the purchase and development of Dorchester House as a national possession to be used 'for the purposes of the Shakespeare National Theatre, and to comprise the various literary and artistic accessories to such an institution'. In some ways this scheme was attractive, and the Committee resolved that it was cordially interested in it, and went so far as to appoint a sub-committee to confer with Lady Beecham. This committee included Mrs. Lyttelton, Sir Frank Meyer, and Sir Robert Donald, who as we know had from the beginning evinced a lively concern with the fortunes of the National Theatre scheme. Unfortunately I can find no details as to what transpired behind the scenes, but at the next meeting of the Committee on 2nd October 1927, Sir Israel made a statement (not recorded), after which it was resolved that 'the Committee decided to disassociate itself from Lady Beecham's proposal. . . .'

At this meeting the Hon. Secretary also reported that before the meeting a gentleman had called to see him on a plan to utilize the site of the Foundling Hospital for the Shakespeare National Theatre, the suggestion being that the Committee might help with the deposit required to secure an option on the site. Although it was decided that the Committee were unable to consider the matter in the form presented, discussions continued for some time between the Committee and the promoters of the Foundling scheme, which, however, for good or evil, came to no conclusion.

Then, in October 1928, the irrepressible Mr. Rowe, nothing abashed by the turn-down of his previous plea for help in the purchase of Sadler's Wells Theatre, came along with a new proposal for a wholesale merger of the S.M.N.T. fund with that of the Sadler's Wells. The advantages of this combination were enumerated in a memorandum which, in view of future developments, is of some historic interest.

The Sadler's Wells scheme will undoubtedly carry out in practice essential objects of the Shakespeare Memorial Fund. Its main purpose is to provide performances of Shakespeare and of such plays, old or modern, as can be claimed to be of permanent value. The historic theatre of Sadler's Wells, with its unique Shakespearian tradition, will be re-established as a tribute to Shakespeare for the use indicated.

By the terms of the Fund's appeal, the work of the Old Vic must be carried on at prices within the reach of what are commonly called the working-classes, but this would allow profits up to £200 per performance. No one with knowledge of the theatre denies that if the drama is to be improved it must rely for support on those with moderate means.

The economic saving of running two theatres on Old Vic lines under one administration will be, as could be shown in detail, very considerable. The Old Vic pays its way, the combined theatres will do more than this, which means more money to be put back into production. The point is emphasized because the greatest of all difficulties in establishing a National Theatre would be to ensure running it without loss, and if this were impracticable the concern could have no permanent existence. For a new concern this risk must be considerable, but starting with the Old Vic as a basis means building on a sure foundation. The initial, successful, organization is there, and has merely to be extended, thus ensuring at least a creditable standard of performance and its continuance. But no one wants to leave that as it is; the aim of the Old Vic has always been progress, both in financial results and artistically, year by year.

The Old Vic is already building up an Endowment Fund, and it should in practice be easier to raise this ultimately to any figure that may be desirable than to create such a fund in advance for any new venture. Without such a fund, or a large reserve to fall back upon, the mere building of a National Theatre is likely to be a waste of money. The alternatives to be considered and compared, are, therefore, an entirely new creation, without experience or organization, and the development of an existing enterprise which has proved its vitality and power of growth. The Shakespeare Memorial Fund has more than enough money, when added to the £42,000 (which includes the cost of the site) of the existing Sadler's Wells Fund, not only to carry out the scheme proposed but to carry it out more effectively and more valuably for the public benefit, than has hitherto been regarded as practicable.

Though not in the heart of the metropolis, Sadler's Wells has a fine situation, where a good building, which is essential to the scheme, would show to advantage. In these days of motor traffic it is easily accessible, being nearer to London north of the Park than is the Strand, and a very few minutes further from the south-west of London. It is remarkably well served by omnibus, tram, and 'tube'. Owing to various circumstances, theatres in central London are becoming more and more restricted to drama of an inferior though popular type, while drama of the better class is more and more, from economic necessity, being pushed further into the field. The process seems likely to continue; and the tendency of businesses of a similar kind to congregate in an area may bring it about that Sadler's Wells will presently be the centre of an important theatrical district.

The opinion of the Charity Commission, unofficially expressed, is that co-operation between the two Funds would be practicable. To carry the matter further, the most effective procedure would be to appoint a small sub-committee, representative of the two Committees, to consider details.

A new Sadler's Wells Theatre, to hold 2,000 persons, has been designed by Messrs. Matcham & Co., and the plans have been passed by the L.C.C. Outwardly it represents the covering of the bare bones of the old theatre quite simply, but the design has dignity and balance. The interior of the house should be as good as any theatre in London, better in practical respects than that of any theatre of the older type. Important improvements could nevertheless be made both outside and inside if a larger sum were available for construction.

It has been provisionally decided that 'The Sadler's Wells Foundation' shall be separate from the 'Royal Victoria Hall Foundation' (the Old Vic), the proposed constitution being so formulated as to secure the smooth administration of the two theatres under one management. It is proposed to include representatives of the L.C.C., the University of London, the Carnegie Trust, the City Parochial Foundation, the Borough of Finsbury, and the Royal College and Royal Academy of Music on its Governing Body. If the suggested co-operation were approved, some modification of this 'scheme' would be necessary to make provision for the interest of the Shakespeare Memorial Committee.

There is no doubt that the Sadler's Wells Theatre is going to play an important part in British Drama. The enterprise will extend very notably the People's Theatre movement of which the Old Vic is the foundation, and its productions should eventually attain as high a standard as is possible in any theatre.

Now, Sir Israel had already taken the precaution of submitting this memorandum to the Charity Commissioners; and in a written reply they had stated that while it did give a correct summary of the view expressed by the Commissioner in charge of the case in a conversation with Mr. Rowe, the memorandum was incomplete in so far as it made no reference to the point, to which the Commissioner drew attention, that the application of the Fund to any purpose other than a Shakespeare Memorial National Theatre could not be sanctioned unless it were admitted that the Trust had failed to such an extent that the objects could not be carried out in their original form. This, of course, was a technical point with which Mr. Rowe, as Treasurer of the Sadler's Wells Fund, was not directly concerned, and the Commissioners agreed that once the failure of the Trust was admitted, the Sadler's Wells scheme might be held to offer a proper *cy près* application thereof. Indeed, the Commissioner acknowledged that it would be difficult to find any other scheme which would carry out so nearly the practical objects aimed at by the Shakespeare Committee. But in view of the Opinion expressed by Mr. Justice Laurence when the case was before the Court in 1923, the Commissioners would hesitate, on the information at present before them, to proceed with the establishment of a Scheme for the *cy près* application of the Fund until the Court had decided such failure existed. The Committee were therefore back where they were in 1923. Should they now at long last admit that the Trust had failed? Once more they replied with no uncertain voice. Someone proposed that the question should be referred to a sub-committee for further investigation, but so strong was the opposition that on the proposal of the chairman, Sir Frank Meyer, the resolution was withdrawn, and there the matter ended, with, I suppose, a polite letter of regret from the Hon. Secretary to Mr. Rowe.

'Broken down', 'turned down', 'negotiations abandoned'—by now the reader, if he has persisted so far, must be tired of the recurrent negatives which have formed the theme-song of this chapter. No wonder that the Committee itself was growing restive, or that Nigel Playfair—of Beggars' Opera fame—felt moved to relieve the growing tension by submitting the following letter for consideration at the next meeting of the Executive:

DEAR SIR ISRAEL,

It might be worth while placing the following memorandum which embodies my own views, subject to correction, as to steps which the Committee might usefully take in the present circumstances.

I believe that, miracles apart, the trust has failed in its specific object, and that no further subscription of any amount worth serious consideration can now be obtained. I consider that the best policy would be to go before the Commissioners with this frank confession, and with a strong recommendation that a new trust, if that is the correct word, should be created with the following conditions:

That the Capital Sum should remain untouched until such time when it can be devoted to its original purpose, the erection of a National Theatre in London and its endowment. That in the meantime, the Committee should be empowered to use such part of the yearly income as is not required for office expenses for the purpose of subsidizing certain performances of Shakespeare's plays in London.

That the conditions of such subsidizings should be as follows:

(1) A sum not exceeding (say) £3,000 may be granted by the Committee in any one year to any *bona fide* management that will undertake to give a performance of one of Shakespeare's plays for not less than four weeks in a theatre and at a season in London to be approved by them, etc. etc.

(2) That the 'producer' of the play shall be named by the said management and approved by the Committee, and that the Management will guarantee that for this production the scenery and dresses will be specially made and designed and the music specially arranged and composed.

(3) That for all these performances after the first four weeks and during the following period of five years a percentage (say $2\frac{1}{2}$ per cent) on the gross receipts will be paid to the Shakespeare Memorial Fund.

(4) That these performances in their initial run shall be announced as 'Shakespeare National Memorial Performances'.

There, surely, spoke the clever Actor-Manager, with an eye to fresh capital for further adventures in the Shakespearian field;

and for many reasons one may wish that Playfair had succeeded in his quest. London, I am sure, would have seen some lovely productions, not only from him, but belike from others too. But, owing to their intermittent appearance, it is hard to see how they could have materially contributed to the main object in view. The permanent National Theatre company would have been brought no nearer. Some of the productions might have proved artistic failures and no good advertisement for the Cause. Apparently this was also the opinion of the Committee, and once again, true to form, 'After discussion,' says the Minute, 'it was agreed not to proceed with the proposal.'

Except for a purely formal meeting in the early spring of 1929, the Committee was not called again until October, and then only three of the members, apart from the Hon. Secretary, turned up—Sir Frank Meyer, in the chair, Mr. Holford Knight, and Mr. S. R. Littlewood. Yet this meeting was of crucial importance, illumined as it was by a new ray of hope from an unexpected quarter. On July 22nd, in the House of Commons, it appeared that Mr. Reginald Young, M.P., had formally asked a question of the Prime Minister, Mr. Ramsay MacDonald: 'Would he, in order to promote the artistic sincerity and dignity of Great Britain and to encourage the best elements in the British Theatre, consider the establishment of a national theatre on lines somewhat similar to those followed in many European countries?'

THE PRIME MINISTER. I have a great deal of sympathy with the scheme which my hon. Friend has in mind. There are, however, serious difficulties arising partly from the number of similar schemes which are put forward. In present circumstances, therefore, I would only be holding out false hopes if I were to answer otherwise than that I regret that I cannot give a promise of a Government subsidy.

MR. HOLFORD KNIGHT. Has it been represented to the Prime Minister that there are various schemes for a National Theatre?

MR. JAMES HUDSON. If those who are pressing various schemes would come to an agreement, would the Prime Minister be prepared to reconsider the answer that he has made?

THE PRIME MINISTER. I think that my answer is partly an invitation for them to do so.

The S.M.N.T. Committee were at once seized with the important significance of this reply, and quickly decided to summon a Conference of Bodies and persons interested in the National Theatre scheme so that an agreed plan might be drawn up for submission to the Prime Minister in accordance with his hint.

At the same meeting a letter from the British Drama League was read urging prompt action, and intimating that in default of such, steps would be taken by the League to initiate it. The Committee resolved to welcome the co-operation of the League, and to explain that already the Committee had decided to summon a conference, at which it was hoped that the League would be represented.

The upshot of all this will be narrated in due course. But now let us retrace our steps a little, and inquire more closely into the nature and origin of this 'Drama League', and its relation with other movements in the post-war theatre which from now onwards were to exercise a growing influence on the National Theatre scheme.

VII

FLYING BUTTRESS

It may have been noticed that hitherto the National Theatre scheme had been mainly supported by members of the aristocracy, the professions—including the dramatic profession—and the academic world. Arguments in favour of the project were chiefly concerned with its value to Shakespearian drama, to forging bonds of Empire, and as an impetus to the progress of dramatic art as such. Little was done to court the favour of the masses, and this may have been a deliberate policy on the part of the organizers; for while the building of the theatre was not yet in sight, it would have been a mistake to rouse popular expectancy with no immediate prospect of satisfying it.

As it happened, however, there were already signs of a spontaneous stir on the part of the people towards a new conception of the theatre. While serving with the army in France, Basil Dean had found time to organize, with the approval of the military authorities, concert parties and stage entertainments behind the lines. At almost the same time, Lena Ashwell, one of the leading actresses of pre-war days, conceived the notion of starting musical and dramatic entertainment in Y.M.C.A. huts at military bases at Havre and elsewhere. Nothing but the best was good enough for Miss Ashwell. Shakespeare and Shaw figured prominently in her programmes, and though at first she had to meet much scepticism, her sublime faith was completely vindicated by the reaction of the soldiers themselves, which showed that in the masterpieces of dramatic literature rather than in the ephemeral frivolities of the day were to be found the source of strength and healing most apt to refresh the minds and spirits of men foredone with battle at the gates of hell.

My friend Eric Patterson, who later became the Principal of Ashridge College, and was then a social worker at the front, has told how Y.M.C.A. huts and similar establishments found themselves suddenly transformed into theatres, though not always of an orthodox kind! The proverbial 'two boards and a passion' had often to do duty for the complete article, and the inconveniences suffered by the performers could be prodigious. *Candida* was one of the first plays produced by Miss Ashwell. It was not too well received. But after a year's interval it was revived, and proved one of the most popular plays in the repertory. And poetry, too, began to raise her head. As an experiment, Penelope Wheeler was persuaded to give recitals of Gilbert Murray's versions of *Euripides*. She was invited again and again.

But what of the future? [wrote Patterson, in 1919]. Is all this progress towards the realization of a national dramatic ideal to be lost with the conclusion of the war? Have all these efforts to create a repertory movement in France merely owed their success to the passing needs of the time? It is true that work in Britain in days of peace, along similar lines, will not be quite so easy in some ways as it was in France; in other ways, it will be more simple.

From that beginning [Patterson continues] resulted a repertory movement which spread to the other bases in France. Better facilities were given and stage conditions were improved as the Authorities awoke to the social and moral value of what was being done. By degrees actresses were sent out from England and later a few professional actors were released from the army. It was now possible to be more ambitious. The drama became part of the life of the base, which was now able to see different types of plays; modern like *Cousin Kate, You Never Can Tell, The Importance of Being Earnest*, Gilbert Murray's version of *Electra*; plays of the Lancashire and Irish schools. The drama also began to influence people whom before it had never touched. Men began to see plays which they had not had the opportunity to see in civil life; and by degrees, too, their taste was developed.

It is a great mistake to suppose that the average man prefers poor to good; if only poor stuff is put in his way he takes it for want of something better, but give him the chance of progress and he will progress to that point where he will refuse the bad and the ugly.

Whether the popular repertory movement will continue to progress depends upon the faith which is in us. Of all the lessons which this war has taught, none is more true than that the people are willing to respond to great ideals, if they are presented to them in a living form and in a way which makes them part of their lives. This war has not only been an age of destruction, it has also been an age of transition and reconstruction. Truth has forced itself to the front. Men have realized new needs because of the artist and spiritual nature within them. That things can never be the same again is a truth which is apt to be forgotten because it is so obvious. Democracy has come to its own; therefore, the theatre of the future must be democratic in its outlook. True democracy implies the enrichment of the common life, therefore the theatre must come to the people, carrying rich gifts in its hands and at the same time receiving from the people in exchange all those treasures of art which life produces.

Abroad, after the armistice, when many thousands of soldiers awaiting demobilization found themselves faced with long hours with nothing to do, the Authorities determined that this enforced leisure must be filled with various activities of an educational, sportive, or social character, and among other subjects the drama was not forgotten. Play-reading circles, amateur performances, and drama-classes were started up, and many a man formerly employed on the professional stage was detailed to supervise them. Outstanding among these was Captain Esmé Percy, who was put in charge of 'Das Deutsche Theater' at Cologne, where he ran a whole repertory season with marked success. As in Havre, no concessions were made to the lower instincts. It was found that the kind of plays that Lena Ashwell had encouraged continued to attract large audiences, and what an eye-witness avows to have been the greatest success of them all was John Galsworthy's *Strife*, staged during the time of the railway strike in England. 'It was well produced', we are told, 'well acted, and provoked a good deal of discussion, and what was most noticeable was that the large cast was representative of almost every rank and regiment in the Army.'

At home, too, the same sort of thing was going on. There was the new 'Army Education Scheme', under which every soldier during his service with the colours was to receive a thorough all-round training in educational and vocational subjects, so that when he returned to civil life he might be qualified to obtain a type of employment much higher than that which had usually been associated with the ex-soldier in the past. It was realized that even the recreation of the soldier could be turned to profitable account, and in this instance the possibilities of the drama were fully appreciated. The War Office School of Education at Bedford was among the pioneers of this movement, and there the practical value of dramatic representations, organized and produced during leisure hours, was clearly demonstrated. At the same time the 'Old Vic' was at the beginning of its most successful period as purveyor of cheap yet first-rate drama to the people of London. Lena Ashwell, too, was putting all her war-time experience at the service of her 'Once a Week Players' who were taking plays of high calibre in weekly series round the Town Halls of the principal London Boroughs. There were difficulties, of course, much inertia to be overcome, all of which moved Patterson to declare, 'Well might one sigh for the comparatively easy days in France. Yet one need not despair, for there are new stirrings in the air, with the promise of big things to come. Municipalities, in spite of the financial outlook and the vested interests, are beginning to take a wider view of their duties to the ratepayer, so that we may even see the English miracle of a Municipal Theatre, and then, perhaps, the State may take the example and we may even have the miracle of miracles, a National Theatre!'

But now you may be wondering what has all this to do with the British Drama League? The answer can best be given in a piece of personal reminiscence, which begins when, in the autumn of 1918, and while still a member of the publishing firm of Chatto & Windus, I found myself delivering a lecture in a temporary wooden hall belonging to the Y.M.C.A. at the Vickers-Maxim munitions works at Crayford. The title of the lecture was 'A Bird's Eye View of the History of the Stage', illustrated by lantern slides, and adapted, so far as I knew how, to the amusement and edification of munition workers. After the lecture I was informed of a surprise item. 'The Crayford Reading Circle' was about to present a one-act play by Stanley Houghton. Would I not stay and hear it?

So I took my seat in the second row and waited events, expecting to be rather bored. But the first thing that happened was that the hall, which previously had been half empty, began to fill. The billiards room was deserted. The refreshment bar soon lacked a customer. The women laid aside their knitting-needles, and the men their newspapers. This was no lecture. This was real and this was earnest. This was a Play. . . .

Yet here were no actors in the proper sense of the word. They just sat, on a semi-circle of chairs. They were not dressed for their parts. They had not even memorized them. With books in their hands, and with a minimum of action, they did not do much more than read the words of the play, pointing them with a few gestures. And yet, through the emotional sincerity of their interpretations, the characters came to life, and as I watched and listened, I felt that I was coming close to the fundamental quality of dramatic art in a way that I had never understood it before. Here was the art of the theatre reduced to the simplest terms, yet in this very reduction triumphant. Devoid of every grace, and of the simplest gadgets of stage appointment, the agonists on the platform found the right echo in the hearts of their audience. And they were in no way expressing *themselves*. They were denuding themselves of all the normal attributes of their selfhood, depending for the effect they made almost wholly on a microscopic rendering of the playwright's thought, achieving at the same time that unity between reader and audience whereby both reverberate in unison as a couple of tuning forks when one is struck. Thus they vindicated the existence of that common soul in which we live and move and have our being. And at Crayford this vindication was achieved for its own sake alone. Not for private gain, not even in the cause of charity, these players were simply following their own instincts, satisfying their own need. That was all they knew and all they needed to know. But in so doing they were satisfying also the need of the community. Givers and receivers were one.

Now this visit to Crayford was also my point of divergence to that new orientation of mind—conversion if you like to call it— which was to result, a year later, in the foundation of the British Drama League. What had been done at Crayford could clearly be done elsewhere, and ignorant as I was of how far similar movements were already in action both abroad and at home, I felt impertinently moved to do all I could to spread the good news. There was no knowing how the idea might 'catch on'. And I felt, too, that here might be the germ of something which, if not exactly the National Theatre of my youthful allegiance, was not wholly unrelated thereto. For what had so distinguished the play-reading at Crayford was the fact that it had been undertaken in a spirit of community enterprise. It was that which had endowed the performance with its peculiar dignity, and was it not precisely this dignity that would characterize the work of a National Theatre? In a flash I saw that a National Theatre, for all its costly elaboration, for all its perfection of professional technique, was no more and no less than a Community Theatre writ large. And for this a democratic background was the first essential, and the creation of a public consciously concerned with the practice of theatre art both for its own sake and as a major factor in the enjoyment of life.

It was wonderful to find that these ideas were endorsed by others, and the Drama League was privately founded in December

1918. A little later Harley Granville-Barker, just returned from the States, became Chairman of the Council, with Lord Howard de Walden as President. The public inaugural meeting took place at the Theatre Royal, Haymarket, on 22nd June 1919, with the support on the stage of Sir Michael Sadler, who presided, J. R. Clynes, M.P., Lady Denman (President of the National Federation of Women's Institutes), Lena Ashwell, the Rev. H. R. L. Sheppard, J. Fisher White (representing the Actors' Association), Ben Greet, Laurence Binyon and John Drinkwater. The Hon. Secretary (your humble historian) briefly described the origin of the League at Crayford a few months earlier, adding his opinion that as this was a time when the art of the theatre as regards the London stage was moribund, the contrast between that deadness and the promise of vitality outside suggested a scheme whereby a theatrical revival on democratic lines might be stimulated in the days to come. Practical work was already being undertaken by many individuals and organizations—by Miss Lena Ashwell, by Miss Baylis, by Mr. Ben Greet and many others—but it was felt that a central organization might do much to help these separate movements and apply their experience and example to the betterment of social life and to the art of the theatre as a whole. The drama was the art *par excellence* of the people, and the theatre everybody's business. It was therefore an essential part of the scheme that it should include representatives of every interest involved—not artists only and not social workers only, and it was on this basis that the League had been founded, and had already undertaken the preliminaries of its programme.

The Chairman, Sir Michael Sadler, speaking from the standpoint of an educationist, said that all through the centuries many of the best schools practised the drama as part of their educational system. Mr. Edmund Holmes had made the English-speaking people realize what part the drama could play even in elementary schools. The practice of acting, combined with the making of beautiful things, the singing of beautiful songs, beautiful gestures and a love of beautiful words, was one of the greatest educational influences at our disposal.

Mr. J. R. Clynes ended an important speech by averring that the League should receive as much support as anyone could give it. He would like to be one of the men claiming to speak and act for organized labour in this country to associate themselves with the British Drama League, and in that way bring it permanently before the millions of men and women whose lives could be made more joyful, their outlook broadened, and their eyes brightened by all the League could do.

Mr. John Drinkwater, in making an appeal on behalf of the League, offered some valuable suggestions regarding repertory work in the provinces, and the way in which the League could best foster it. He said that in his view the future of English drama depended on the standard of provincial repertory theatres at least as much as upon any other form of theatrical activity. All that was required to establish a repertory theatre in any centre was a guarantee of £5,000 a year for five years. In Manchester, where he had lectured on this subject, the objection was raised that the money could not be obtained—£5,000 a year could not be obtained in Manchester! and for a thing which was going to work right down to the roots of the life of the whole place; it was tragic! It was the duty of the Drama League to see that Manchester got its £5,000 a year, and that had to be done too all over the country. Failing the establishment of Municipal Theatres, and this was a long way off, here was the chance for private enterprise, which the League might hopefully stimulate. First of all, the League must force support from rich people, and then encourage the proletariat to support it with their weekly shillings.

The Rev. H. R. L. Sheppard (Vicar of St. Martin's-in-the-Fields) also spoke in support of the League, saying that he realized that the drama and his own profession must go hand in hand. He deplored the fact that the Christian Church did not possess its own theatre in London. What the ordinary man wanted from the theatre was to be sent home with a restful feeling in his heart, and with the knowledge that he had learned something, and that he had been made to think a little more deeply. He wanted to be lifted out of the rut of his ordinary monotonous daily life.

Miss Lena Ashwell said that the League was desperately needed because there was no apprehension at the present time of the power of drama for good or evil. This aspect of things was regarded with most extraordinary indifference. No other nation would allow its people to eat mentally what this nation was eating. She had lately had occasion to visit every place of entertainment in most of our large cities, and nothing could be imagined more rotten, low and suggestive, or more detrimental to wholesome life than the entertainments through which she had to sit. If the nation allowed its people to feed on that sort of stuff, we should not long remain one of the greatest Empires the world had ever seen. The meeting terminated with various words of encouragement from Fisher White, Ben Greet, Lady Denman, and Mr. Laurence Binyon.

And now I am tempted to follow up the fortunes of the League still further, and tell the tale of all that it was to do, or try to do, between then and now. But that is another story. Nevertheless, it may not be quite irrelevant to reprint here a leading article from the *Times Educational Supplement*, reviewing many years later a brochure published by the League on the occasion of its Silver Jubilee in 1945. In a surprisingly small space the article sums up the main results and purposes of our endeavour.

'The theatre is irresistible,' said Matthew Arnold; 'organize the theatre.' But the theatre was still unorganized in 1919 when another believer in the theatre declared: 'The theatre is everybody's business.' Of the two, the later dictum, which was delivered by Mr. Geoffrey Whitworth at the inaugural meeting of the British Drama League, carries the greater weight of high explosive. The theatre—the professional or 'commercial' theatre—has always stuck out for being nobody's business but its own. Wittingly or not, that independence was challenged by a voice of the new League. Yet on its first list of officers and committee members there were no fewer than fifteen professional actors and actresses—some, no doubt, leaning towards the left, or highbrow wing, but others well to the right, and one of them openly representing the Actors' Association. It seems to suggest that from the start the League was tactful in its handling of a very difficult problem—the extent or nature of the right of everybody to make the theatre his business, beyond the obvious right to go and see plays and players that he likes and to stay away from those he does not. By 1922 we find the League joining with the Actors' Association in an attack on the bogus manager, and the Actors' Association asking the League to help them keep an eye on outstanding performances by actors in touring companies.

What Mr. Whitworth—the first honorary secretary and later the director of the League—really meant to say, no doubt, was that the drama—not the theatre—was everybody's business. And, as we may learn from the proud but unassuming record of twenty-five years of striking progress (not without some very narrow squeaks in it), the British Drama League left the professional theatre pretty much alone and set hard to work on 'everybody'. It proceeded to collect, to permeate, in the nicest possible way to get at the public in all its guises—Government departments, local authorities, societies and clubs, schools and colleges, and especially the small community, the village and the home. It undertook all that business of conferences, committees and the rest at which artists of any kind are seldom any good, and which even enthusiasts can find an intolerable bore. It undertook also to encourage and instruct the amateur actor, producer, dramatist, stage designer and—not least—hearer and spectator, and to increase their respect for themselves and for the arts they cultivated.

To make 'everybody' so drama-minded and so knowledgeable in the drama that he could be trusted to manage that business of his was a high aim, and a much wider aim than the foundation of a National Theatre, which the League appears rather to fancy, or any sort of nationalization of the theatre, which it inclines to reject. Even the effect (if any) of the British Drama League on the professional theatre is a matter of less moment than its actual achievement, into which it seems to have been drawn step by step by purely empirical incitements. It has found itself bringing the drama into thousand of lives that lacked it, and thus enriching both 'everybody' with the drama and the drama with the inexhaustible powers of 'everybody'.

All very gratifying. In one phrase only, perhaps, did the writer of the article do the League less than justice: 'A National Theatre, *which the League appears rather to fancy*' was certainly an understatement. For, as a matter of fact, this objective had been primary from the start; and after the Haymarket meeting was over, I was anxious at the earliest possible moment to face our infant membership with a challenge that should leave no room for doubt as to where the League stood in this relation. The opportunity soon came. By the good advice of Elsie Fogerty, Principal and founder of the Central School of Speech and Drama, the League held its first Annual Conference at Stratford-on-Avon in the August immediately following the Haymarket meeting. Our 'platform' was a distinguished one. The proceedings opened with a message of goodwill from Ellen Terry, and the speakers included William Archer, Granville-Barker, Lord Burnham, Bridges Adams, Edith Craig, Ben Greet, Norman Wilkinson, Lewis Casson, Viola Tree, Sir Israel Gollancz, Gwen Richardson (representing the Old Vic), Miss Horniman (of the Gaiety Theatre, Manchester), W. S. Kennedy (of the Incorporated Stage Society), and Alfred Lugg (the Secretary of the Actors' Association). This, I believe, was the first occasion in history when a representative gathering of amateur theatrical societies, of professional actors, managers, producers, scene designers, educationists, social workers, and members of the general public had gathered together for free discussion on problems confronting the theatre in its artistic and social aspects.

It was at the opening session of the conference that Sir John (then Mr.) Martin-Harvey moved the first resolution, which took the form of a call to the Drama League to make its chief aim the foundation of a National Theatre. After referring at some length to what he regarded as the parlous state of the English theatre, and to the difficulty there would always be in finding managers who could afford to 'muddle through' by doing the distinguished thing on a basis of commercial speculation, he went on to ask:

FLYING BUTTRESS

Is there a remedy? Yes, I believe there is. I know there is. We are here to-day to discover it, if possible. I do not believe that the remedy will be found in the activities of the many societies which are co-operating at this Conference unless these activities are combined with one single ultimate end in view, and that is the foundation and endowment of a State Theatre. If the eleven points which define the object of the British Drama League can be pursued with this *one object*, I believe that the League will attain that object and confer a lasting blessing on our people. I venture to think that many of the objects laid down in your 'eleven points' will be found to be superfluous. I doubt whether the country needs educating to an appreciation of great drama. I have found that Maeterlinck, Sophocles, Shakespeare, will draw crowds to the theatre. I do not think children need educating—drama is inherent in them—Shakespeare they take to as a duck to water. It is the *poor* and the children who support Shakespeare. If the aim of the British Drama League is to confine its activities for the benefit of small groups and *coteries* of what for want of a better name one may call 'intellectuals' I confess that I am out of sympathy with that aim. It is the working classes—forgive me for using the objectionable expression—who need the beauty in their lives which great drama brings to them. It is the most extraordinary thing to me that no Government has ever had the vision to perceive the necessity of *beauty* in the lives of the poor. It is true that some glimmering of this need is seen in the plans of the Government in relation to better housing of the workers—plans involving the expenditure of millions. But who has the vision to see that great drama at cheap prices is the most potent instrument for the refinement of the working-classes, an instrument ready to their hands at the cost of a few thousands. Let us then concentrate upon the necessity of founding a great National Theatre, build a big one in the midst of the great labouring classes, admit them to great productions of the finest work at small prices. You will have less labour unrest if you remember that man does not live by bread alone, but by beauty in his life and food for his imagination. And if this should appeal to you as the widest and broadest course to pursue, and should you seek to carry it into effect, where will you find a machine better fashioned than the carefully considered scheme of the Shakespeare Memorial National Theatre? That is the scheme which has always had my devotion, and always will have, and in so far as the eleven points of the British Drama League can be utilized to further this end, they shall have my support to the best of my ability.

FLYING BUTTRESS

It is useless to say that because the Shakespeare Memorial National Theatre has not yet had the support of the great public it is a sure proof that it is not wanted. In these cases the public is not articulate. The public does not always voice its need. I never heard that a deputation waited on the Government with a desire for public baths. It has not clamoured for museums, for picture galleries, or for many things which, at the same time, it was only right for their well-being and their enlightenment that they should have. Ladies and gentlemen, I fear I have kept you too long and addressed you in far too didactic a spirit. If you have felt this I can only ask your pardon and excuse myself on the strength of my intense convictions—my deep love and respect for the art I follow, and my very ardent hope and belief that all that is so fine and worthy in it may be placed on a sure and honourable basis. This I firmly believe will come, and if the old parties do not seize the opportunity of doing something towards this end, the Labour Party will.

The speaker's eloquence and transparent sincerity left a deep impression on his audience, though he had, perhaps, gone rather far in asking that *all* the activities of *all* our members should henceforth be *solely* directed towards a single object. However, as a forthright challenge to the Drama League, the speech did nothing but good, and it is significant that at the close of the conference ten days later there was no dissent from the following 'summary resolutions' which were proposed and carried with acclamation:

I. That this Conference urges the importance of establishing:
  (*a*) A National Theatre policy adequate to the needs of the people.
  (*b*) A faculty of the Theatre at the Universities of the country, with the necessary colleges.
II. That this Conference pledges itself to promote and help forward collective and individual efforts for the development of the art of acting, the drama, and of the theatre, as forces in the life of the nation.

No time was lost in making the most of the mandates obtained from the Conference, and the two 'Summary Resolutions' were submitted to the President of the Board of Education, Mr. H. A. L.

Fisher, by a deputation introduced by Mr. Charles Tennyson
(Chairman of the League's Executive Committee), together with
Mr. W. L. Courtney, Sir Sidney Lee, Dr. Boas, Dr. Borland,
Captain Maurice Colbourne (President of the OUDS), Miss Elsie
Fogerty, Mr. Ben Greet, Mr. J. C. Squire, Mr. J. Fisher White
(representing the Actors' Association), and the Hon. Secretary
of the League. Among those intimating their sympathy with the
aims of the deputation and their regret for their inability to be
present were Lord Burnham, Sir Walter Raleigh, Messrs. William
Archer, Martin Harvey, Norman McKinnel, John Masefield, E. J.
Dent, and Professor William Rothenstein.

Mr. W. L. Courtney, speaking on the first resolution, said that
a great deal depended on how we regarded drama; was it a
necessity or a luxury? If a luxury, then there was no need for
further action; but if a necessity, then it should form a part of the
whole educational, social and artistic life of the nation. He mentioned the orgy of commercialism which was then so inimical to
dramatic art in this country, and instanced the different attitude
which prevailed abroad. In conclusion, Mr. Courtney commended
to Mr. Fisher's favour dramatic art as a part of national life and
as a necessity of future education.

After Sir Sidney Lee had spoken on the second resolution,
Mr. Fisher gave a lengthy and encouraging reply. But on the
question of a National Theatre policy he was more wary.

I do not know whether the deputation has any views as to the particular form that the policy should take. As I have already said, our
system of education is on a local basis, and it would be the course most
consonant with our political tradition that any step which the Government might take in the way of helping the theatre should be in aid of
schemes initiated by local enterprise and assisted by local contributions.
I am, of course, giving no pledge as to the attitude which the Government might take up if such a course were adopted by the local
authorities, but I should imagine that if anything were done the initial
steps would be taken locally.

I have said enough to show that I am greatly interested in this subject, that the Board of Education is alive to the importance of cultivating the dramatic instinct and realizes that the merely literary treatment of drama is quite inadequate in any true conception of the education to be derived from it.

Mr. Fisher could, when he liked, adopt a somewhat piscine mood, and on this occasion his words had been so carefully considered that they offered little comfort. However, a *rapport* had been established with the Board which was to bear fruit later on; and, to anticipate a little, it can be recorded that in 1926 the League received an invitation from Mr. Charles Douie, secretary of the Board's Adult Education Committee, to submit evidence for the 'Report on the place of Drama in Adult Education' which was then being prepared. Granville-Barker and the League's Hon. Secretary were called as witnesses, and on the publication of the Report we had the pleasure of reading the following passage dealing specifically with the National Theatre.

While we wish to commend in every way the work of the Shakespeare Associations in furthering the study and production of Shakespeare's plays, we feel unable to offer any detailed comment on the proposals for a Shakespeare National Theatre. We considered from the first that this subject involved so many difficult issues, and might lead to so much controversy that we would not attempt to consider it within the limits of this Report. We should not, however, be giving a fair presentation of the views of some of our witnesses, if we did not mention that some of them in the course of their evidence referred to the establishment of a National Theatre as an essential condition of the advancement of the drama, both as a form of art and as an instrument of education, in providing an inspiration for such dramatic enterprises as we have mentioned in this Report. Mr. Granville-Barker and Mr. Whitworth, the representatives of the British Drama League, for instance, laid great emphasis on the point. In a pamphlet issued by the League, the concept of a Shakespearian Memorial is placed side by side with the need for a theatre which should build up a repertory of modern masterpieces.

The proposals for a National Theatre appear to contemplate some measure of support from the Exchequer. So far as this point is concerned, it was pointed out that virtually every nation in Europe, other than our own, has a National Theatre, and that many have municipal theatres. Another memorandum includes this passage: 'If the objection to a National Theatre endowed or assisted out of State Funds is purely financial, it seems odd that money can be found out of the National Exchequer for the support of collections of savage implements such as flints and poisoned arrows, and of the relics of dead civilizations, but none for the encouragement of the greatest of living arts.'

We cannot debate the merits of these arguments. We wish, however, to make one suggestion. We have found that, under right conditions, the drama can be a most potent influence of moral, intellectual and artistic progress. Some of our witnesses contend that these conditions can best be brought about by the establishment of a National Theatre. We suggest that their contentions should be made the subject of enquiry by a Committee better qualified than this Committee to undertake the task.

In the National Theatre, Exemplary Theatre, Ideal Theatre, by whatever name the institution is called which is to bring drama to its consummation as a form of art, what place has the amateur, and of what significance is the amateur movement, which we have been at pains to describe? We are inclined to think it has the highest significance. For in Mr. Granville-Barker's words, the perfect theatre could never exist without the perfect audience. And the amateur movement, in giving an ever-increasing number of men and women an acquaintance with the art of the theatre, and a capacity for the keenest critical appreciation, is providing that audience.

Turning to the future, we ask what may be the outcome of this dramatic movement which we have surveyed? Surely it will grow; and giving to an ever-growing number the gift of imaginative sympathy and the sense of comradeship, will bring some element of healing and of reconciliation into the warring elements in our national life.

It seems strange, does it not, that no move was made by the League, or for that matter by the S.M.N.T. Committee, to follow up the suggestion of a further departmental inquiry into the National Theatre project on its own account. It was feared, perhaps, that such an inquiry would have revealed as much antagonism as approval. The commercial theatre would have naturally been invited to give evidence; and their reaction to State subsidy was in doubt. But reverting to the year 1922 and thereabouts, let us see how the League in other ways was pulling its weight in the National Theatre cause.

William Archer's Dream

In that year William Archer, who was becoming dissatisfied with the slow progress made by the S.M.N.T. Committee, began a considerable flirtation with the League. On his behalf, we issued an anonymous booklet, written by him and printed at his own expense, under the title *The Foundation of the National Theatre: a Chapter from the History of England After the Great War*, and purporting to have been first published in 1950. The fabulous historian begins by summarizing the events which are already known to readers of this book, and then goes on to describe the money-raising scheme which Archer was unavailingly at that very time endeavouring to persuade the S.M.N.T. Committee to undertake.

In the year 1922 we are told:

The resources of the Committee were too scanty to enable them to place even the New Shakespeare Company upon a permanently satisfactory basis. It was recognized that, if the movement was to be carried forward at all, more money must be raised; and it was fortunately determined that an appeal should be made on behalf of the whole enterprise rather than of any partial and tentative advance towards it. After much deliberation, it was decided that the sum of half a million should be the object first aimed at. It was only, so to speak, a half-way house; but there could be little doubt that, when once attained, the ultimate goal would be, not only in sight, but easy of achievement. Five hundred thousand pounds was not enough to create the whole National Theatre—site, building, and endowment fund—and on the other hand it was considerably more than ought ultimately to be required for the Endowment of the National Theatre alone. . . . The capital was to be strictly tied up in the hands of trustees; only the revenue was to be available; and on this basis an Interim National Theatre was to be established in some existing building. It was recognized as more than likely that a whole year's income would have to be devoted to structural alterations (especially behind the scenes) necessary to render the building approximately fit for repertory uses; but these changes once effected, it was thought that, even with the burden of rent to be borne, the theatre could be worked in a manner not *too* remote from the ideal to be ultimately realized. This ideal, of course, was not for a moment dropped out of sight. The temporary and preparatory nature of the enterprise was emphasized in its official style and title, the 'Interim National Theatre'. But it was believed that, as soon as the institution had proved its value, the Government would awaken to its duty of offering a site, and private munificence would not be slow to supply, not only the bricks and mortar, but the granite, the marble and the bronze.

The first step taken was to draw up a concise and carefully worded statement of the urgent desirability of a National Theatre, and to get this 'confession of faith'—or at any rate of hope—signed by, as nearly as possible, all the leaders of the national life and thought: statesmen, churchmen, authors, artists, actors, journalists, lawyers, doctors, soldiers, sailors, representatives of capital, of labour, of the great provincial cities, of schools and universities, of, in short, the whole intellectual and economic life of the country. The signing of this pronouncement involved no pecuniary or other responsibility. It meant merely the acceptance of a principle, the endorsement of an idea.

While this document was being circulated and signed, the Committee occupied itself in drawing up such a Constitution for the theatre as should clearly differentiate it from all private and profit-making enterprises. It was felt that a governing body, prefiguring, at any rate, the authority to be ultimately created, ought at once to come into operation. The permanent authority, as everyone knows, is now vested in a Council, nominated by the Government, the Universities, and other public bodies. This Council elects a Board of Control, fifteen in number; and the Board appoints the Director of the theatre, receives his periodical reports, and, by approving or disapproving them, continues him in office or requests his resignation.

The Constitution being drafted and the Statement of Principle very influentially signed, the next step to be taken was eagerly debated. Many were in favour of at once calling in the aid of the Press, and setting afoot a great national subscription. It was ultimately decided, however, that a private or semi-private endeavour ought to be made to secure the indispensable foundation of the enterprise—the Endowment Fund—before appealing to the generosity of the public at large.

There followed a lengthy analysis of individual income-groups as disclosed by the Inland Revenue surtax assessments for the year 1918–19. It was apparent that for the year in question there were no fewer than 7,000 persons in receipt of annual incomes of £10,000 and upwards. If 18 per cent of these would each contribute the sum of £1,000 to the fund, the desired total would be obtained.

It was no easy matter to put this 'Theory of the Thousand-pounders' to the test. The first great point was to find representative men in the six or eight different classes among which the wealth of the country is divided, to head the lists and set the ball rolling. When this was done, however, the good example was freely followed. On Shakesspeare's Birthday, 1923, it was possible to make the welcome announcement that a capital sum of £50,000 had been vested in trustees. . . .

The next step was obvious . . . to organize and launch the Interim National Theatre. . . . The history of this preparatory enterprise is full of interest, but would take too long to recount in detail. Suffice it to say that during the six years which elapsed before the National Theatre was ready for occupation, the Interim Theatre recruited an excellent and homogeneous company and a most efficient staff; taught everyone concerned, from the Director downwards, many valuable lessons: and enabled the National Theatre to present from the outset a seasoned organization, instead of a raw levy of unharmonized talents.

The Board had now to mature plans for raising the additional £50,000 for acquiring a suitable site and erecting the permanent home of the institution. Arrangements were therefore made for a private conference between the Board and the leading newspaper proprietors and editors, at which measures should be concerted for initiating the great campaign on 23rd April 1924. The meeting assembled, but the Chairman of the Board who was to have presided, had not arrived. Five minutes passed, and then the Secretary was called to the telephone. He returned with the announcement that a very important communication had reached the Chairman just as he was starting for the meeting; that he was now dealing with the matter; and that he would arrive without fail in a quarter of an hour. For that space the assemblage possessed its soul in patience, and at the stated moment the Chairman appeared. He felt sure, he said, that the meeting would pardon his unpunctuality when it heard the reason. Just as he was stepping into his car, he was hailed by a well-known solicitor, who desired five minutes' conversation; and it then appeared that the solicitor represented a certain noble lord who desired to have the honour of building the Shakespeare Memorial National Theatre, at the cost approximately of £250,000. No doubt, said the Chairman, the site still remained to be secured; but he thought the meeting would agree with him that this generous offer created a new situation which must be fully examined before any plan of campaign could be profitably discussed. There being no dissentients from this view, the meeting, after expressing its sense of the donor's munificent public spirit, adjourned *sine die*.

It was never reassembled. As luck would have it, the reconstruction of the Trafalgar Square district necessitated by the building of the new Charing Cross Bridge, and the removal of the South-Eastern terminus to the south side of the river, gave the Government control over a large area of ground; and the site where the noble theatre now stands was allotted to the Governors on such favourable terms that only a small additional subscription was required. This was raised without difficulty; competitive designs for the fabric were invited; the choice fell on those submitted by Messrs. Mortiss and Vernier; and the foundation stone was laid by King George V on 23rd April 1926— just 310 years after the death of Shakespeare.

It is scarcely necessary at this time of day to argue that the National Theatre has amply fulfilled its purpose. It has not escaped criticism, sometimes just, sometimes unjust. Mistakes have no doubt been made —in what great enterprise are they ever avoided?—but they have seldom or never been ignoble errors. The Theatre has done all that came within the definition of its duties. It has kept Shakespeare constantly in its repertory, its statutes demanding that no week should pass without the performance of at least one of his plays. It has cultivated a thoroughly intelligent method of Shakespearian presentation, avoiding equally the bombast of the eighteenth century, the over-adornment of the nineteenth, and the pedantry of the early twentieth. It has kept alive many of our best modern plays which, without it, would have remained unknown to the younger generation of playgoers. It has produced many new plays of great merit. It has offered its artists far healthier and more dignified conditions of life and work than are possible in the long-run theatres, with their precarious engagements and their ever-shifting personnel. It has formed a highly valued social rendezvous for people of intelligence and culture. It has given, in each season, many educational performances at reduced prices. And it has offered a model and set a standard for the Repertory Theatres throughout the country, which have contributed to the now admittedly flourishing state of the British drama.

These are great services: but they are far from being all that the National Theatre has done for us. It has freed us from the reproach of neglecting and undervaluing the great heirloom and asset of the English-speaking race:

> *Our Shakespeare on whose forehead climb*
> *The crowns o'th'world.*

It has made London—much more truly than it ever was before—a place of pilgrimage for all who speak Shakespeare's tongue. It has relieved us from the humiliating necessity of owning to our European neighbours the hopeless inferiority of our theatrical organization. It has, in a word, removed a stigma from the national character, a blot from the imperial escutcheon. Better late than never.

What a vision! In some ways so prophetic, though in others very wide of the mark. That scene, for instance, where the private press conference hears the news of the noble lord's £250,000 donation—a piece of drama worthy of the author of *The Green Goddess!*

It must be noted that the idea of initiating a new appeal for funds by way of a 'Statement of Principle' to be signed by a limited number of influential people, had already been submitted by Archer to the S.M.N.T. Committee. His disgust at its turndown was communicated in a letter to Granville-Barker from which I am sorely tempted to quote, so humanly does it reveal the personal tensions which find no place in official records.

MY DEAR H. G.-B. [he writes on 21st July 1922],

The Old Vickers—whom Satan fly away with—have had the unspeakable audacity to turn down my proposal at the Executive that we—the Sub-Comm. of Ways and Means, should be empowered to collect signatures privately for the enclosed Declaration. Really life is impossible with these people. They assemble outside, march in military formation with Bourchier at their head, and sit in a solid body. I expect them to turn up at the next meeting with a fife and drum band playing 'See the Conquering Heroes Come!' . . . I expect they were specially disgruntled to-day, for we succeeded in cutting down from five years to three the term during which we engage to give £1,000 a year to an already largely subsidized Old Vic. . . .[1] The division on my proposal was a tie—5 to 5—and Courtney in the chair ruled that I ought to withdraw the motion, in which I suppose he was right. If I hadn't acted with extreme magnanimity we should have won. X was on the point of going away before the division, when I begged him to remain and hurried up the vote, feeling that we oughtn't to take advantage of the fact that one of the enemy had to catch a train; but I don't believe the nobility of my conduct was in the least appreciated. . . .

Enough for to-night. If you have any good and sufficient reason against my proposal, of course I shall bow to it—especially if you can substitute a better. But don't let the mere Capuan mood inhibit you.

Granville-Barker replied five days later, saying that he thought Archer's treatment by the S.M.N.T. Committee made a good deal of difference, and counselling him to go ahead with his plan, but to cut out the Preliminary 'Declaration'.

This by itself will be of no use. Fine words butter no parsnips. But clearly I think, you have to capture the Executive. . . . The way you will capture them will be to bring them some promise of money (I remember that after the Sir C. M. gift, Mrs. Lyttelton had the whole body for a time in the hollow of her hand). They have no scheme for getting any. You have. The advantage is with you so far. . . . I shove, as you see, all the work on to you, but not in a merely Capuan mood. I believe I am right in recommending a start straght away with conditional thousand pounders. No more words. And you are undoubtedly the person unaided to catch 'em.

As to the scheme in general, he had already written on July 17th:

MY DEAR W. A.,

I think it is awfully good—the Chapter itself and the Scheme. Moreover, I believe the Scheme is perfectly and immediately practicable.

[1] This of course, was some time before the Charity Commissioners decided that no National Theatre funds could be used for any outside purpose. See pages 120-2 passim.

I have independently become strongly persuaded of this during the last two or three months. . . .

I talked to Whitworth at some length upon the immediate practical issue, and we are agreed that the Drama League must place itself unreservedly at your disposal for what its activities are worth. So far we have done *this* (I remind you);—staved off an attack on the N.T. Committee by the wilder spirits in our midst with a resolution pledging our support to the said N.T.C. But clearly if something on your scale isn't attempted, the attack will materialize again, and next time I shall personally make no attempt to check it, so strongly do I feel that the N.T.C. *must* move, and forward something upon a scale which will excuse this pampering of the Old Vic and the neglect to nourish the Bridges Adams' enterprise. And though the D.L. may seem something of a stage army, I am now convinced that it does stand for, even if it can't fully represent, a very real and enthusiastic movement which at any time may be made to concentrate itself temporarily upon a demand for the N.T.

The League asked nothing better than to go forward under the conditions laid down by its Chairman. As already mentioned. we circulated Archer's 'Chapter' among our members and among a number of important people, most of whom endorsed it out of hand. But at this point Archer seemed to vacillate, discouraged by his Committee's lack of support and not daring to cut himself off from them altogether. In this decision he was probably influenced by Granville-Barker, who on July 26th had written:

I think there *are* circumstances under which you and I might act together alone about the Declaration, but I strongly feel that you ought to keep your hold on the official Committee and that, at the moment, this might prejudice it. Also my immediate past action in telling the Drama League (and carrying my point) that they must support the official Committee instead of rivalling it, stands a bit in the light.

So, on 25th August we find Archer writing to Mrs. Lyttelton, his confidante and great ally on the Committee:

My mind is a sort of maelstrom of conflicting ideas and suggestions as to the National Theatre. I think we ought to send £100 to Germany (where it would be equivalent to several millions of marks) and in a few weeks they could ship us a National Theatre in sections, with Director and all complete. Why is it that they can do these things there and we can't?

For the present the essential points before the sub-Committee are these: (1) Is the principle of *provisional promises* a sound one? (2) Ought we to try to raise the Guarantee Fund by a semi-private appeal to rich people to give provisional promises of substantial sums—£1,000 and such like? If these questions are answered in the negative, all my speculations fall to the ground, and the field is open to another plan of campaign. If the questions are answered in the affirmative, we must act 'in a concatenation according'.

But there is, I admit, one more question to be answered; supposing the above principles to be right, have we, so to speak, the spring-board off which to jump? If we can get promises of £50,000 I am confident that we can get £5,000,000—but can we get the intial £50,000? Here I am useless. I can hammer a type-writer to any extent; but when it comes to sending round the hat, I turn tail and run away. If other people can't step into the breach here, there is 'nothing doing'. We are wrecked (I verily believe) in sight of port.

It was not until June 1923 that the next move was made by the Drama League. It happened that the well-known American actor, James K. Hackett, was in London; and, introduced to us (I think) by William Archer, he disclosed a plan for raising the major part of a million pound fund on the basis of the sale of shilling shares to the public. When the theatre had been built coupons for these shares were to be cashable at the box office for a rebate of one shilling on the price of each seat purchased. Each coupon would apply to one performance only, and not for first nights or gala performances. By this means constant attendance at the theatre would be encouraged, and the rule whereby only one share could be used to secure a rebate on one ticket would prevent the theatre being swamped by the owners of shilling shares, thus depriving the theatre of any actual revenue for a considerable time. Donations up to five pounds would carry with them their equivalent number of shares. But after five pounds no more than a hundred share coupons would be supplied.

This ingenious scheme was fully outlined in a memorandum forwarded by the League to the S.M.N.T. Committee, together with a detailed proposal for the future Constitution of the National Theatre, and a plan for a money appeal to the wealthy on much the same lines as those suggested by William Archer. The whole thing, it was recommended, should be linked with the British Empire Exhibition at Wembley Park, then in process of organization.

In this connection [says the Memorandum] the Drama League has been lucky enough to secure an extensive gallery in the Fine Art Palace at the Exhibition. We had meant to use this Gallery for a retrospective Exhibition of British Theatrical Art, but if the present suggestions, or some agreed modifications of them, be adopted, we should be prepared to consider the utilization of the entire space which the Authorities of the Exhibition have placed at our disposal for an intensive Exhibit designed to illustrate the past, present, and future of the National Theatre Movement. A model of a National Theatre could be on view, together with plans for the building, in the production of which the leading Architectural Bodies might be invited to assist by way of organizing competitions for Models and Plans or otherwise. The whole Exhibit would centre, or rather circle, round the National Theatre scheme, and we need not emphasize the high publicity value of such an Exhibit, both for our own general public, and for the wealthy and influential overseas visitors who will come to Wembley Park during the course of the summer.

Finally [concluded the memorandum] to avoid any possible mis-conception, we should state quite plainly that the wish of the Drama League is simply to offer assistance to the S.M.N.T. Committee. Competition in regard to such an object as the foundation of a National Theatre would be as absurd as it would be disastrous to the end in view, and we trust that our proposal may be considered in the same spirit as that in which it is offered—namely, a single-minded effort to help in the work which the S.M.N.T. initiated and exists to carry on to a successful issue. The proposal is not made because the League is a wealthy organization, or one which has before undertaken work of this kind, but because it has ready to hand the skeleton of a machinery which could undertake the work more easily, as we believe, than any other body. In this case it would not be a case of improvising the machinery. This, as already noted, exists already to hand in the shape of nearly three hundred affiliated organizations[1] scattered through the length and breadth of England, and ranging from small village acting societies to such important bodies as the Actors' Association, the Royal Academy of Dramatic Art, the Manchester Playgoers, etc. The League, it will be seen is nothing more nor less than a Federation of theatrical organizations, amateur and professional, and we are confident that the majority of the bodies forming this Federation would be induced to throw themselves into the scheme with the utmost enthusiasm.

The League has at present adequate offices at 10, King Street, Covent Garden, and for the extension of work which would be involved, further accommodation could be obtained in the same building. Our present staff would, in the initial stages, be at the service of the National Theatre Campaign, but soon extra help would undoubtedly be required. But we believe that if the Shakespeare Memorial Committee could see its way to render financial assistance for a definite period the raising of further funds for propaganda purposes would not be necessary. In the event of such financial support being forthcoming, it would of course be understood that money voted by the Shakespeare Memorial National Theatre Committee should be used for no other purpose than for the National Theatre propaganda and always under the supervision of a special committee on which the S.M.N.T. should be adequately represented.

Could one speak fairer than that? But there was nothing doing so far as the S.M.N.T. Committee was concerned; as will appear from the following item in the minutes of their meeting on 10th July 1923:

The appended communication from the British Drama League, comprising details of a scheme by Mr. Hackett, was considered, after reference to the relevant committee, and the following resolution was adopted: 'The Executive, having carefully considered the scheme submitted by the British Drama League, as also Mr. Hackett's plan, is of the opinion that the present time is not favourable for the success of these schemes, and is not prepared to countenance the proposals.'

Though abandoning all idea of making an appeal for money on its own, the League, nothing daunted, and in association with

---

[1] Today there are over six thousand.

Country Life, went on with its competition for architectural designs for a National Theatre. The panel of judges included Mr. Alfred Gotch, President of the R.I.B.A., Sir Edwin Lutyens, and Granville-Barker, the result being announced at the Annual Meeting of the Drama League held in the summer of 1924 at the British Empire Exhibition. The successful competitor was Mr. W. L. Somerville of Toronto, and the generous donor of the £250 award was Mr. James K. Hackett. A full report of the competition with reproductions of the winning plans was published in the League's journal *Drama* for July 1924, and again in December 1929 a special National Theatre number of *Drama* was issued, containing an illustrated analysis by Granville-Barker of Mr. Somerville's designs, and a list of over 170 important people who had favourably responded to a questionaire circulated earlier by the League.

This manifesto followed a well-attended National Theatre Demonstration held during the tenth annual conference of the Drama League at Northampton on October 25th of the same year. During a Gala Performance at the Opera House, and in the presence of Colonel Malone, M.P. for Northampton, the Mayor and Mayoress, and other distinguished guests, Lord Lytton delivered a powerful address on the need for a national repertory theatre. Referring to the pioneers of the repertory movement, Miss Horniman, Miss Lilian Baylis, Miss Lena Ashwell, and Sir Barry Jackson, 'The only proper apex for this movement is', he said, 'the establishment of a National Repertory Theatre in the capital of the Empire.' Lord Lytton expressed the hope, too, that the scheme would be sufficiently comprehensive to enable half the company to be always on tour so that the chief provincial cities and the Empire could have the opportunity of seeing the actors.

Next day, at the Conference itself, there was a lively debate on a Resolution moved by Mr. Robert Young, M.P.:

'That this Conference of the British Drama League, believing that

FLYING BUTTRESS

the Government is in sympathy with the idea and establishment of a National Theatre and would favourably consider a practical and agreed scheme to this end, requests the Council to take early and energetic measures to achieve this great object.'

In speaking to this motion Mr. Young stated that a certain amount of scepticism had entered the minds of most people when considering the question of a National Theatre. He read a letter from Mr. Bernard Shaw, stating that no one cared tuppence about a National Theatre, and he could not honestly advise Mr. Young to put his shoulder to it— he would be baffled by the national cold shoulder. For twenty years the Shakespeare Memorial Committee had been begging for subscriptions with no result. This letter Mr. Young interpreted as a plea to 'get a move on'. He explained that he had brought this resolution forward in consequence of the Prime Minister's reply to a question about the National Theatre in the House of Commons last July. This reply was undoubtedly an invitation to those interested to 'get together'. Unfortunately, the British Theatre was in the grip of commerce, and until it could free itself from this commercial tyranny, it would not be able to reveal itself as a thing of beauty and a joy for ever. There was little hope of our being able to interest the vast number of our population in the National Theatre, but as a minority we could achieve our object and the majority would then look on this achievement with pride. We were doing an honourable and worthy things to press for a National Theatre. There were two practical ways by which the cause could be furthered:

(1) by defining what is meant by a 'National Theatre';
(2) by propagating the idea.

Mr. Young stated that he hoped and believed the necessary money would be forthcoming from the Government, but no Government would provide money for a National Theatre, unless it were pushed by a strong volume of public opinion. The League had not yet realized its potential power—its 1,600 affiliated societies represented many thousands of individuals outstripping in its influence the Professional Theatre. In conclusion, Mr. Young urged the Conference not only to pass the Resolution, but to follow it up with propaganda in every direction.

Mr. Norman Marshall, in seconding the resolution, stressed the importance of the workshop as an integral part of the National Theatre.

Before opening the discussion, the Chairman, Mr. Geoffrey

171

Whitworth, read a letter from the Home Secretary, Mr. J. R. Clynes, supporting the motion:

DEAR MR. WHITWORTH,

I hope you will have a very successful Conference at Northampton. I would welcome the prospect of an agreed scheme to promote the establishment of a National Theatre. We already have a variety of Municipal and State Institutions, which altogether render substantial service in the sphere of science and art. Libraries, Art Galleries, Orchestras, and extensive provisions for sports and recreation have become a Municipal or National charge. The Drama, first because it is Drama, and secondly because of its far-reaching educational value, deserves not merely recognition but co-operation and honour. In the last ten years dramatic enterprise must have poured into the Treasury many millions of pounds, and must have made a widespread, if indirect, contribution to improved National character and understanding. It would be enough if in exchange for the service which the Drama renders to our country, the cause of a National Theatre could receive but a fraction of its own contribution. The subject is, however, more than one of finance. It is one of Public opinion and Parliamentary disposition. I hope your Conference will do something to create the National support which is necessary for your purpose.

Yours sincerely,

J. R. CLYNES

Mr. Holford Knight, M.P., stated that there were certain facts which should be made clear. Mr. Bernard Shaw was becoming a perennial fount of inaccuracies. The Shakespeare Memorial Committee had not asked for donations for fifteen years. The Committee had met the previous week and was taking immediate steps to collect all friends of the National Theatre in the most catholic sense, and they were proposing to revive the deputation to the Prime Minister which had been inaugurated in 1924. The Committee would welcome every possible help that this League could give in achieving its great object. He concluded by cordially supporting Mr. Young's resolution.

Mr. Weston Wells said that it would depend very largely on the public whether the Theatre would be dull and run for school children. This was not an argument against the National Theatre.

Mrs. Porter protested against this slur on school children.

Mr. Sladen Smith feared that the National Theatre would be dull and inefficient, an eyesore and an earsore.

Mr. C. B. Purdom thought that it would be a good idea if the British Drama League could formulate a scheme, but it had a very difficult task to make its propaganda successful.

The Chairman explained that the chief reason for the scheme being brought forward now and from a somewhat different angle than hitherto, was the encouraging answer of the Prime Minister to Mr. Young's question in the House. What was lacking at the moment was a definite scheme, and this the Council would engage themselves to draw up. He further suggested that a permanent centre, and a tradition, must be established before a Travelling Company could be sent out.

The motion, on being put to the vote, was carried by 62 votes to 10.

As a result of this meeting, the Council of the League took immediate action, and on 29th October a letter was sent to Sir Israel Gollancz informing him of the Northampton resolution, and stating that a Committee consisting of Lord Lytton, Sir Kenneth Barnes, and the Hon. Secretary had already been appointed by the Council to draw up a new National Theatre scheme.

But, since we naturally desire to act in harmony with the Shakespeare Memorial National Theatre Committee [the letter continued], I am asked to enquire if your Committee would be disposed to appoint three of its own number to collaborate in the work? By this means it is felt that the danger of over-lapping would be obviated, and collaboration from the start secured. It would, of course, be understood that any scheme agreed on by the Joint Committee would be referred to our respective Councils for their approval before being sent up as an agreed scheme to the Prime Minister.

On November 1st there was a meeting of the S.M.N.T. Executive at which the above letter was duly considered. It appeared that on October 23rd, prompted perhaps by an earlier letter from the Drama League, which had asked for an expression of goodwill from Sir Israel Gollancz to the forthcoming conference at Northampton, the Committee realized the need for some kind of colla-

boration with the League, if their position as the official pro-
tagonists of the National Theatre was not to suffer. It was therefore agreed to accept the League's offer of co-operation, and
explaining that they had already decided to summon a Conference, the S.M.N.T. Committee invited the League to take
part in it. In the event, the conference was convened at the
House of Commons on 25th November 1929, and was attended
by representatives of the various bodies interested in the proposal
to establish a National Theatre in London. It was unanimously
resolved, on the motion of Sir Johnston Forbes-Robertson, Chairman of the Conference:

> That a selection panel, consisting of two members of the Shakespeare
> Memorial National Theatre Committee, two members of the British
> Drama League, and two members of the Parliamentary Committee
> (formed for the purpose of furthering the National Theatre project)
> should be appointed to frame an agreed scheme, and to bring this
> scheme before the Conference at the earliest possible date.

This selection committee met without delay, and appointed
the following to frame an agreed scheme, namely, the Earl of
Lytton, Miss Lena Ashwell, Sir Kenneth Barnes, Sir Israel
Gollancz, Mr. Percy Harris, M.P., Major Hills, M.P., Professor
Allardyce Nicoll, Mr. Walter Payne, Sir Nigel Playfair, and Mr.
Geoffrey Whitworth. The Earl of Lytton was appointed Chair-
man, and Sir Israel Gollancz the Hon. Secretary.

Their report, when completed, did not materially differ from
earlier proposals, except that for the first time two theatres, a large
and a smaller one, were specified, and that fifteen Governors,
appointed by the Prime Minister, were to nominate an Advisory
Council to co-operate with the Director, and be responsible with
him for the general policy of the theatre. This Advisory Committee was to consist of three of the Governors, three experts in
theatrical work, who should receive a fee for attendance, and
ex officio the Director, Treasurer, and Literary Adviser. The need
for such an advisory body was, I remember, particularly stressed

by Sir Nigel Playfair, since he thought that among the active stage producers at the time there was no one who could be trusted to take full responsibility as Director.

It must be admitted that by now the Drama League had fairly earned its recognition as a powerful instrument for spreading the National Theatre idea in quarters scarcely touched by the official propaganda, and accorded at last and on its own merits an integral position in the National Theatre movement. Only on one further occasion did the League act without reference to the S.M.N.T. Committee. That was on 31st January 1930, when it organized a large and enthusiastic demonstration at the Kingsway Hall, with Lord Lytton in the chair.

The speakers included Mr. Bernard Shaw, Miss Lena Ashwell, Mrs. Philip Snowden, Sir Donald Maclean, M.P., and Sir Israel Gollancz. It would be pleasant to print a full report of all the speeches, which were on a high level and displayed a greater degree of confidence than had lately been the custom. However, we will confine ourselves to the following contribution from Mr. Shaw:

England [he said] was always a curious place in which to raise any question of fine art. He did not want to be committed for contempt of court and hoped the audience would not let this go any further. But *was* acting a fine art? According to the rules by which our public officials were governed, fine art in this country was anything connected with the Art Union founded by the Prince Consort in the time of Queen Victoria. Therefore, he hardly dared to say in the presence of Miss Lena Ashwell that acting was not a fine art. Wherever you travelled on the Continent you found State or Municipal theatres. Maybe they hadn't any plays, for they built theatres because it was the custom. When one of his plays was being produced at the Burgtheater in Vienna, he tried to impose certain conditions under which the play was to be performed, but found himself in correspondence with a gentleman of the rank of Count, who told him such a thing was without precedent. The regulations had come down from apostolic times; they could no more be changed than the laws of the Medes or Persians. He had retorted: 'Politically, no doubt your Emperor is the Emperor of

Austria-Hungary, but from the dramatic point of view I am the Emperor of Europe and I insist on my treaty.' The Count was a man of tact and produced the piece without any agreement at all. He afterwards wrote and said what a success the play had proved. 'An English or American producer,' continued Mr. Shaw, 'would have told me under the same circumstances, that my play was a sanguinary frost.'

Mr. Shaw talked for a few minutes about the medieval attitude towards the theatre. Molière was buried by night in an unknown grave! Shakespeare was buried in consecrated ground, it is true, but his monument had no connection with the stage. He was there as William Shakespeare, Gent! There was never any official recognition in this country. On the Continent there was.

Concerning the eloquent case recently put forward by Mr. John Drinkwater against a central theatre as suggested, advocating in its place municipal theatres, Mr. Shaw remarked: 'I entirely agree as to the enormous importance of municipal theatres, but I think Mr. Drinkwater was too hasty in saying, "Let us have many municipal theatres and therefore no central one." I want a central theatre in London as a monument. He added, to the evident amusement of his audience, that he doubted very much whether his plays would be performed at a National Theatre in London. Very likely, if it were under any sort of direct State regulation, they would be thought too dangerous and advanced. But, after all, that did not matter. There was sufficient admirable dramatic art which did not terrify the Governments to keep the theatre going. Without having regard to strict commercial considerations, a National Theatre should be able to do the best work in the best way and not go in for that horrible policy of giving the public what it likes. Nobody knew what the public liked. Take his own play, *Man and Superman*, for example. He had put into that play a third act, which everyone connected with the theatre said it was impossible to perform. He himself had not expected it to be performed. His friend, Mr. Esmé Percy, had insisted on learning the act and playing it. The public liked it and now they always wanted it. He had tried to sit through it once, and had nearly died afterwards. This had induced him to write *Back to Methuselah*, which lasts a week. The English people wanted three-and-a-half hours of solid entertainment and not one-and-a-half hours, with long intervals for going to the bar. There were very few who could afford 5s. for a seat. The public needed plenty of 2s. 6d. seats, and for the snobs, the real out-and-outers, some seats at 5s.

A site was wanted for this theatre. They wanted the Government to give them one, as well as a lot of money. All the efforts for obtaining money had been heart-breaking. The position, however, was now more hopeful than ever before. The B.B.C. were spending thousands a year, but the only complaints were that the programmes were too good. It was the old cry of 'Give 'em mutton.' We wanted a theatre which refused to give the people merely what it wanted. There was needed some institution to give the public the best until they learned to like it. Mr. Shaw finished by saying, 'I want the State Theatre to be what St. Paul's and Westminster Abbey are to religion—something to show what the thing can be at its best.'

He then formally moved the following Resolution: 'That this meeting convened by the British Drama League registers its support of the project to establish a National Theatre in London, and welcomes the present effort to promote an agreed scheme for submission to the Prime Minister.'

During the meeting the Hon. Secretary read out various messages of sympathy and support which he had received from abroad, including one from M. Einarson, of the National Theatre of Iceland, which was being built but had not yet opened. It was to be financed from a tax on cinemas, and its prospective leading actress, Mlle Kalman, was present on the platform, and was presented with a bouquet. The following extracts are drawn from the other principal messages received:

From M. Gemier, *President of the French Section of the Universal Society of the Theatre:*

The civilized world, all the friends of England, will be grateful to the British Government, to the Municipality of London, when they have established a theatre—National and generously endowed to preserve the treasures of dramatic art from Shakespeare to Bernard Shaw. This is a patriotic duty of the greatest urgency. All the members of the Universal Society of the Theatre send to the British Drama League, to Granville-Barker, to all those who are at the head of this movement of generosity and patriotic justice, their most ardent wishes for its success.

FLYING BUTTRESS

From ÉMILE FABRE, *Administrateur Comédie Française:*

Your idea of founding a National Theatre in London is excellent. Your dramatic literature is rich in masterpieces, but the performances of them are infrequent. A National Theatre, where they would be played regularly, would be a Theatre which every educated person would welcome with joy.

From PROFESSOR MAX REINHARDT, *Deutsche Theatre, Berlin:*

In England it seems to me a circumstance of peculiar significance that through a National Theatre the formation of a close association of actors would become possible. The conception of a community is, in my experience, inseparable from the art of theatrical production. Only from community consciousness can grow the team-work of which the theatre stands in need. The actor in the National Theatre would have his duties clearly prescribed. With an assured income he would be spared the pressure to accept employment for purely pecuniary reasons; a sense of peace would be borne into his life and thence into his art. If public interest be sufficient and be skilfully guided, it will soon come about that an engagement in the National Theatre will be the highest aim of every actor. In the project for an English National Theatre I greet one of those valuable ideas from which later generations will trace the dawn of a new era in art.

From ERIK WETTERGREEN, *Royal Theatre, Stockholm:*

Let me at once state that I greet this idea with the greatest joy. The expressionistic line that flourished during and after the Great War is now going to fade, and our epoch is asking for a new realism working with simple but well modulated means. In this style of acting England is the great master. This fact is not as yet sufficiently recognized on the Continent, certainly owing to the fact that the London theatres, from commercial reasons, generally have a repertory much inferior to the acting. A National Theatre with a sufficiently strong financial base need not be the victim of these considerations but can carry the noble English art of acting to that level where it is rightly at home. May the new National Theatre be the bearer of the world's greatest dramatic traditions and of that new truth and sincerity for which the world is longing.

At this meeting Sir Israel Gollancz had been at the top of his form. To him fell the task of proposing the vote of thanks to the

Chairman, and thus an opportunity was given him to review the work of the past and to foresee a grand future for the project under the inspiring guidance of Lord Lytton. Of this opportunity he took full advantage, concluding his speech with a ringing peroration worthy of the best days of his eloquence. But not long afterwards, when I had occasion to call on him at King's College, I noticed a change. Friendly as ever, he manifested a sense of anxiety which in him was most unusual. So resilient he had always been, so humorous, and agile both in gesture and in thought. If now the end was not far off, it might come as a disaster to the Shakespeare National Theatre with which he had been associated from the very beginning, loyal to it through every chance of fortune, and though criticized by some, the axle round which the whole wheel turned. His last words to me that day were of a strange foreboding, mingled with a hint of benediction that made me gravely ponder as we said good-bye.

VIII

THE NINETEEN THIRTIES

Sir Israel Gollancz passed away on 23rd June 1930. The Executive Committee did not meet until November 6th. There were present Sir Frank Meyer in the chair, Mr. Bernard Shaw, Sir Robert Donald, Sir Archibald Flower, Mr. Alfred Sutro, Mr. Holford Knight, Mr. Acton Bond, Mr. Hamilton Fyfe, and Sir Nigel Playfair. Their first act was to pass a resolution expressing their deep regret and sense of the loss sustained by the movement by the death of their late Honorary Secretary.

It was then moved by Mr. Bernard Shaw, and seconded by Sir Robert Donald, 'That Mr. Geoffrey Whitworth be invited to become Honorary Secretary of the Committee.' When informed of this invitation, I cannot pretend that the recipient was not pleased, though his pleasure was mingled with a sense of trepidation. Reading through the minutes of past meetings of the Executive, I was astonished by the mass of work which had been accomplished or attempted. The complexity of the situation was borne in on me, and I realized that many of the ideas already burgeoning in my mind would seem no novelty to the Committee, since most of them had already been tried and found wanting. Henceforward committee meetings were held at the headquarters of The Drama League, at 8, Adelphi Terrace (now, alas, no more), within a stone's throw of the flats of Barrie and Bernard Shaw, just round the corner in Duke Street. We met in a green-panelled room overlooking the Thames, with a fine view of the tumble-down South Bank, and in the foreground over a belt of trees, the broad and silver highway of the river. Turning our eyes eastward to the Shot Tower at the southern end of Waterloo Bridge, we did not foresee that on that precise spot would arise one day the theatre of our dreams.

This site, as a matter of fact, or one very near it, had been suggested by Granville-Barker in a new book on the National Theatre which he brought out in 1930. 'The site facing the river', he wrote, 'between County Hall and the Surrey Approach to the new Charing Cross Bridge, is about all that one can wish for; a National Theatre could hardly be better placed. A National Opera House could find a place opposite.' Transfer the site a little further East, and for 'Opera House' read 'Concert Hall' and you have a shrewd anticipation of what the womb of time would one day bring forth.

Granville-Barker's New Plan

And now it will be well to pay some attention to this revised scheme of Granville-Barker's, for its effect on opinion was prompt and permanent. The book was really an up-to-date sequel to that earlier volume which he had written with William Archer, a sequel that was badly needed; for much in the first plan was already out of date, particularly in the sphere of financial estimate. Granville-Barker, we may note in passing, had by now retired from active work on the stage, and was living in Devonshire, busy with Shakespearian criticism, and collaborating with his wife in translating Spanish plays into English.

In spite of this, he must have spent a great deal of time in preparing the new National Theatre book, which, short as it was, contained an intensive study of the whole set-up of the theatre and of the organization which he now felt to be necessary.

The chief and most controversial aspect of his report was a novel insistence on the need for *two theatres under one roof*, not as a mere luxury, but as a necessary condition if the theatre were to pay its way. Unfortunately, at the moment of writing, this book is out of print, but I am permitted to quote at some length from those pages which deal specifically with the size of the company and with the need for a two-stage theatre. In the first place he lays it down that to cope with an annual repertory of some 49 plays, the strength of the company must be in the region of 63 actors and 27 actresses. He goes on to say that:

> This number depends upon the impossibility of the actors, even of small parts, rehearsing daily and playing eight or nine times a week all the year round. Nobody should be in more than six performances a week, and actors of important parts in not more than four or five. The 'eight performances a week' custom is comparatively new; and it is one at least of the causes of the decline of quality in modern acting. It is bound to lead to automatism. It has a peculiarly disastrous effect upon the younger actors playing the smaller parts (and just at the time when they are most impressionable). With the best will in the world they cannot give variety—eight times a week!—to their thirty or forty lines. And even the long parts fall into mechanical repetitions; spontaneity becomes trick, however cleverly disguised. As to great parts; no man can *act* Hamlet or Othello or Macbeth eight times a week. He would kill himself within a month if he tried to. Garrick, Kemble, and Macready would have been shocked at the notion. . . .
>
> The number of the company yet further depends upon two considerations which the theatre will ignore at its peril. There must be no play in the normal category of plays which cannot be played because it cannot be cast. *King Lear*, for an instance, cannot be long left out of the bill for lack of a Lear, or *Antony and Cleopatra* for lack of a Cleopatra. And there must be none of that playing of 'lines' of parts (First Old Man, Second Old Woman, Singing Chambermaid) which was the curse—and at last the doom—of the old stock companies. Nor, when it comes to modern plays, can there be a necessitous thrusting of square pegs into round holes. The modern author must have a reasonably wide field for the casting of his play, or he will not bring it to the theatre. Full freedom he cannot have; if in theory he has it now, in practice it is largely illusory; the coherence and better general quality of the company should be full compensation for loss.
>
> Nor, were there one stage to play on instead of two, could the number of the company be very greatly reduced. Since this may seem

a very obvious economy to make, let us look into the fallacy of it with some care.

With one stage only, a representative repertory of plays would still ask for a company of not less than sixty-six. That at least is the figure which William Archer and I arrived at when we drew up our *Scheme and Estimates*. We went into the matter very thoroughly, casting every play in the year's list of productions, with each play's needs and with actual individual actors in mind; and forty-two men and twenty-two women were needed for adequate casting. See now what might well happen, with one stage only to play upon. In the specimen repertory set down hereafter there are *Antony and Cleopatra* and *Henry V*. There is also *Peer Gynt*. The first will absorb thirty-four men and four women, the second about forty men and four women (some parts can be doubles, but too much doubling is an undesirable form of thrift), and the third something like thirty men and twenty women. There is also Flecker's *Hassan*. And if we happen to be considering *Cyrano de Bergerac*, here are forty-two parts for men and thirteen for women. These, and plays which make like demands, must be acted, and the company must be measured for their needs. But they might in any year be acted for comparatively few performances, and the successes might be such plays as the *Importance of Being Earnest* (with its cast of nine) or even *The Mollusc* (with its cast of four). These certainly are extreme instances; but even the normal chances of an extended repertory must, it is easy to see, keep far too many actors standing idle if there is only one stage upon which they can be acting. I turn back to the *Scheme and Estimates* to find that in its season of forty-six weeks no actor played more than one hundred and sixty-nine times and no actress more than one hundred and six (except the players of quite small parts). That is well enough if they are constantly rehearsing too. But one actress only played forty-one times and several others less than seventy times; one actor only seventy-two times and nine of them less than one hundred. This was a serious flaw in the scheme; none the less because the lower scale of salaries of those days enabled one to overlook the waste of money involved.

The standing idle should not have been overlooked. Good actors will not stand idle, even if they are paid to. And the waste of money we cannot now overlook. Turn this two-house estimate into a one-house estimate, reduce the company by a third (this, without calculation to that end, turns out to be the exact difference between the needs of one house according to the old *Scheme and Estimates* and the two as now presented) and the waste in salaries paid to actors left standing idle for lack of a second stage would be something like £46,000 a year. That clearly is intolerable; and the provision of two houses, by which the margin of idleness can be reduced to as near vanishing point as possible, is the obvious, is really the only remedy. There is none in the employment of actors who do not care if they stand idle and will do it cheaply, or whom nobody else will employ; this would be reduction in quality. Nor is there in the anarchy of a company with half its members for half the time occupied elsewhere.

The actor's work is, of course, not to be thought of wholly in terms of performances; the study and preparation of plays (something more comprehensive than mere rehearsing) and, as importantly, the keeping of the current of repertory fresh and interesting will be as predominant a part of it. With everything reckoned in there should be very little standing idle. At times the plays in both houses might happen to have small casts; at times a little contriving would be needed to prevent plays with large casts clashing. But, in general, the flow of work should be fairly steady, and the margin of unemployment a narrow one.

All very interesting. And to my mind quite convincing, though the picture wants filling out with details of the kind of programme policy envisaged for a company of players founded on such generous lines. Luckily, with his usual thoroughness, Granville-Barker leaves us in no doubt as to what he intended, and it seems desirable that we should remind ourselves of what is, so far as I know, the only extant blueprint for an all-embracing British National Theatre repertory. Possibly it is a counsel of perfection, but none the worse for that!

Here [writes the author], *for the sake of illustration merely*, are forty-nine plays which might well make up the repertory for any year, once the theatre were well established. This number of one less than fifty has been somewhat fortuitously arrived at only by the inclusion of the History cycle. If we think of that as four plays in one, the number becomes one more than forty-five. The repertory would normally run to between forty-five and fifty plays a year, probably.

THE NINETEEN THIRTIES

NEW PLAYS

Large House	Small House
Saint Cecilia	The Trumpet of Peace
The Flight of the Duchess	These Bright Young Things
The Chiltern Hundreds[1]	Peradventure
	The Man who would be King
	The Long Road
	Here We Are Again

The titles are, of course, invented for this occasion, or borrowed. They stand for new plays, but not necessarily for new productions; four of them at least may be counted for successes of last year carried on. Among the authors should be some of the younger dramatists who are not represented in the list of modern revivals below.

SHAKESPEARE

Large House	Small House
Hamlet	The Comedy of Errors
Antony and Cleopatra	The Tempest
Othello	
Richard II	
Henry IV (parts 1 and 2)	
Henry V	
Romeo and Juliet	
Twelfth Night	
A Midsummer Night's Dream	

Twelve plays out of forty-nine may seem too high a proportion for Shakespeare. But the historical series, which would usually be played as a series (not necessarily on four consecutive performances), may in a sense be counted as one. . . . The theatre should, moreover, be under an obligation to have at least one play of Shakespeare's in the bill each week, and to give not less than one hundred and fifty performances of his plays in the year. But a number of these performances might be specially organized for students and schools; and this is one of the reasons why these plays are set down predominantly for the large house. But if they were played in a more or less conventionalized setting (and, personally, I should hope they would be), they, and other plays so treated, could very simply be transferred from one house to the other.

[1] A curious anticipation of the title of a recent successful comedy by Mr. Douglas Home.

CLASSIC, MEDIEVAL, MINOR ELIZABETHAN

Large House	*Small House*
The Agamemnon	The Faithful Shepherdess
Everyman	The Feast of Bacchus (arranged from Terence by Robert Bridges)

These imply student and school performances too.

EIGHTEENTH-CENTURY COMEDY

Large House	*Small House*
The School for Scandal	Love for Love

REVIVALS OF MODERN ENGLISH PLAYS

(or, to avoid controversy, call them plays written in the English language)

The Admirable Crichton	Preserving Mr. Panmure
John Bull's Other Island	An Irish Triple Bill
Strife	(Yeats, Synge, Lady Gregory)
Hassan	The Faithful
The Importance of Being Earnest	Jane Clegg
The Mollusc	The Constant Wife
The Return of the Prodigal	The Great Adventure

One is immediately struck by the omissions from this list. There could be no better proof of the wide field of choice for plays which could command good audiences for from ten to thirty performances in any year (granted good performances of them), plays which, if this is all they can command, are at present left in oblivion.

TRANSLATIONS

Le Bourgeois Gentilhomme	The Thieves' Comedy (der Bier-
Peer Gynt	pelz)
The Kingdom of God	Pelleas and Melisande
The Wild Duck	The Three Sisters

There are Crimes and Crimes

Here, besides the recognized classics, we have, as in the list of English revivals, some plays of admittedly minority appeal, and some which need such quality of performance as only a theatre devoting as much care to the play that will not earn large profits, as to the play that will, can give. There will be no lack of material for the repertory, that is evident. Any play that was good of its kind would have a claim to be admitted and any kind of play that the theatre could cast and stage.

For the benefit of those who do not easily visualize the working of a repertory here are two specimen fortnights. The first falls in the winter holiday season. The large house is given up mainly to Shakespeare, and is playing no less than four matinées a week. This, of course, is exceptional. But even the small house is giving three. The bracketed figures show roughly the number of actors and actresses employed in each performance.

Large House	*Small House*

Wednesday, January 1

Twelfth Night (matinée)	The Importance of Being Earnest
(14 m., 3 w.)	(matinée) (5 m., 4 w.)
Antony and Cleopatra	The Long Road
(34 m., 4 w.)	

Thursday, January 2

A Midsummer Night's Dream	The Great Adventure
(matinée) (13 m., 4 w.)	(15 m., 3 w.)
Peer Gynt	
(30 m., 22 w.)	

Friday, January 3

Antony and Cleopatra	The Long Road (matinée)
(34 m., 4 w.)	The Thieves' Comedy
	(9 m., 4 w.)

Saturday, January 4

Antony and Cleopatra	Irish Triple Bill (matinée)
(34 m., 4 w.)	(12 m., 8 w.)
A Midsummer Night's Dream	The Long Road
(13 m., 4 w.)	

Monday, January 6

| Twelfth Night | The Importance of Being Earnest |
| (14 m., 3 w.) | (5 m., 4 w.) |

Tuesday, January 7

The Magnet (matinée)	The Long Road
Antony and Cleopatra	
(34 m., 4 w.)	

Wednesday, January 8

A Midsummer Night's Dream
(13 m., 4 w.) (matinée)
The School for Scandal
(12 m., 4 w.)

The Great Adventure (matinée)
(15 m., 3 w.)
Irish Triple Bill
(2 m., 8 w.)

Thursday, January 9

Antony and Cleopatra (matinée)
(34 m., 4 w.)
The Magnet

The Importance of Being Earnest
(5 m., 4 w.)

Friday, January 10

The Admirable Crichton
(13 m., 10 w.)

The Comedy of Errors (matinée)
(14 m., 5 w.)
The Long Road

Saturday, January 11

The Magnet (matinée)
Antony and Cleopatra
(34 m., 4 w.)

The Long Road (matinée)
The Thieves' Comedy
(9 m., 4 w.)

Monday, January 13

The School for Scandal
(12 m., 4 w.)

The Long Road

Tuesday, January 14

The Admirable Crichton (matinée)
(13m., 10 w.)
Hamlet
(22 m., 2 w.)

The Great Adventure
(15 m., 3 w.)

Antony and Cleopatra, we may suppose, a recent and successful revival. It is given six performances in the fortnight. For the rest, Shakespearian comedy is in the ascendant, *A Midsummer Night's Dream* being particularly a holiday play. But *Twelfth Night* would be never long absent from the repertory, nor *Hamlet*. *The Magnet*, a new play, occupies the large house for three performances; it may be a successful production now some six months old. *The Long Road* has seven performances in the small house; this stands for a new play more recently produced and very fairly successful. *The School for Scandal* would never be long absent from the bill. The modern revivals speak for themselves.

The numerical capacity of the company is never very hardly strained. On the evening of January 2nd forty-five men and twenty-five women are acting in the two houses together, forty-six men and twelve women on the evening of Saturday January 4th.

For a second specimen fortnight:

Large House	*Small House*
Wednesday, October 1	
The Chiltern Hundreds	These Bright Young Things (matinée)
	Love for Love
	(10 m., 6 w.)
Thursday, October 2	
The Chiltern Hundreds (matinée)	These Bright Young Things
Othello	
(18 m., 3 w.)	
Friday, October 3	
The Chiltern Hundreds	The Long Road
Saturday, October 4	
Agamemnon (matinée)	Love for Love (matinée)
(21 m., 2 w.)	(10 m., 6 w.)
The Chiltern Hundreds	The Tempest
	(1 m., 7 w.)
Monday, October 6	
Romeo and Juliet	The Wild Duck
(21 m., 4 w.)	
Tuesday, October 7	
The Chiltern Hundreds	These Bright Young Things
Wednesday, October 8	
John Bull's Other Island	The Feast of Bacchus (matinée)
(10 m., 2 w.)	The Wild Duck
	(20 m., 3 w.)
Thursday, October 9	
Richard II (matinée)	Love for Love
(36 m., 4 w.)	(10 m., 6 w.)
The Chiltern Hundreds	

Friday, October 10

The Chiltern Hundreds	Peradventure

Saturday, October 11

Henry IV, Pt. 1 (matinée)	The Return of the Prodigal
(35 m., 3 w.)	(10 m., 5 w.)
Henry IV, Pt. 2	These Bright Young Things
(44 m., 4 w.)	

Monday, October 13

The Chiltern Hundreds	The Long Road

Tuesday, October 14

Henry V	Love for Love
(45 m., 4 w.)	(10 m., 6 w.)

The Chiltern Hundreds is a new play and is a success. It is drawing full houses, and is being acted, for the moment, as often as is compatible with the interests of the rest of the repertory. It is given eight performances in the fortnight. There is no reason why more matinées should not be acted. In the small house another new play, *These Bright Young Things*, is fairly successful, and is given four performances in the fortnight: yet another, *Peradventure*, is (as befits its title) a more doubtful affair, and it has only one. *The Long Road*, which was being played in January, is still alive: we may suppose that there is a steady three parts of a houseful for it once a week. *Love for Love* looks like a recent revival; if really well done it will gather audiences, though not in crowds, about twice a week for a month or so. Good acting granted, an occasional revival of *The Wild Duck* will not lack support, nor will a performance of St. John Hankin's admirably bitter-sweet comedy; nor a few, even more than a few, of Bernard Shaw's masterpiece. *The Feast of Bacchus* is an experiment. *Agamemnon* and the Shakespeares stand for the steady 'classic' repertory—kept from becoming too steady by occasional changes of cast. The inclusion of the history cycle should be noted, with the complete *Henry IV* given on the Saturday. Devotees may find a meal in the theatre's restaurant between the performances.

If the modern revivals in this sample repertory seem a bit old-fashioned, one must remember the date at which Granville-Barker was writing. Barrie was still a living force in the theatre, and the Manchester school of dramatists, and the Irish, were still fresh in the public memory. To-day, no doubt, he would have included more recent work like that of Noel Coward and T. S. Eliot.

On the whole, though, it would be true to say that Granville-Barker, though in his time a great innovator, had never tried or wished to break with tradition. His small theatre would never have been allowed to become the playground of *avant-garde* producers. Half-baked or tentative productions would have been relegated to their proper place, the Little or Studio theatres where the public could enter at their peril and under no misunderstanding that they were being invited to assist at anything more than an *experimental* production, amusing perhaps in itself but quite unsuited to a national theatre.

Return to our Story

I remind myself that of the members present at the first Committee Meeting which I attended as Honorary Secretary, Sir Frank Meyer, the Chairman, I had known from Oxford days, and Bernard Shaw, of course, needed no introduction. With Holford Knight I was already acquainted, since he was also a member of The Drama League Council, and a constant speaker from our platforms on behalf of the League and of the National Theatre. A popular Labour M.P., he was filled with boy-like enthusiasm, which sometimes led him into indiscretion; but he was very much of a 'live-wire', a fine speaker, and quite unsparing of his time and energy. Of Hamilton Fyfe it may be said that he concealed vast experience of life and journalism under a gently satirical façade. Then there was Sir Archibald Flower, kindly and urbane as ever, and a valued link with the Stratford-on-Avon Memorial Theatre, with which there was never a hint of rivalry. Acton Bond was also there, an actor of the old school, who, with his wife, was running a dramatic Academy in the north of London. Subsequent meetings brought me into pleasant contact with other regular attendants at the Committee: Sir John Martin-Harvey, one of our ablest public orators, S. R. Littlewood, the genial dramatic critic of the *Morning Post*, Nigel Playfair, Dame Edith Lyttelton, staunch protagonist if ever there was one, and last yet foremost, the Earl of Lytton, Knight of the Garter, Imperial Statesman, Beau, Trustee of the National Theatre and Chairman of the Executive.

I do not want to weary the reader with endless details of the Committee's activities between the end of 1930 and the end of 1934. The history of these is sadly reminiscent of the similar more or less abortive activities of the 1920s. But useful experience had been gained, and now there was undoubtedly a new sense of urgency and a more unanimous agreement on the need to acquire a site for the theatre as the preliminary for renewed appeals to the public. During this period, countless meetings of the Executive took place and, amongst others, the following sites or existing theatres were carefully considered as being chiefly within the range of possibility: The 'Prince Edward Theatre' (now the London Casino), a site in Leicester Square adjacent to the Alhambra, Norfolk House, the New and Wyndham's Theatres (to be rebuilt as a single block), the Phoenix, the Saville, and the Cambridge theatres, a site in Hart Street, Bloomsbury, St. George's Hospital, and a site adjacent to the National Gallery.

Although the Granville-Barker twin-stage theatre was freely acknowledged to be the ideal, most of the sites or theatres mentioned above would have been inadequate to that arrangement. The consequences, I think, were never squarely faced by the Committee. But certainly to comply with the Granville-Barker scheme would have been to restrict the field of choice somewhat severely. At least an acre of land would have been needed for the two theatres—almost exactly the area occupied by the Theatre Royal, Drury Lane. Granville-Barker was disappointed, and did not fail to say so. But with his characteristic generosity of mind he continued to give his advice freely, although I do not think that he could ever have been persuaded to throw his whole weight into any scheme which did not satisfy the conditions which he had laid down, and which he thought essential. This, indeed, proved to be the case, as will be seen when he was invited to be the first Director of the theatre to be built on the South Kensington site in 1937.

Investigation of some of the theatres already mentioned was carried to considerable lengths, particularly in the case of the Phoenix and Cambridge theatres, which formed the Agenda for no less than nine meetings between January and June 1934.

In the meanwhile further discussions were once more being sought by the Old Vic. Lord Lytton, as Chairman of the Old Vic Governors, may have sometimes found himself in a somewhat equivocal position, but the redoubtable Mrs. Alfred Lyttelton, who represented the S.M.N.T. Committee on the Old Vic board, valiantly stood her ground and was able to save the situation time and again.

Earlier on in my secretaryship, The Drama League, at my instigation, offered to start a National Theatre Guild on the basis of the collection of a hundred thousand members, each paying a token fee of one shilling. The object of this Guild was not so much to raise a vast sum of money, as to provide an impressive façade of individual support throughout the country. This suggestion was made in 1930, but a little later, in view of the 'economic blizzard' then sweeping the country, I felt it incumbent on me to advise the abandonment of the scheme, somewhat to the disappointment of the National Theatre Committee.

Still, we kept eyes open for any chance to publicize the movement. The anniversary of Shakespeare's birthday in April 1934 seemed to Holford Knight an appropriate time for a National Theatre Drama Festival. The Committee agreed, and an attractive scheme was drawn up for submission to the Charity Commissioners. They intimated, once again, that the question would have to be referred to the Court, and might entail some modification to the Trust Deed. Certain members of the Committee were doubtful as to the advisability of speculating in such a season of plays, and as the Honorary Secretary pointed out, even if the proposed Festival were a success, any enthusiasm and interest aroused by it would soon evaporate if the Festival were not quickly followed by some definite and practical step towards the realization of our objects.

By now, the Committee had been strengthened by the addition of Messrs. Lewis Casson, R. A. Scott-James, Sidney Bernstein, and Sydney Carroll. The two latter were particularly helpful over the negotiations with the owners of the Phoenix and Cambridge theatres. Mr. Bernstein had great experience in the building of cinemas, being Managing Director of the Granada Group. He had built, and at one time owned, the Phoenix Theatre itself. Sydney Carroll, of course, was a prominent stage impresario and a dramatic critic of high authority. He had strong opinions which sometimes outran the discretion of his colleagues, but his dynamic and zealous personality was at all times a challenge to action, and this was just what was needed at a time when the next move was always in doubt.

Negotiations for the purchase of the Cambridge Theatre were very nearly completed by June 1934, protracted as they had been by a lengthy haggle over the price; and it was agreed to accept the owner's offer of an option on the theatre, and to seek the Charity Commissioners' agreement to its purchase at a figure not exceeding one hundred and fifty thousand pounds. To this end, Lord Lytton visited the Charity Commissioners in company with Sir Frank Meyer. The Commissioner intimated that this amount would be available for the purchase of the Cambridge Theatre, as it complied with all the conditions of the Trust, except that there would be nothing left for endowment. Lord Lytton explained that while it was hoped ultimately to achieve a theatre on a really national scale, and to raise a genuine endowment fund, operations could at once begin if adequate working capital were provided outside the Trust for an experimental period at the Cambridge Theatre. Should this working capital become exhausted, it would be necessary either to raise more money or to sell the theatre and thus conserve the capital now in the hands of the Trust.

Yet again, for one reason or another, negotiations for the Cambridge Theatre hung fire, and for a time the flighty favours of the Committee strayed towards the Alhambra, St. George's Hospital, and Messrs. Hampton's premises in Trafalgar Square, all of which, it was rumoured, might soon come on to the market. At the same time, another appeal campaign was discussed. It was suggested that this might be launched as the nation's gift to King George V on the occasion of his Silver Jubilee; but it was found that no official approval to this scheme would be forthcoming. Mr. Carroll, however, insisted that an appeal must be made without delay, and there seemed no reason why the National Theatre should not run its own 'Jubilee Gift' even if it lacked official status. Special offices for the Organization of the Appeal were taken at 50, Pall Mall, from which address all further operations were carried on. Much of the equipment and furniture for these offices was obtained in the form of free gifts from various friendly firms through the mediation of Mr. Carroll.

The expenses consequent on this development were heavy; but convinced that a serious effort was being undertaken to raise the money for an object well within the definition of the Trust, the Charity Commissioners consented to allocate an annual sum of two thousand pounds from the interest on the fund for the purposes of appeal. Moreover, Sir Oswald Stoll, who before the War had contributed a couple of thousand pounds for an architectural competition (abandoned at the outbreak of war), expressed his willingness for the residue of the fund, £1,616, to be used for any purpose approved by the Committee. It was decided that for the moment this sum should be held in reserve. The Appeal Committee now included Lord Lytton as Chairman, Mrs. Alfred Lyttelton, Sydney Carroll, Sidney Bernstein, Nicholas Hannen, Holford Knight, and the Honorary Secretary. Major Long-Innes (late private secretary to Granville-Barker) was appointed Assistant Secretary.

So far, so good, but a few months later, in the early spring of 1935, the Committee, and indeed the movement generally, suffered a severe loss. Riding one morning before breakfast in fields near his home in Hertfordshire, Sir Frank Meyer fell from his horse which had stumbled, to die within a few hours from the effects of the fall. Still in the prime of life, he was a reserved, proud man, clean-cut as a diamond, and as a Trustee, it was he who since the end of the war, had been mainly responsible for the investment of our funds. The original seventy-five thousand pounds, with the addition of ten or twelve thousand pounds-worth of donations had, at the time of his death, well-nigh doubled itself, and by 1936 had miraculously reached the grand total of £150,000, all in gilt-edged stock. But Sir Frank had proved himself to be much more than a clever financier. He presided at meetings with dignity and resource, and was often able to redress a balance of opinion which threatened to become dangerously weighted on one side or the other.

In spite of this sad event, the Appeal Committee carried on at an ever-increasing pressure. Indeed, by this time it, rather than the Executive Committee, became the mainspring of the movement. To the appeal staff was now added a resourceful and zealous Organizer, in the person of Mr. Harvey Lloyd.

Soon the Committee was involved in the consideration of several new sites, including the premises of the Junior United Services Club, the Lyceum Theatre, a site in Wilton Place at the back of Victoria Station, Aldridge's Repository near Garrick Street, Charing Cross Hospital, His Majesty's Theatre, and Drury Lane itself. On all these investigations much time and energy was spent; but some of them were leasehold properties and on that account not very eligible, and the remainder much too expensive.

Many and various were the schemes entertained for the raising of funds, and two or three of them met with success. Harvey

Lloyd, for instance, had a bright idea in connection with the Silver Jubilee Celebrations in 1935. He acquired the rights in over seven hundred seats overlooking the route of the Jubilee procession, which he subsequently sold at a considerable profit, a balance of eight hundred and thirty pounds accruing to the Appeal. The same idea was revived on the occasion of the Coronation of George VI in the following year, resulting in a final nett profit of £2,366.

And then, in the autumn of 1935, there was an exciting Shakespeare Matinée at Drury Lane, under the direction of Mr. Ivor Novello and Mr. Sydney Carroll, with a galaxy of stars. This showed a profit of over eighteen hundred pounds; and while on this subject of matinées and royal celebrations, we may anticipate the future by a mention of the magnificent Coronation Ball which took place at the Albert Hall on 13th May 1937. This was held under the patronage of the King and Queen, and though they were themselves unable to attend, owing to a State banquet on the same night, their Majesties intimated that the guests who were attending the banquet might be invited to the ball, which would also be graced by the presence of the Duke and Duchess of Gloucester. In the event, this Ball turned out to be one of the big events of Coronation year. Besides affording unique publicity for the National Theatre, a net profit of £4,500 was realized. This, together with earlier profits from the matinée and sale of processional seats, amounted to a considerable total, but was still not enough to add materially to the central funds. Nevertheless, the Appeal could be said to be paying its way. Its heavy expenses could be met for a while longer, and prospects generally seemed brighter against the day when the ideal site should have been discovered, and that not impossible he or she should loom on the horizon bearing the longed-for bags of gold.

By June 1936 the Cambridge Theatre proposal was finally abandoned. It is true that a resolution to the effect that a sum not exceeding one hundred and twenty thousand pounds should be offered for the theatre had been carried by five votes to four, but in view of the cleavage of opinion exhibited in the Committee and of the absence of several members who normally attended, the Chairman, Lord Lytton, gave an undertaking that no action should be taken on the resolution until a further meeting had again been called.

I well remember the feelings of despair almost, which were aroused in me by this further procrastination. I was aware that forces were at work in a section of the Committee which might soon succeed in a definite acceptance of the view that the Trust had failed of its original intention, and that the Court might once more be approached for a definite permission to use the fund for some cognate purpose or purposes. I felt in my bones that on the day when the fund found itself at the mercy of applicants for help —however worthy—the National Theatre for our generation would be as good as dead, for where the corpse lies, there the ravens are gathered together.

Just in time, however, the thoughts of the Executive Committee were diverted to the consideration of a new site which appeared to be free from most of the faults which hitherto had stood in the way of complete approval. On 2nd February 1937, the Honorary Secretary reported to the Executive Committee that in a private conversation, Athole Hay, the Registrar of the Royal College of Art, had informed my wife that the French Institute in Cromwell Gardens was about to be removed elsewhere, and that the Office of Works, the owners of the site, would probably wish to dispose of it. Mrs. Whitworth had communicated this information to Miss Elsie Fogerty, principal of the Central School of Speech and Drama, in the belief that the site might be large enough for a National Theatre and for the premises of the Central School as well. But Miss Fogerty soon came to the conclusion that the area of the site (16,000 square feet) could not possibly accommodate both school and theatre, and generously agreed to waive all claim to it.

This idea had already been considered by the Appeal Committee, and the Honorary Secretary had himself inspected the site and was of the opinion that it would make possible a theatre slightly larger and with a better stage than the Cambridge. The firm of architects, Messrs. Wimperis, Simpson & Guthrie, had been asked to survey the site and to provide some preliminary details of the form of theatre that could be erected thereon. This report had been encouraging, and it was there and then decided by the Executive Committee, to send a letter to the Office of Works intimating that the Committee were prepared to buy the site, and would be glad to negotiate on the same terms as those which had been previously suggested by the Office of Works to the Royal College of Art.

These negotiations were soon opened on an official basis. The Committee hoped that their private offer of £50,000 might be acceptable, but the Ministry of Works soon made it clear that they felt obliged to dispose of the site by public tender. This did not involve an auction in the ordinary sense of the word; but it did mean that the highest offer received by a certain date would acquire the site. There was much discussion within the Committee as to the amount which should be offered. Some went so far as to recommend a maximum of £90,000. Others would not go beyond sixty thousand. Finally, a compromise figure of £75,000 was agreed to. There followed a period of suspense, which culminated at a meeting of the Executive Committee held on the 23rd July 1937, the very day on which an announcement appeared in *The Times* to the effect that the Cromwell Gardens site had been sold to a client of Messrs. Harrods, for £85,000.

But this had not been the end of the matter. Lord Bessborough informed the Honorary Secretary that there was reason to believe that the "client" might be prepared to consider a resale of the property to the National Theatre Committee, at the price which he himself had paid, and Lord Lytton strongly urged the Committee to enter into further negotiations on this basis.

However, this did not prove to be necessary. At the next meeting of the Executive held on the 21st September, Lord Lytton reported that since the last meeting he had been informed by the Office of Works that the client for whom Messrs. Harrods were acting, had defaulted in the payment of his deposit, and that if the National Theatre's tender for £75,000 was re-submitted it would be accepted. Owing to the urgency of the affair, Lord Lytton, after consultation with the Honorary Secretary, had agreed to make this offer, and had been subsequently informed by the Office of Works that it had been accepted. The site was ours!

It is only fair to remember that before ever their final offer for the site was made, the Committee had been fully aware of most, if not all, of the objections likely to be raised by the public. It was frankly realized that the scheme for a twin-stage theatre was ruled out, and Mr. Lewis Casson, particularly, was doubtful if sufficient storage accommodation for a true repertory theatre policy could be guaranteed. Fears were also expressed on account of the site's proximity to so many museums. Mr. Bernard Shaw, however, weighed in with a precisely opposite argument; that the museum district was, in fact, a positive advantage since, if nothing else, the National Theatre would in itself most surely fulfil the object of a Museum of Drama, and that the site therefore was appropriate to an academic atmosphere. It was also evident that far from being out of the way, the theatre would be extremely accessible, owing to its proximity to the underground station at South Kensington, and to many lines of buses. Finally, the theatre plans, which were inspected by the Committee, showed that while the entrance-hall and foyers might be constricted, the auditorium of the theatre could accommodate at least 1,200 people, and that the stage itself would be the largest in London. Storage space completely adequate to the purposes of a repertory theatre would be available beneath the auditorium. The Hon. Secretary was also able to state that he had recently conversed with several important people resident or connected with the Royal Borough, among them Sir William Davison, Member for South Kensington. On all sides he had found great enthusiasm for the idea of a National Theatre in that quarter, and he believed that the acquisition of the site would open up a new and special field for raising the balance of the money required. The Committee found further justification of their courage when permission was obtained to build a *porte-cochère* over the road separating the site from the triangular garden to the east of it, thus providing the opportunity for a spacious restaurant without any limitation of the space to be occupied by the theatre itself. Arrangements with the London County Council and the Town Planning Authorities were successfully concluded. It now only remained to go ahead with the Appeal, with the knowledge that an adequate site for the theatre was in the possession of the Committee together with the sum of £75,000 of the original capital now intact.

There arose the question of the architect. This indeed proved a knotty problem. Two main alternatives presented themselves: (1) To hold an open competition; (2) To appoint a definite individual. Stressing the need for a building which would be truly monumental, and likely to stand the test of time, Lord Lytton pointed out that though there was certainly an off-chance that the ideal design might result from a competition, the major practising architects would not be likely to compete. The other side argued that public opinion demanded that the young, and possibly unknown architect, should be given his chance, and urged the interest and publicity which would accrue if a public competition were held. In he event, however, Lord Lytton's view prevailed. A list of some six eminent architects was drawn up, and the Hon. Secretary was asked to interview them, and to inquire if the architect selected would give his services free (apart from overhead expenses) since with such a public-spirited example, it was not unlikely that various contractors, through the good offices of Mr. Montgomery, of the Building Trades Exhibition, might be induced to donate a large amount of the material for building and decorating the theatre. There was one complication. None of the six architects chosen for interview had had any personal experience of building a theatre. Technical advice would clearly be necessary; but it was thought that this difficulty could be overcome if the services of a technical architect could be retained who would act in collaboration with the main architect of the building. In the event, Sir Edwin Lutyens accepted the Committee's invitation on the conditions laid down, and he was good enough to welcome the collaboration of a technical expert in the person of Mr. Cecil Masey, F.R.I.B.A., who could point to a long experience in the construction of cinemas, and had been the architect of the Phoenix Theatre in Shaftesbury Avenue.

The collaboration between these two men turned out to be a very happy one. Each was the perfect complement to the other. Sir Edwin brought all his genius to the common task, and Masey his talent for inventive adaptability. The site itself was difficult to cope with. One end was a good deal wider than the other; and the sides were out of alignment. Nevertheless, when the final model was on view, almost everyone agreed that the problem had been admirably solved.[1] The exterior was in the main tradition of English architecture, yet simple and up to date. The interior a marvel of concentrated amenity. Everything fitted like the mechanism of a watch. With no sense of cramping, there remained not an inch to spare.

Some of my happiest memories recall the meetings of the Building Committee, which provided the technical specifications, and approved or improved the resulting sketch plans. Ashley Dukes, Sidney Bernstein, Bridges Adams (of Stratford fame), Lewis Casson, and Nicholas Hannen were the most constant and zealous attendants. For lunch we would often adjourn to Rosa's Edwardian restaurant in Jermyn Street, to resume more light-heartedly the

[1] Four of the plans for this theatre are included among the illustrations to Vol. III of the "Architecture of Sir Edwin Lutyens", Country Life Ltd., 1950.

discussions of the morning over plates of succulent beef and glasses of undiluted ale.

As to the Appeal itself, this clearly must now be promoted on a new and more professional basis. Miss Elsie Fogerty and Mr. Ashley Dukes consented to joint the Appeal Committee, whose next task would be to consider the appointment of an expert Appeal Organizer. On their recommendation, Mr. Richmond Temple was appointed to the post. He was a man of proved ability in this and other fields and from now onwards the Appeal was conducted with a drive and impetus hitherto to seek. But about the same time Mr. Sydney Carroll tendered his resignation from the Committee, saying that he did so with regret and for purely personal reasons, in no way connected with any lapse of interest in, or sympathy with the National Theatre. This resignation was received with regret by the Committee, though they felt it no matter for surprise that a man of so many responsibilities and with so many 'irons in the fire' could no longer find time to attend so many meetings, and to give so much thought to our concerns as Carroll had given in the past.

With a view to enhancing still further the attractiveness of the Appeal, it was felt that the Committee should now be in a position to announce the name of the Director to be. Everyone agreed that Granville-Barker was the man, and steps were taken to discover whether he would look with favour on such an invitation. He was now resident in Paris, where he held the position of Chairman of the British Institute in that city. Lord Lytton agreed to approach him on the matter, but as I feared, the reply was in the negative. Granville-Barker recapitulated the arguments for the twin-stage theatre which have been already quoted

Every sort of enterprise [he concluded] has its most favourable economic dimensions. In my 1930 book, I set out to discover, if I could, what these would be for a National Theatre with quality and variety demanded of it, and I was driven to the conclusions I reached. One warning is worth issuing. If comparison is to be made with foreign theatres it should be, not with their paper constitutions but with the actual conditions under which they are kept alive to-day, barely and often with little credit; i.e. 'The economic dimensions' in which they are presumed to exist are no longer practically valid. You will not think that all this is mere carping, I hope, but it is better to criticize, and even to carp, betimes.

To which Lord Lytton replied:

DEAR GRANVILLE-BARKER,

Thanks for your letter, which is rather discouraging. Your arguments apply with great force if we were obliged to engage and maintain a stock Company large enough for all our requirements. This, however, is not contemplated at present, and we hope to be able to make other arrangements.

I am very sorry that in the circumstances you cannot give us the start we require by becoming our first Director, but of course I cannot press you to accept responsibility for an enterprise of which you do not wholly approve.

At about this time, true to form, the Old Vic submitted a further proposal, on this occasion for a complete amalgamation between the two bodies. Financial assistance was to be offered to the Old Vic forthwith, and a combined appeal at some future date was to be made for the endowment of a new National Theatre south of the river under the auspices of both bodies. It was hard to see what precisely could emerge from these discussions, in view of the fact that we were already committed to build our theatre at Cromwell Gardens. Nevertheless, negotiations were continued, but ended with nothing more definite than that the S.M.N.T. agreed to suspend its appeal for a month or two so that the field might be left clear for the Old Vic to launch its own appeal for £30,000 in memory of Miss Baylis, whose death had occurred in the year 1937. This decent arrangement was ratified by two letters which appeared in *The Times* of 10th and 11th March 1938. They cleared the air somewhat, and with a clear conscience, each side was enabled to continue its own Appeal with no sense that it was trying to queer the pitch of the other.

THE NINETEEN THIRTIES

To the Editor of *The Times*

Sir,

In view of the forthcoming banquet to be held at the Mansion House on March 15th to further and perhaps consummate the appeal on behalf of the Old Vic and Sadler's Wells, my committee wish it to be known as widely as possible that they are in the fullest sympathy with the appeal. They believe that the establishment of the Old Vic and Sadler's Wells on a sound financial basis is indeed a first call on the generosity of London theatre-lovers, and that such a memorial to Lilian Baylis is the one that she would have desired.

My committee would like to take this opportunity of reasserting that when the building of the National Theatre is completed it will in no way compete with the Old Vic. The policy will be widely different, but no doubt means will be found whereby constant and most friendly co-operation will ensue.

Yours faithfully,

GEOFFREY WHITWORTH,
*Hon. Secretary, Shakespeare Memorial
National Theatre Committee*

Sir,

As managing governor of the Old Vic and Sadler's Wells and hon. secretary of the Lilian Baylis Memorial Fund, I wish to say how gladly I reciprocate the sentiments expressed in Mr. Geoffrey Whitworth's letter on behalf of the Shakespeare Memorial Theatre Executive Committee. In doing so I feel sure that I speak for the governors of our two theatres and for the committee of the Lilian Baylis Memorial (Vic-Wells Completion) Fund. When the time comes for co-operation in the activities of a national theatre Mr. Whitworth and his committee may rely on the friendliness and sympathy of those in charge of the great work which Lilian Baylis created.

Yours faithfully,

REGINALD ROWE

*Lilian Baylis Memorial (Vic-Wells Completion) Fund,
19, Old Buildings, Lincoln's Inn, W.C.*

Now we have arrived well into the year of Munich—not the best atmosphere, one must admit, for an attempt to raise money on behalf of a cultural purpose. Arguments based on the noble example which Germany had set the world by way of State endowment for the theatre tended to fall on unsympathetic ears, and the newspapers were filled with war-like anticipations. Mr. Richmond Temple, however, stiffened his campaign, and introduced to our meetings his colleague, Sydney Walton, brimming with ideas, and with a long record of successful enterprise since the days when he had worked with Lloyd George at the Ministry of Munitions during the first war, to become Director of Publicity for the Victory Loan, in 1919. Any number of activities were undertaken by the Appeal Committee—meetings and lectures all over the place, *Thés Dramatiques* at Claridges, Shakespeare stamps. But the most remunerative of all was the seat endowment scheme, whereby Counties, County Boroughs, institutions of all kinds, and individuals, were invited to promise donations of £100 in return for which a small plaque would be placed on a seat in the theatre bearing the name of the donor, together with that of the locality dramatist, actor, or actress, whom he wished to be associated with his gift. In all, over eighty endowments were made on this basis, the result either of personal invitation or of public meetings held in various likely centres. Then there was the Public Interest Committee under the chairmanship of Lord Esher (by now a member of the Executive), with Mr. Osbert Sitwell as Vice-Chairman. This Committee was concerned not with the actual raising of funds, but with publicizing the project through meetings, personal contacts, and otherwise.

With the help of Nicholas Hannen, a midnight supper-party was held at the Savoy Hotel, the guests being confined to members of the acting profession, whose sympathy with the movement it was hoped to re-kindle. Among the speakers were Mr. John Gielgud and Miss Lena Ashwell. Many misconceptions were removed at this party, though we were reminded that the younger members of the acting profession had begun to feel rather 'out of it', being insufficiently informed of the nature of a National Theatre, and how it was being brought nearer to accomplishment.

It may be interesting at this point to recall some of the adverse opinions which were appearing in the press or bandied from mouth to mouth. Some showed a fundamental difference of outlook which one had to respect. But most of them were quite frivolous, being based on lack of knowledge, or a wilful misinterpretation of the facts of the case. However, here was plenty of material for the Appeal Committee to work on. They counterattacked with every means in their power, and when it was proved that the National Theatre people really meant business, much of the criticism evaporated.

I like particularly the categorical negative which Lord Lytton published in the *Evening Standard* in reply to a correspondent who, in a sprightly attack on the scheme, had gone, perhaps, a little too far.

It is not true [he wrote] that the site in South Kensington for the National Theatre is the site of an old plague pit.

It is not true that Sir Carl Meyer's generous contribution was given to Sir Herbert Tree. It was given to the National Theatre Committee (of which Sir Herbert Tree was at that time a member) and forms part of the funds now in trust with the Charity Commissioners for the National Theatre. It is not true that, when he made his contribution, Sir Carl Meyer was expecting it to be used for anything but the building and endowment of a theatre which should be a worthy memorial of Shakespeare, and in which a company of the best players available would act a repertory of the best plays—objects which are still those of the National Theatre Trust Fund. If it had not been for the war in 1914 this theatre would now be in existence.

Your correspondent asks, 'Has there been since 1910 no theatre that could have been leased or bought to be the home of British drama?'

The answer is 'No', for the following reasons: There is no existing theatre in London with sufficient storage accommodation for the scenery of a repertory company, and this fact alone has necessitated the erection of a new building. His Majesty's Theatre is not a freehold, and the price of the Lyceum, about £500,000, was at no time within the reach of the National Theatre Committee. Moreover, the Lyceum was acquired and is to be demolished by the L.C.C. for a street widening scheme.

Of other hostile criticisms the following may be taken as typical:

'Even as a gift the South Kensington site would be unacceptable.'

'No site at all is wanted. It should be a National Touring Company.'

'Danger of museum surroundings.'

'To have no National Theatre is a tribute to our liberty.'

'The existing West End theatres provide all we desire or deserve.'

'No demand for such a theatre except from a few well-meaning amateurs.'

'The Public do not want Shakespeare or any other classics. The few who do are adequately served.'

'How can the theatre cater for the Provinces?'

'Why not the Surrey side, near County Hall?'

'Only one theatre instead of two as originally planned.'

'It will be an academic thing which will not do any good. Bound to be a very dull affair, very conventional and very safe.'

'Site should be sold and wait till a National Theatre can be built that will rank with the great institutions of the past.'

'Will only achieve an elegant mausoleum recording the demise of a once virile art.'

'Disliked by every actor and actress.'

'Design if "in keeping with its surroundings" will be an architectural tragedy.'

'Give Miss Baylis her £30,000 and subsidize her as long as she alone retains the ultimate say in all matters connected with the house she has created.'

'The White elephant in Cromwell Road which will not earn its keep.'

This final *coup de grâce*, believe it or not, emanated from the revered dramatic critic of *The Times*!

Stimulated rather than daunted by these squibs of disapproval, the Appeal went forward with added zest, and from the beginning of 1938 to August 1939 the frequency of Executive, Appeal and Building Committee meetings exceeded all previous records. By this time for half each day I was to be found at 50, Pall Mall, where the committee meetings were held, and where Major Long Innes was working whole time, as Appeal Secretary. The money-raising schemes discussed and sometimes operated were innumer-

The Rt. Hon. the Earl of Lytton, K.G.

The Ceremony of the Twig and the Sod. Bernard Shaw hands the symbol of ownership to Geoffrey Whitworth, as representing the Trustees. Cromwell Gardens, 23rd April 1939

able, but the reader shall not be worried with their details. One item, however, deserves more than a casual reference, since it was the major feature of our publicity campaign, and the first intimation to the world at large that things were really on the move.

Sydney Walton it was who insisted that the handing-over of the title deeds of the Cromwell Gardens site to the National Theatre should be accompanied by some kind of demonstration. This, he suggested, should take the form of a ceremony on the site itself where, according to ancient custom, a sod of earth taken from close by, should be delivered into the hands of the new owners. The date of the ceremony was fixed for the eve of Shakespeare's birthday, 1938, and at the appointed hour a large concourse gathered together. There we stood, within the site—much of its surface obscured by rubble and other waste products—a somewhat dismal prospect it must be admitted, and with a threat of rain. That, however, we were mercifully spared, and at one end of the site a fine pavilion had been erected, gay with scarlet trappings, where the chief actors in the ceremony would stand to play their several parts. In the foreground were ranged a battery of cameras, film-cameras, and microphones, for the voice of the American Ambassador was to be transmitted to the States. Further off were the loudspeakers, through which the voices of the orators would be magnified above the boom of passing traffic so that the goodly crowd of onlookers who had by now assembled should not miss a word.

Next day lengthy accounts, in most cases accompanied by pictures, appeared in the national press, from which we quote the following from *The Times*:

The deeds of the site of the projected National Theatre in South Kensington were handed to Mr. Bernard Shaw at a ceremony yesterday at which the American Ambassador, members of the acting profession, dramatists and leaders of British national life were present. The proceedings were broadcast to America.

Sir William Davison, M.P. for the division, first passed the deeds to Sir Robert Vansittart. A sod of Kensington earth and a twig from a Kensington tree, the traditional symbols of an exchange and possession of landed property went with them.

Sir Robert Vansittart in turn handed the deeds and the symbols to Mr. Shaw with the words, 'You shall now take seisin from me of this land', and Mr. Shaw replied: 'We are now lawfully seised and possessed by right of the National Theatre.' The deeds were finally received by Mr. Geoffrey Whitworth, on behalf of the trustees for safe custody.

Mr. Shaw said they were so far on the way to having a National Theatre that they now possessed, and had paid for, the site, and they were not at an end of their resources. People sometimes asked him: 'Do the English people want a national theatre?' Of course they did not. They never wanted anything. They had got the British Museum, the National Gallery, and Westminster Abbey, but they never wanted them. But once these things stood as mysterious phenomena that had come to them they were quite proud of them, and felt that the place would be incomplete without them.

What they had to do was to start the phenomenon, because, although they could go ahead for some distance, in the long run the Government would have to keep on its feet this great national institution. The way that phenomena, such as the National Gallery and the British Museum, came about was by a small group of persons who understood the national and cultural importance of these institutions making a start. After a time the beginning they made became a necessity. Then the created institution stood in the way of the Government who never wanted it, but felt that for some reason or other they had to keep it going. They had to carry this project to the point at which the Government would be up against it. They must remember that the group of cultured people who started it were not too numerous in this country. They were gratified, therefore, to find that the American Ambassador was present. This country owed several of its institutions to the contributions of America.

At a reception held later at the Rembrandt Hotel, Lord Snell read a letter from the Poet Laureate (Mr. John Masefield) welcoming the National Theatre and wishing it happy fortunes. Lord Snell said that the position of the National Theatre to-day was one of great hope and encouragement. The project was not a State enterprise, although the State would benefit from it. It was not supported by the Board of Education, though scholarship would be enriched by it. A nation might be either ennobled or debased by the quality of its culture, and if its spirit were to be kept alive, if it was to be a growing, living thing, it could not be left entirely to the hazards of private enterprise. A national theatre could do what the private theatre could not always do; it could work to a predetermined standard of selection and of excellence.

Sir William Davison said that it had been pointed out that a national theatre was not merely one more London theatre, but a national centre and focus for the drama in Britain. No fewer than 10,000 amateur companies were producing plays in various parts of this country. All of these associations would be able to look to the national theatre for inspiration.

Dame Edith Lyttelton said that she wanted the National Theatre to be free from the fear of financial failure which hampered managers. There were many plays which, however beautifully written and played, did not appeal to a sufficiently large number of persons to cover theatre rents and costs of production in London. They wanted not only to build a National Theatre but to endow it; to be able to send touring companies to the county towns, to dominions and colonies, and to India.

Mr. Geoffrey Whitworth said that last year the fund stood at £150,000. In August £75,000 was paid to the Office of Works for the site. They hoped to raise at least another £200,000, but their present appeal was for £100,000 which, with the sum they had in hand, would enable them to build and equip the theatre.

Dame Sybil Thorndike appealed for gifts of £100 units for the endowment of seats. Promises already received, or made at the meeting were as follows: Liverpool Repertory Theatre, the proprietors of the *Hereford Times*, Lady Muspratt, Miss Viola Tree, Sir Charles Mander, Mrs. Mary Ralli, two friends of Lady Gollancz, Mr. Barrow Cadbury, Mr. Clifford Bax, Sir Robert Mond, Lord Camrose, Lord Kemsley, Sir W. Davison, Mr. and Mrs. Owen Nares, Mme Genée, Sir John Martin-Harvey, Dame Sybil Thorndike, Mrs. Holford Knight, Mr. Harcourt Williams, and on behalf of Mr. Geoffrey Whitworth. In addition many London boroughs have undertaken to organize appeals for the endowment of seats in their names.

Old English madrigals were sung before the ceremony at the site by the Fleet Street Choir, under the direction of Mr. T. B. Lawrence.

Altogether this was a famous occasion, marred, however, by the absence of Lord Lytton, who unfortunately had been called away for important business in Palestine. And this was not the only disappointment. Though no word was spoken, some of us began to feel the pressage of a storm which might, sooner perhaps than later, cast a shadow over all our undertakings. We tried to keep up our spirits with the wishful thought that it was incredible that history should repeat itself so exactly that what had happened five-and-twenty years ago should again dash the cup of victory from our hands at the very moment when all seemed hopeful.

Messrs. Temple and Walton, however, from now onwards stepped up the appeal campaign to a breath-taking intensity. And as the summer wained, more plans were made for the autumn, and we were told of mysterious millionaires who might at any moment transform the shadowed scene into a glorious finale. What had been done hitherto, was mere spadework. The seeds that had been scattered so opulently would now begin to fructify. And so it might have been, had not our secret fears proved to be justified, and had not fate intervened with a far different climax, in which not only the National Theatre project but the world entire was overwhelmed.

IX

THE DARK DAWN

And darkness was upon the face of the earth, and in September 1939 the Committee met again for the sorrowful business of disbanding the staff and closing down the appeal. Several suggestions were made and repeated at subsequent meetings for keeping the National Theatre in recollection. Naturally, the Old Vic came along with further requests for help, and there were other suggestions for the formation of a National Theatre Touring Company to be sent around the country under the auspices of the Committee. This might have been legalized by recourse to the Court; but without it, the Charity Commissioners would not give their consent. In view of the financial position of the country, the capital assets of the Trust were also a cause of anxiety, and as a precaution it was decided that the Trustees should be asked to transfer the long-term investments of the Fund to short-dated stock. A little later, the South Kensington site was offered on loan to the Government for the period of the war, and the L.C.C. were glad to make use of it for one of those fire-fighting water reservoirs which were now appearing on almost every vacant space in the London area. At the same time the chairmanship of the Committee was accepted by Dame Edith Lyttelton, for, to everyone's regret, Lord Lytton had felt moved for personal reasons to resign that office at the beginning of the war. However, he still remained a Trustee, and continued to give attention to the work of the Committee as occasion arose.

At a meeting held in May 1940 it was reported that the first term of the lease of the offices at 50, Pall Mall was shortly due to expire. It was decided that the lease should not be renewed, and that the office of the Committee should be transferred to the headquarters of the British Drama League in Fitzroy Square. Some of our furniture and effects went there too—but the bulk of them to a repository in Pimlico, which, in the middle of the war, went up in flames together with some important records belonging to the Committee. Among these was the list of seat-endowments; a loss which was to give much trouble when we were endeavouring, after the war, to distinguish those seats which had actually been paid for from those which had only been promised.

To finish with these relics of happier days, let me add that at a meeting held on 9th June 1941, the Hon. Secretary reminded the Committee of Mr. Badger's fruitful bequest of £3,000 which, it will be remembered, had started the whole movement, and had been given on the understanding that a statue of Shakespeare should form part of the National Theatre when finally erected. On the death of Mr. Badger his executors, seeing no sign that the theatre would ever come to pass, took upon themselves to apportion the legacy between three missionary societies. As a result of negotiation, however, these worthy societies were persuaded to relinquish one half of the legacy, and the sum of £1,500 was duly credited to the National Theatre Fund. Lord Esher proposed, and it was unanimously resolved that this sum should be retained and earmarked for the provision of a statue of Shakespeare when the theatre was built.

Meanwhile things were happening outside the particular field of the National Theatre which yet were to have an important bearing thereon. I refer to the creation of 'The Entertainments National Service Association' and to that of 'The Council for the Encouragement of Music and the Arts' soon to be known more familiarly as E.N.S.A. and C.E.M.A. The former owed its existence to Basil Dean who some months before the outbreak of war had reminded the War Office of the music and drama work which he had organized under the Navy and Army Canteen Board in 1915. The Authorities were at once convinced of their obligation in this new emergency. Plans had already been drawn up by Mr. Dean and within a fortnight of the new war's outbreak, Drury Lane Theatre had been taken over for E.N.S.A's head-quarters, and its first concert for the Forces had been given at a Southern camp. Soon the E.N.S.A. concert parties were visiting war-centres in every part of England and abroad. The statistics of the organization are astronomical. It has been said that over three million people must have been entertained at E.N.S.A. shows by the end of hostilities, and though, on the drama side, a distinctly 'popular' type of entertainment was the rule, there was also a sprinkling, small at first, but gradually increasing, of serious plays. Strange to relate, these plays were often more warmly appreciated than the lighter stuff, and many of our most eminent actors took part in them. A small charge was made for admission, the ultimate financial responsibility being shouldered by the Navy, Army and Air Force Institutes.

C.E.M.A., concerned mainly with the maintenance and diffusion of high artistic standards, was set up by the President of the Board of Education in January 1940, to administer a grant of £25,000 from the Pilgrim Trust; and in the following April the Coalition Government, impressed by the need to nourish the flickering flames of culture, agreed to give pound for pound with the Pilgrim Trust and any other gifts which might come to hand up to a total of £50,000. The Government again combined with the Pilgrim Trust for the following year, but the Trust retired in April 1942, and thereafter all the funds for C.E.M.A. were found by the Exchequer. Between the years 1940–50, no less than £2,095,000 of public money had been spent on C.E.M.A. and on its successor, the 'Arts Council of Great Britain', incorporated by Royal Charter in 1946. These grants, it must be remembered, were expendable not only on the drama, but on music and the

visual arts as well. But considerable sums have always been devoted to the theatre, including £25,000 for the purchase of the
derelict Theatre Royal, Bristol, and annual subsidies to the Old
Vic Trust, amounting (in the year 1948–9) to £26,000.

Separating the two organizations there was of course a basic
difference. E.N.S.A. was born of a war-time emergency, and derived its funds from the profits of the Navy, Army, and Air Force
canteens. C.E.M.A. was conceived on more idealistic lines,
which were intended to lead to a permanent institution, entirely
supported on direct grants from the Exchequer. With such a
precedent, the claims of a National Theatre for State aid could
never again be refuted out of hand, and one immediate result of
C.E.M.A's benevolent intervention was that the S.M.N.T. Committee found itself enabled to refuse with a clear conscience the
many pleas for assistance which continued to arrive from the Old
Vic and other bodies who began to see their future seriously
imperilled by the stress of war.

But the outlook for the National Theatre was by no means a
bright one. On his eighty-sixth birthday Bernard Shaw felt it
incumbent upon him to resign from the Executive Committee,
conveying his decision in a letter to the Hon. Secretary dated
26th July 1941. 'I am acting', he wrote, 'after the most careful
consideration, and beg the Council to accept my resignation as
inevitable and my decision as unchangeable. My name can remain
in the bill as a member of the General Committee. I shall thus be
available for consultation if any occasion should arise. Please
convey to my late colleagues my regret at losing the very enjoy-
able contacts with them which our meetings secured for me.'

After that there was nothing more to be said. But the Committee fully realized that they were saying 'Good-bye' to one who
in spite of years remained their youngest member, and one who
in a very special degree had won their respect and their affection.

And all the while Sir Edwin Lutyens and Mr. Cecil Masey were
doggedly at work on the completion of the theatre plans. Sir

Edwin was even turning his attention to the interior *décor* of the auditorium. When suddenly, like a comet in the dark night sky, to a meeting of the Committee held in March 1942, came Trustee Alderman Blake with a proposition so revolutionary as to change the whole face of the future.

He told us that plans were under consideration by the London County Council for the post-war development of the Surrey side between Westminster and Waterloo bridges, and that if the Committee so desired, an application to the Council for a National Theatre site in that area might not be inopportune. The Committee immediately perceived that here was a matter of critical importance. Despite the many advantages of South Kensington, we had always known that the site there was on the small side, and though some, like G.B.S., had regarded the museum atmosphere of the district as a positive asset, there were others who had their doubts. Paramount, however, was the feeling that if the L.C.C. became implicated in our scheme, their moral backing would be of supreme value in other and even more august quarters. Nevertheless much, of course, depended on the area and situation of the Council's site, and on the terms offered for its acquisition. Mr. Blake having given some tentative assurances on these points, it was resolved to pursue the possibility he had unveiled, and to ask him to arrange a meeting as soon as might be between Lord Latham (Leader of the Council), and the five Committee members present. It was also decided that Mr. Bernard Shaw should be invited to attend.

Owing to the indisposition of Lord Latham, the meeting had to be deferred till June 9th, when it took the form of an informal discussion in Mr. Blake's private room at County Hall. The S.M.N.T. representatives included our host (at that time Chairman of the L.C.C.), Mrs. Lyttelton, Sir Barry Jackson, Mr. Ashley Dukes, the Hon. Secretary, and Mr. Bernard Shaw, whose appearance was something of a surprise, since he had at first refused the Committee's invitation, and had moreover indicated that he was

217

frankly opposed to the South Bank scheme. For the County Council appeared Lord Latham, Sir Harold Webbe, Professor Lascelles Abercrombie, Mr. Forshaw (Architect to the Council), Mr. Silkin, and several other officials.

Lord Latham opened the proceedings by emphasizing that this was only a private conversation, with no powers to take action or to commit the parties in any way. The speakers were asked to remain seated and to chat as informally as possible. We were soon made aware that the Council was flirting with the idea of making us an offer of land on the South Bank *in exchange* for our site in South Kensington. This was excellent. But to our consternation, Bernard Shaw metaphorically leapt to his feet, advanced all the possible objections to the river-side site, and seemed to infer that if the L.C.C. were trying to induce us to 'swap' our South Kensington site for such a manifestly inferior one on the South Bank it could only be with some ulterior motive. 'Clearly', Shaw continued, 'our policy is to hold on to our site and keep it vacant until we are given Thurloe Square in exchange; a very advantageous bargain for us.' He went on to elaborate his theory that the West End was moving further west, that in the not far future the Albert Memorial would become the cultural mecca of London, and that therefore the right place for the National Theatre was somewhere in that vicinity. Horrified as at first they were, the National Theatre delegates could only sit bemused and fascinated by the brilliance with which their whole case was being torn to shreds. Nor later on did they fail to appreciate the paragraph in a private report of the meeting which Shaw circulated among his colleagues, to the effect that 'Sir Harold Webbe, on leaving, rose smiling broadly and said that he had come to the meeting as leader of the Council Opposition, but his presence was superfluous, as the opposition was safe in the hands of that sound old Tory, Mr. Bernard Shaw.[1]

[1] With his usual blend of generosity and realism, Mr. Shaw ultimately changed his mind. On October 17th, 1946, Mrs. Lyttelton reported to the

On this almost hilarious note, the talk ended, and having taken tea with Mr. Blake, some of us boarded a motor-boat for a river trip that provided us with an alluring view of the South Bank and its amenities. A report of the proceedings was laid before our Committee in due course, and after some further consultations with out architects, the Hon. Secretary was instructed to send the following letter to the Clerk of the Council.

17th November 1942.

DEAR SIR,

Consequent on the Discussion which took place between representatives of the London County Council and of the Shakespeare Memorial National Theatre Committee at the County Hall on June 9th, my Committee have requested me to inform you that at their last meeting held at this address on Wednesday, November 11th, the following resolution was carried unanimously:

That this Committee will be willing to negotiate for a site suitable for the National Theatre on the South Bank of the Thames between County Hall and Waterloo Bridge on a minimum area of one acre, in exchange for the present site at Cromwell Gardens, South Kensington.

The reader shall not be worried with details of the elaborate negotiations which ensued. The fact was that the L.C.C. had not as yet made up its mind as to the precise nature of their contemplated development of the South Bank. First, we were asked to submit plans for a theatre at the southern end of Waterloo Bridge. Sir Edwin Lutyens and Mr. Masey went so far as to design a completely new theatre for this site, taking advantage of the larger area now available to include the two theatres which had always been regarded, since Granville-Barker's book, as

---

Executive Committee that she had lately seen him, and that he was now in favour of the theatre on the South Bank, and thought that a beautiful smaller theatre should also be built on the North Bank. Moreover, some months previously, Mr. Shaw had offered the fine bust of himself by Sigmund Stroble to be placed in the Foyer of the theatre when erected. In the meantime the bust was accepted on loan by the London County Council for display in the ambulatory of the Council Chambers at County Hall.

the well-nigh necessary ideal. These plans were shown at a Drama League twenty-fifth aniversary exhibition at Burlington House early in 1944. But yet again these plans had to be scrapped, for the Council were now envisaging the theatre as the centre-piece of a row of commercial or official buildings to occupy the entire tract of land between the Waterloo and Hungerford bridges.

On the death of Sir Edwin Lutyens in 1944, Mr. (now Sir) Hubert Worthington was consulted by the Committee on the design of a theatre in this central and spectacular position, and he actually produced a drawing which sketched a truly magnificent façade both for the theatre and for the office buildings on either side. Nevertheless, the Committee were not quite happy about this scheme. They were aware that in such surroundings the National Theatre would be positioned in a dead area so far as its appeal to the public was concerned. At night-time especially there would be nothing to enliven the dark and dismal aura of the deserted offices in whose neighbourhood the theatre would find itself. It was a very different proposition when the Council began to consider a much more attractive layout for the whole area—a great Concert Hall by Hungerford Bridge, and the National Theatre on the site now occupied by the old Shot Tower, with a gracious open space between.

But this is to anticipate a series of events of prime import which began in the winter of 1944, when a few weeks before Christmas I was rung up on the telephone by Sir Reginald Rowe who asked me if I would go to see him. Not knowing what I was in for, but expecting the usual thing, I accepted the invitation, and on a night of pitch black-out found myself lost and wandering in the precincts of Lincoln's Inn. There was no one about from whom I could ask the way, but, at last, with the aid of a torch, I found his staircase at the end of a little court. The numbers over the doors were invisible. Almost at hazard I knocked at the first which confronted me on the second

floor. The door opened at once, and Sir Reginald himself
ushered me into the warmth and light of his heavily curtained
sitting-room.

It was an invalid who confronted me, though for most of his
life he had been a man of magnificent physique. A foremost
rowing-blue at Oxford, his abilities had afterwards promoted
him to the office of Treasurer of Lincoln's Inn; and for many
years his spare time had been devoted to philanthropic work
among the boys of London, and to the Hon. Treasurership of
the Old Vic and Sadler's Wells combination, which many a
time he must have saved from financial failure by his business
acumen and his whole-hearted enthusiasm. Now he told me
quite frankly that the Old Vic company, temporarily banished
to Liverpool, were doing good business, but that their post-
war future was a matter of grave concern. The Old Vic itself
had, of course, been put out of action early in the war. To re-
construct the building was a task quite beond its resources.
He fully realized that the S.M.N.T. had by now gone too far
with the London County Council even to listen to a further
appeal for assistance. But might there not be a way open to some
kind of co-operation that could prove, at this critical moment,
equally beneficial to us both?

Pressed for something a little more definite, he informed me
that the Old Vic, as well as ourselves, had been in touch with the
London County Council, with what object he did not reveal,
leaving me to form my own conclusions. But he went on to say
that he felt the time had come to consider whether it might not
be advisable for the Old Vic to seek amalgamation with the
National Theatre, with a view to a concerted policy based on the
acquisition of the South Bank site. Now we were talking! And
I instinctively replied that I would be glad to hear from him
further on the matter if and when he was in a position to lay
before us an outline of what was proposed. To this Sir Reginald
readily agreed. But alas, it was not to be. A few days later,

stumbling in the dark, he suffered a shock which swiftly brought his life to an end.

But evidently there had still been time for him to communicate the result of our interview to his colleagues. Early in the New Year, I received a letter from the Secretary of the Old Vic asking the National Theatre Committee if they would agree to discuss possible collaboration at a joint meeting between the two bodies. Having deeply pondered the problems raised in my talk with Sir Reginald Rowe, I prepared the following statement giving a purely personal view of the situation as I saw it. This was duly laid before the meeting of the S.M.N.T. Executive which I summoned for 7th February 1945:

From a conversation I had with Sir Reginald Rowe, at his request, shortly before Christmas, it was evident that the Old Vic was putting out feelers for a possible amalgamation with the National Theatre. It appeared that this suggestion might involve a *real amalgamation* under which the Old Vic would become, in fact, the National Theatre; or some looser form of association under which the Old Vic Company would perform, on certain conditions, in a National Theatre building to be provided by our own Committee.

The latter alternative appears to me to be of no interest to us. It could not eventuate for some years, unless in the meanwhile the Old Vic desired us to become responsible, financially or otherwise, for its present programmes. But I take it that our Committee would not desire to contribute finance to the Old Vic Company, since our capital fund needs husbanding for future operations, while our income may hardly suffice for our headquarters expenses between now and the opening of the Theatre.

What are the advantages and disadvantages from our point of view of what I have called a *real amalgamation*? If this could be announced in the near future, the chief advantage would be that we should secure a new impetus of public approval at a time when support of the National Theatre idea, particularly in the provinces, shows signs of failing. Moreover, the goodwill of the Government, of C.E.M.A., and other important bodies might be attracted, whereas we might even find some hostility in these quarters should the idea get about that we were trying to found a National Theatre in opposition to, or in competition with, the Old Vic. (Such an idea, of course, may be quite unfounded, but the later developments in Old Vic propaganda have been well designed to nourish such a misconception.)

A further advantage of amalgamation is that we should be associated with a live company which offers the nucleus of a National Theatre Company as good as any we could ourselves hope to create when the time for opening the Theatre came. Amalgamation would also counter the view, often expressed, that the National Theatre Committee is concerned with nothing but bricks and mortar, and is incompetent to provide the actual performances by which the National Theatre must stand or fall. Lastly, it would be of manifest advantage to the National Theatre project if the Old Vic would put its capital assets (e.g., the value of the Waterloo Road theatre) into the common pot.

On the debit side, amalgamation would undoubtedly tie our hands to some degree. We should not be so free to lay down the general policy of the National Theatre when it started, and we might even be associated in the public mind with a standard of performance which stems from an earlier period when the Old Vic was more a charit- able institution than a first-class theatre. In other words, it is some- times dangerous to pour old wine into new bottles, and the opening of the National Theatre would be deprived of the lure of novelty if its company was already known to the theatre-going public.

Nevertheless, on a long view, the prospect of amalgamation may be worth pursuing, but only on two fundamental conditions.

(a) The Old Vic should agree to the complete merger of its title and constitution in the National Theatre of the future. This, surely, can be legitimately expected if the Old Vic is honest in its desire to assume the position of a National Theatre. It cannot both have its cake and eat it. Though, of course, due acknowledgment to Miss Lilian Baylis and her pioneer theatre could, and should, be made in the Constitution, and worthily commemorated somewhere in the Theatre itself. Such merger should be the more acceptable to the Old Vic when it is realized that it would not be swallowed up by our own National Theatre Committee, but that a newly constituted Committee would swallow up both of us. For I believe it has always been recognized by the present National Theatre Committee that the time would come when it should give place to a new and nationally constituted body. It is into this new body that the Old Vic Committee would be merged, together with ourselves.

(b) An amalgamation on the lines suggested should be subsequent to an assurance that both the present committees were substantially agreed on the policy to be adopted by the National Theatre. Not every detail of organization need be gone into, but I think there is one condition that is paramount, and that is that apart from the touring companies which the Old Vic will probably desire to be included in a National Theatre policy, the Number One National Theatre Company should itself be centred in London for not less than nine months in any one year. Without some such safeguard, the aims of our own Committee, as stated constantly from the inception of the movement to the present time, would risk being lost sight of, to the detriment of that high standard of production and performance which can be achieved only by a company for the most part resident at the centre.

Discussion then ranged over a variety of topics, but in the end the policy outlined in my memorandum was endorsed, and it was resolved that the invitation of the Old Vic should be accepted, and that a joint meeting should be arranged as soon as possible. Our representatives were to be Mr. Oliver Lyttelton, Lord Esher, Mr. Lewis Casson, Mr. J. P. Blake, and the Hon. Secretary. Any proposals put forward at this meeting were to be referred back to our respective Committees.

We met again on 14th March, and considered the report of the joint meeting which in the meanwhile had been held at the Ministry of Production, under the authoritative yet tactful chairmanship of Mr. Lyttelton. The Governors of the Old Vic, it appeared, had met a few days earlier, and a letter was read from their secretary, saying that they had unanimously welcomed the report and the opportunity to explore the suggested co-operation. As their representatives at a further meeting, they had nominated Viscount Hambledon, Mrs. L'Estrange Malone (L.C.C.), and Mr. Tyrone Guthrie. After further discussion it was finally proposed by Mr. Hamilton Fyfe, seconded by Lord Esher and resolved 'that the S.M.N.T. Committee unanimously welcomes the report of the meeting held at the Ministry of Production to

The Rt. Hon. Oliver Lyttelton, D.S.O., M.C., M.P.

View of the South Bank with the Royal Festival Hall and, to the extreme left, a section of Waterloo Bridge. The site of the National Theatre is indicated by the Shot Tower, to be demolished at the close of the Exhibition

discuss the possibility of amalgamation with the Old Vic, and also the opportunity to explore further co-operation between the two bodies and to frame the Constitution.' The following were appointed to represent the Committee: Lord Esher, Mr. J. P. Blake, and the Hon. Secretary. As before, any proposals made at joint meetings were to be referred back to the Executive.

Subsequently several such joint meetings were held under the chairmanship of Mr. Lyttelton which served to clarify the situation and to allay whatever hesitations still remained in the minds of the more die-hard supporters of either party. The way was now open to a final fusion between the National Theatre and the Old Vic, which Mr. Lyttelton happily characterized as a 'contract of betrothal' pending the consummation of the 'marriage' which would not actually take place until the National Theatre building had been erected and a Royal Charter of amalgamation obtained. In the meantime the machinery of co-operation and the terms of mutual responsibility were outlined and ratified in a formal document:

ABSTRACT OF AN AGREEMENT made the Twenty-fifth day of January One thousand nine hundred and forty-six BETWEEN THE GOVERNORS OF ROYAL VICTORIA HALL (hereinafter called 'the Governors') acting by THE RIGHT HONOURABLE VICTOR ALEXANDER GEORGE ROBERT EARL OF LYTTON, K.G., P.C., G.C.S.I., G.C.I.E., their duly authorized agent of the one part and the TRUSTEES OF THE SHAKE-SPEARE MEMORIAL NATIONAL THEATRE (hereinafter called 'the Trustees') acting on behalf of the Shakespeare Memorial National Theatre Committee and by Geoffrey Whitworth the duly authorized agent of the Trustees of the other part.

WHEREAS:

1. Royal Victoria Hall is a Charity constituted under a Scheme dated the eleventh day of September One thousand nine hundred and twenty-five of the Board of Charity Commissioners for England and Wales.

2. The Shakespeare Memorial National Theatre is a Charity constituted by Deed Poll, dated twentieth day of May One thousand nine hundred and nine.

3. The Governors and the Trustees consider it in the best interests of the said two Charities and the expansion and development of the objects thereof to effect an immediate co-operation of the said two Charities and ultimately an amalgamation to the intent that they shall then become and be administered as one body under the name of the National Theatre with the following objects:

To provide in London, being the capital city of the British Commonwealth and Empire, a Theatre conducted on a repertory basis where the people may have continual opportunities of seeing the best drama, past and present, produced with the utmost distinction, played by actors of the highest merit, and at admission charges as moderate as may be consistent with the fulfilment of these aims; to serve and promote the art of the theatre by providing opportunities for its exercise in its highest classical departments; to keep the plays of Shakespeare in frequent production; to foster whatever is vital in British Drama; to prevent recent plays of merit from falling into oblivion; to produce new plays and to further the development of modern drama; to produce translations of representative works of foreign drama, ancient and modern; to organize National Theatre Tours throughout this country and Overseas; in short to stimulate the art of the theatre by every possible means.

Now it is Hereby Agreed by and between the parties hereto as follows:

1. The Governors and the Trustees shall use their best endeavours to effect an amalgamation of the said two Charities but no such amalgamation shall take place until the National Theatre building which is the principal object of the Trustees shall have been erected.

2. The Governors and the Trustees have appointed a Joint Council of nine persons with co-ordinating functions (hereinafter referred to as the Council). The first members thereof whose appointment is hereby confirmed are:

Chairman	The Right Hon. Oliver Lyttelton
Representative of The Governors	The Earl of Lytton
	Viscount Hambleden
	Mrs. L'Estrange Malone
	Sir Ernest Pooley
Representative of The Trustees	Viscount Esher
	Mrs. Alfred Lyttelton
	Mr. J. P. Blake
	Mr. Geoffrey Whitworth

The Governors and the Trustees shall respectively have power to appoint any person to fill a vacancy upon the Council in respect of their representative members thereon. The Council shall have power to fill a vacancy in the Chairmanship. Each member present at a meeting of the Council shall have one vote and the Chairman shall have a second or casting vote.

3. THE Council is hereby authorized to represent itself as a joint Committee appointed by the Governors and the Trustees respectively for the purpose of appealing for funds to be devoted either to the building equipment or endowment of a National Theatre or to finance theatrical productions.

4. UNTIL the National Theatre Building has been erected and the amalgamation of the two Charities effected by Royal Charter or otherwise there shall be no blending of the assets and funds of the said two Charities for any purpose or in any manner whatsoever.

5. THERE shall be two Sub-Committees of the Council as follows:
(a) An Old Vic Sub-Committee consisting of:
      Five of the present Old Vic Governors to be nominated by the Governors
      Mr. John Burrell
      Mr. George Chamberlain
      Viscount Esher
appointed to represent the Council.
(b) A National Theatre Building Sub-Committee consisting of:
      Five persons nominated by the Shakespeare Memorial National Theatre Committee
      Mr. M. MacOwan
      Mr. John Burrell
      Sir Ernest Pooley
appointed to represent the Council.

6. VACANCIES on the Old Vic Sub-Committee will be filled by the Governors and vacancies on the National Theatre Building Sub-Committee will be filled by the Trustees. The Council shall have the power to appoint additional members of the National Theatre Building Sub-Committee.

7. IT shall be the duty of the Old Vic Sub-Committee to carry out the plans and policy of the Governors. This Agreement shall in no way interfere with the various activities in London and elsewhere of the Old Vic Theatre Company which shall if circumstances permit con-

tinue to function and develop until the National Theatre Building is erected. The Old Vic Theatre Company and any other similar under-takings present or future of the Governors shall, until the National Theatre shall have been erected, be presented by 'The Joint Council of the National Theatre Committee and the Governors of the Old Vic'.

8. IT shall be the duty of the National Theatre Building Sub-Committee to negotiate with the London County Council and any other bodies or persons public or private in regard to the site on the South side of of the River or elsewhere, and to proceed with the plans for building the National Theatre.

9. THE two Sub-Committees will report to the Council and the Old Vic Sub-Committee will also report to the Governors and the National Theatre Building Sub-Committee will also report to the Trustees. Each Sub-Committee shall annually appoint its own Chairman and shall make rules for the conduct of its business. The Secretary of the Council shall act as Secretary of each Sub-Committee.

10. WHILE the National Theatre is in course of erection, the Council will use their best endeavours to procure a Royal Charter providing for the amalgamation of the Old Vic with the Shakespeare Memorial National Theatre to the intent that they shall become and be ad-ministered as one body under the name of the 'National Theatre'.

11. ONE or more further Sub-Committees may be instituted by the Council for special purposes other than those covered by the two Sub-Committees above mentioned.

12. THE Council shall keep the Arts Council informed of these arrangements and the Sub-Committees shall be at liberty to apply to them for advice and assistance as required.

As WITNESS the hands of the Right Honourable Victor Alexander George Robert Earl of Lytton on behalf of the Governors and of Geoffrey Whitworth on behalf of the Trustees the day and year first above written.

As secretary of the new Joint Council was now appointed Mr. Kenneth Rae, who during the war had been at the Ministry of Information, and before that had been attached to the firm of Cobden-Sanderson, thus maintaining the long connection be-tween publishing and the National Theatre started by Mr. Britton in 1813. At first the operations of the Joint Council were con-ducted from the office of the Old Vic in St. Martin's Court, but in 1950 they were transferred to a separate office in Goodwin's Court nearby. I myself continued as Hon. Secretary of the S.M.N.T., and it is a pleasure to affirm that Kenneth Rae turned out to be a tactful and pleasant colleague. He proved not only effective and accurate in all sides of his work, but enterprising and originative.

One of the first tasks confronting the Joint Council was the appointment of an architect in place of Sir Edwin Lutyens. It was decided to seek a way out of the dilemma by taking advice from a panel of experts consisting of Sir Patrick Abercrombie, Mr. J. H. Forshaw, Mr. William Holford, Mr. Charles Holden, Professor Sir Charles Reilly, and Mr. N. Pevsner, Editor of the *Architectural Review*. These gentlemen, under the chairmanship of the Earl of Crawford and Balcarres, Chairman of the Fine Arts Commission, were immured for luncheon at the Savoy Hotel on 10th July 1946, when they unanimously decided to recommend the appointment of Mr. Brian O'Rorke, F.R.I.B.A., to the vacant post.

Mr. O'Rorke hailed from Australia, though he had resided in this country for some years. His name was unknown to the Joint Council; but they were enabled to inspect photographs of buildings for which he had been responsible in Australia, and of the attractive planning and decoration of ship saloons which he had designed for the Orient Line. In finally appointing Mr. O'Rorke the Joint Council may have made a venture of faith, but it was a faith well-grounded on the recommendation of a group of experts second to none, and in all subsequent dealings with Mr. O'Rorke and after inspecting his model of the theatre, the Council has felt fully justified in its choice. Some while later, Cecil Masey found it necessary to terminate his collaboration in the planning—an event which cause me much sorrow.

Urgent as it now was to be able to proceed with the Theatre at the close of the 1951 Festival of Britain, or at such time as a licence could be obtained for its erection, the Building Committee began a series of frequent meetings, and the architect, in company with Michael MacOwan, Norman Marshall, and the Secretary undertook a visit to several Scandinavian theatres to investigate some of the more recent examples of theatre construction. They were interested and heartened by what they saw, and returned impressed with the advice received that twin theatres were indeed desirable for economical administration, and that although such a theatre as that at Malmo had an immense auditorium, a capacity of 1,200 or 1,250 seats was everywhere regarded as the ideal maximum for the larger house.

The L.C.C., be it noted, had by this time changed its mind as to the appropriation for the Theatre of a midway site between the two bridges, and the scheme for Government or business offices on either side had been abandoned. The Theatre was now to occupy a site adjoining Waterloo Bridge at the extreme eastern edge of the arc, while at the western end, shadowed by Charing Cross Bridge, was to rise the great new Concert Hall for which the Council itself would assume entire responsibility. Between the two buildings would be a garden and an open approach for traffic. This arrangement was far more to the taste of the Joint Council than the former one had been, for now the Theatre would find itself in the midst of an entertainement area, instead of being flanked by austere official buildings little calculated to provide an atmosphere of social enjoyment or to attract the passing pleasure-seeker.

At this juncture, it may well be asked what steps were being taken to finance the heavy building costs which Mr. O'Rorke now estimated to be in the neighbourhood of a million pounds or more. The funds remaining at the disposal of the S.M.N.T. Committee would go nowhere for such an expenditure, and they fully realized that the L.C.C. might be not well pleased if their proffered site of an acre and a bit more were left too long in a state of dere-liction after the close of the 1951 Festival of Britain. Had it not been for the hope of Government support, the prospect would have been bleak indeed. Let us see what basis there was for the Joint Council's optimism.

It will be remembered that earlier in this chapter we alluded to the change in the official attitude to the Arts which became noticeable at the beginning of the war, as witnessed by the formation of E.N.S.A. by the War Office, and of C.E.M.A. by the Board of Education. In 1942, in pursuit of this policy the British Drama League had drawn up a Memorandum under the title of the 'Civic Theatre Scheme' which in 1942 was submitted to the Prime Minister (Mr. Churchill), to the President of the Board of Education, and to C.E.M.A., some extracts wherefrom are here reprinted with the omission of recommendations which concern the detailed administration of the plan as being irrelevant to our main theme.

THE CIVIC THEATRE SCHEME

In common with other aspects of the national life, British Music and Drama are now the subject of post-war planning. This memorandum deals with but one branch of the subject: The problem of State Aid for the Drama.

We cannot deal here with the general theory of State Aid. It is sufficient to record that the English Theatre had its origin in municipal and ecclesiastical enterprise during the Middle Ages; and that later, David Garrick, Bulwer-Lytton, and Matthew Arnold were at one in believing that the State had a real responsibility for the promotion of the art of the Drama on a national basis. The grounds of this belief have never been better stated that in the Report on 'The Drama in Adult Education' issued by the Board in 1926.

'Drama is at once a most vivid and most subtle artistic medium for the conveyance of ideas. In consequence drama, under right conditions, can be a most potent instrument of moral, artistic and intellectual progress. . . . The conditions under which drama is presented are, therefore, a matter of the greatest interest to all concerned in Education.'

The extent to which normal theatre-managements have contributed to the maintenance of the drama on this lofty plane is a matter of legitimate pride to us all. But many leaders of the professional stage, from Irving downwards, have been the first to admit that they have carried a burden which has been well-nigh insupportable. In most Continental countries this burden has been shared to a larger or lesser degree by the State. Here in England it is now widely acknowledged that in the public interest the Theatre deserves support from the community on the same lines as those on which assistance is already accorded to the arts of Literature (through the public Libraries), Painting (through the Public Art Galleries), and Music (through Municipal Orchestras, etc.).

It is a notable and encouraging fact that during the present war the provision of the peripatetic entertainment for troops, war-workers, and the civilian population has been actively sponsored not only by the Board of Education, but by the War Office and by the Ministry of Labour and National Service. The methods adopted have been eminently appropriate to current conditions. But it is, to say the least, doubtful whether the emergency support of war-time touring companies should be taken as an adequate precedent for the days of peace. The hope of those responsible for the present memorandum is that Government assistance will be forthcoming after the war for a scheme more closely related with the theatre as a permanent cultural institution. This, indeed, will be an urgent necessity if the creative gifts of dramatic art in its higher ranges are to be preserved for the benefit of all classes, and fairly distributed among those centres which are waiting to receive them. Thus the benefits of the scheme should be available throughout the entire country, not only in the larger cities but in the towns and rural areas. With a view to engaging the invaluable resources of local patriotism and initiative, each unit should be mainly responsible for implementing the scheme in its own district.

If there be any danger in State-aid to the Arts, it is to be found in the uniformity which is liable to result from State control. Methods of centralized or mass production are therefore to be deprecated; if for no other reason than that referred to by the Minister of Labour when addressing the inaugural meeting of the newly formed Provincial Theatre Council. '*I have no doubt*', said Mr. Bevin, '*that the theatre, like all other institutions, will undergo great changes before the end of this titanic struggle. I hope it will. In this mechanical age we look to the theatrical world to preserve the characteristics of our people—not merely national characteristics but (and that is what most appeals to me) local characteristics. In the British people there exist great divergencies of character which are endangered by the current tendency to uniformity, and*

THE DARK DAWN

I look forward, at the end of this great struggle, to the living theatre not only coming into its own as a means of livelihood, but to its becoming one of our great national institutions to convey to the peoples of the world the real character of the ordinary British people.'

Before any Civic Theatre can qualify for State aid, a Budget of Estimated Expenditure and Revenue during a three-year period shall be submitted to the competent authority. If approved the required funds shall be guaranteed as to 50 per cent by the Government, and 50 per cent by a Local Trust which shall be empowered to raise its quota from the Rates, or from voluntary subscription or by a combination of both: provided always that voluntary subscriptions be paid to the Local Trust and not directly to the Theatre. The Director of each Civic Theatre shall have complete control over the artistic management of the theatre, and the engagement of company and staff.

It will be obvious that London occupies a special position in relation to the Civic Theatre scheme. Already it is served by a large number of theatres, and, whatever may happen hereafter, not many municipal authorities in the metropolitan area would probably desire to establish a Civic Theatre on the scale envisaged in the plan. Nearing achievement, however, there is one theatre which by reason of its resources both moral and material, and its potential status as the imperial symbol of British Dramatic art, will claim on every ground to participate and benefit from the scheme. We refer, of course, to the National Theatre which in view of its constitution and declared artistic policy must clearly be regarded as the model and example of all State-aided British theatres.

The League made a special effort to obtain endorsement of this memorandum by those who at that time were representative of all schools of thought . . . and the list of names finally attached to the printed manifesto included British Actors' Equity Association, the Archbishop of Canterbury (Dr. Temple), Viscount Esher, Sir Percy Harris, Bart., M.P., The Hon. Mrs. Alfred Lyttelton, G.B.E., Dame Elizabeth Cadbury, Sir Barry Jackson, Sir Edwin Lutyens, O.M., P.R.A., Col. Sir John Shute, M.P., William Armstrong, James Bridie, Ashley Dukes, T. S. Eliot, Dr. Julian Huxley, F.R.S., Will Lawther, Kenneth Lindsey, M.P., Desmond MacCarthy, Dr. J. J. Mallon, C.H., Norman Marshall, Dr. Gilbert Murray, O.M., J. B. Priestley, Alec. M.

Rea, Dr. Malcolm Sargent, G. Bernard Shaw, Dr. Edith Summerskill, M.P., Geoffrey Whitworth.

Although the scheme was not adopted by the Government there and then (and this was hardly expected), there seems no doubt that it had some influence upon their future action. It was presented in person to Lord Keynes by a League deputation to C.E.M.A., who approved it in principle, while in Section 132 of the Local Government Act, 1948, as recommended in our scheme, Local Authorities were empowered to provide and maintain theatres and were given a mandate to incure expenditure not exceeding in any one year the product on a rate of sixpence in the pound. As noted in *Dobson's Theatre Year-Book for* 1948–9, 'About eight million pounds is therefore now available in any one year to subsidize music, drama, cinema, and other forms of entertainment. No one expects that more than a few local authorities will prepare schemes immediately, but all are able to go ahead with plans, to experiment, and finance initial losses and, if necessary, make a continuing payment or grant-in-aid towards a project which cannot for some years be on a surplus earning basis. The year 1948, therefore, brings to an end a phase of the work of those who have recently been urging civic opera, theatre, and music in this country. To the future remains planning and inauguration.'

Meanwhile, from 5th to 8th February in this *annus mirabilis*, 1948, there took place at the Caxton Hall, Westminster, what its Chairman, Mr. J. B. Priestley, described as 'easily the most representative conference the theatre had ever had'. Unfortunately the Society of West End Theatre Managers and some kindred bodies held aloof, but apart from them, practically every organization of standing in the theatre world took part, including the British Actors' Equity, the Conference of Repertory Theatres, the Federation of Theatre Unions, the League of British Dramatists, the British Drama League, the Shakespeare Memorial Theatre, the Joint Council of the National Theatre and the Old Vic, and the Little Theatre Guild. A number of theatre managers also joined in the debates as individuals.

Among the ninety-odd resolutions submitted was one which welcomed the statement of the Minister of Health that he would shortly move the insertion of a clause in the new Local Government Bill permitting local Authorities to run Civic Theatres, as above noted, at the same time accepting the Drama League's Civic Theatre Scheme submitted to the Prime Minister in November 1942, as a useful basis for discussion. A second resolution, which will interest our readers even more, was moved by Mr. Norman Marshall (representing the Drama League) and seconded by Mr. Michael MacOwan (London Mask Theatre), to the effect that 'The British Theatre Conference endorses the current and already well-established National Theatre Scheme.' Both these resolutions were carried unanimously, which is more than can be said for several of the other motions submitted for debate.

It is not without significance that Sir Stafford Cripps consented to address the final Plenary Session of the Conference, and did so in the most encouraging and sympathetic terms. In the course of his speech the Chancellor gave the following remarkable account of the policy of the Government of the day in relation to the arts in general and to the theatre in particular:

Though I do not profess to have any special knowledge of the theatre, or even now to attend performances as I should like, yet I have a deep interest in matters theatrical because I realize to the full the value of the drama in our culture and education. I am therefore delighted to have been invited to come here to-day to say a few words—I hope of encouragement—in the work that has been undertaken by the British Theatre Conference.

It would be deceptive if I were to suggest that I could give you at this time any answer on behalf of the Government to the many implied questions and perhaps even criticisms which are contained in your resolutions. I hope you expect nothing of that sort from me. I am sure that you here would be the first to protest against the imposition of policies by such unknowledgeable people as a Government administration, until, at least, they had put before them the considered and, I should like to think, unanimous opinions of those directly concerned with the theatre. What I can and will say is that any unanimous opinions of those directly concerned, coming from such a representative and well qualified conference as this, will be taken into serious consideration by the Government. It is difficult perhaps in these times of great economic difficulty and urgency to devote as much time as one would like to cultural matters, but I can assure you that both I and the Government attach very great importance to these matters and we regard it as an essential part of the Government's duty to the people to give them full consideration.

We are convinced that in these days of growing education and progress, and of the shortening hours of labour, culture and entertainment must be prepared to help in their development in whatever way is decided to be best. The field of culture is a difficult one for Government interference, since we should all agree that the freest possible expression is needed for a healthy growth of the Drama. Government help is liable to be connected with Government control, or at least with some body of appointed individuals, and such controls are apt to destroy the initiative and the inventiveness which lie at the root of all artistic accomplishment. The first great experiment that we made largely had its origin with Dr. Thomas Jones and was developed by the late Lord Keynes—the setting up of the Arts Council, wholly financed by a Treasury grant. That was a new idea for this country, and for the first time brought the Government directly into contact with the problems of cultural development. We want to develop, I think, the Arts Council as a flexible living and dynamic organization, not the dictator of the Arts but the wise patron ever ready to encourage new movements and fresh developments.

When we come to consider the difficult question of the availability of theatres and their rents, we must, I think, be careful not to interfere with the freedom to show any play at any theatre, which, theoretically at least, at present exists. I shall be glad to see your recommendations as to theatre rents, but I am sure you must think many times before suggesting that all theatres should be owned by the State, unless your object is to get a State censorship upon all plays! As to municipal theatres which can be run by local authorities, this is a matter which has recently come up in the House of Commons, and you will have seen in the Press that the Minister of Health proposes to include in the Local Government Bill now before Parliament, a clause giving the local authorities the necessary legal powers.

This does not mean, of course, that there is no place for National Theatres. Indeed, I greatly look forward to the time when our economic situation will allow us to get on with the building of the first in London, to be followed, I hope, by others, as your chairman has suggested in his *Theatre Outlook*.

Spoken thus on a public occasion, these words could not fail to be accepted as an official commendation of the National Theatre and, in their context, as a hint that Government assistance might one day be forthcoming. It is only right, therefore, to explain that the Joint Council had previously empowered Lord Esher to approach Sir Stafford's predecessor, Mr. Dalton, and that he had shown himself most favourable to the idea. On the retirement of Mr. Dalton, Lord Esher had visited the new Chancellor with an even more encouraging result. To him—as also to Sir Ernest Pooley—much thanks are due for tactful intervention behind the scenes.

As things turned out, Sir Stafford Cripps proved even better than his words to the British Theatre Conference. On 23rd March of the same year, in reply to a question in the name of Mr. Oliver Lyttelton, the Chancellor of the Exchequer made the following statement in the House of Commons:

I understand that the L.C.C. are willing to reserve space for a National Theatre on the site which they propose to develop on the South Bank as a cultural centre, and to make the land available rent free in exchange for that already acquired by the National Theatre Committee in South Kensington. But they have asked for an assurance that the necessary funds will be forthcoming to build the theatre. The National Theatre Committee so far have some £70,000 in cash, but this will be quite inadequate to meet the cost of building a theatre which is now estimated to be in the region of a million pounds. There can obviously be no certainty of their being able to raise the rest of the money from private sources. The Joint Council of the National Theatre and the Old Vic have therefore approached the Government with a request that the Government would stand behind the project so that the necessary assurance can be given to the L.C.C.

The Government take the view that the establishment of a theatre to be operated under public auspices, which will set a standard for the production of drama in a setting worthy of Shakespeare and the British tradition, is a scheme to which the State should contribute. I am, therefore, proposing to ask for powers to provide a substantial part of the capital cost from public funds. Since, however, it is most unlikely that it will be possible to make a start on the building within the life of the present Parliament, I propose to introduce legislation during the present Parliament to the effect that, if the L.C.C. provide a suitable site for the purpose of a National Theatre, the Treasury may make a contribution not exceeding £1 million towards the cost of building the theatre. If the House is willing to pass such legislation, the requisite powers will be on the Statute Book to be used by the Government of the day as soon as it becomes possible to start on the scheme. The actual amount to be provided by the Treasury would, of course, depend upon the total contributions which may have become available from other sources at the time.

The arrangement for the operation and management of the theatre will need further consideration. My purpose in making this announcement at the present time, and in taking the steps I have stated, is to give assurance to the parties concerned so that they can proceed with their plans in the knowledge that they have the full sympathy and practical support of His Majesty's Government and of this House.

It seemed a shame that Lord Lytton was not still alive to read these words of comfort and good cheer. He had died in the autumn of 1947, an irreparable loss which was soon followed by the resignation of Dame Edith Lyttelton from the chairmanship of the Executive Committee. The reason given was ill health; but happily this remarkable and courageous woman lived on in full possession of her faculties till the summer of 1948, fully aware of and almost girlishly delighted at, as I myself can testify, the certainty of the achievement of the cause which she had served so long, so valiantly, and not in vain.

At the first S.M.N.T. Committee meeting over which Lord Esher presided (he had been unanimously voted to the chair at a meeting on 2nd December), a proposal was made by Mr. Lyttelton that Sir Anthony Meyer should be offered the position of third Trustee in place of Lord Lytton. Sir Anthony, it will be remembered, was grandson of the first baronet who had originally put the movement on its feet by his famous donation of £70,000. Then, at a meeting of the Executive held on 20th April 1948, Mr. (now Sir) Bronson Albery was unanimously welcomed as a new member of the Committee, and some months later was chosen to fill the S.M.N.T. vacancy on the Joint Council resulting from the lamented death of Dame Edith Lyttelton.

The story of these personal losses and reinforcements may be fitly brought to an end by some reference to the meeting of the executive held on 25th November 1948, when the Hon. Secretary reported that Lord Esher had consented to become a Trustee of the National Theatre, thus permitting him to act, together with the three other Trustees, on the highest level in any further negotiations with the Government. This would be an obvious advantage.

At the same meeting, Sir Kenneth Barnes raised the question as to who would finally approve the Constitution or the terms of the Royal Charter which, he understood, would soon be drawn up by the Joint Council? The Hon. Secretary said that he presumed that in the first place the document would be submitted to the Treasury. But after considerable discussion the Chairman proposed and it was resolved: 'That this Committee desires that the Constitution should be shown to the two constituent bodies of the Joint Council before it is shown to the Treasury or to the Arts Council.' In the same connection Sir Kenneth Barnes inquired if stage training would be officially undertaken or sponsored by the National Theatre? The Chairman replied that hitherto no mention had been made in any document concerning the National Theatre of an official training school, and should such a question arise, the views of Sir Kenneth would be taken into consideration.

THE DARK DAWN

In fact, the time was ripe for an official lead on this important problem, for both the public and the experts had for many years been wondering what solution, if any, would be found for it.

The precedent of the Paris Conservatoire suggested that a dramatic school should form an integral part of a National Theatre's work. Yet many were of the opinion that conditions in this country were not favourable to an enclosed college or academy of the kind we find in France. The question naturally arose as to whether one of the excellent schools already in existence might not be picked out for special contact with the National Theatre, and the whole matter was thoroughly debated at a private conference called by Lord Esher in March 1950, at the request of the Joint Council.

At this conference the Royal Academy of Dramatic Art, the Central School of Speech and Drama, and the Old Vic School were represented respectively by Sir Kenneth Barnes, Miss Gwynneth Thurburn, and Mr. Glen Byam Shaw. Though interrupting the normal course of our narrative, it may be convenient to dispose of the matter here by printing the report of the Conference in full.

It was agreed by all present that none of the existing Theatre Schools should have any direct connection with the National Theatre. The suggestion that a Finishing School or Academy should form part of the organization was discussed, but it was felt that an alternative suggestion put forward by Sir Kenneth Barnes would be in every way preferable. Sir Kenneth suggested that a number of ex-students who had already received training at Theatre Schools should be attached to the National Theatre and be used for crowd work. These apprentices would receive a minimum wage and would, in addition to their practical work 'walking-on', receive instruction. This method would have the advantage of attracting to the National Theatre not only students coming straight from school but also any actors or actresses who had already had some experience in the theatre and who were anxious to join this body of apprentices with the hope of ultimately being recruited to one of the National Theatre companies.

The Director of the National Theatre would have the power of

240

selection with no prejudice towards any one school. Some three teachers (perhaps, for some classes, actors in the company) would be required to give instruction in Acting, Movement, Production, Diction, etc., during four afternoons a week. This would mean the engagement of such teachers on a part-time basis.

It was thought that the maximum number of apprentices should be 40, divided into two classes of 20 each, with an annual intake of 20 recruits at the end of each year. The better apprentices would be chosen at the end of each year to join, as junior members, one of the National Theatre companies, and would be obliged to accept a contract for a minimum of two years. Those who, after two years, wished to leave the company in order to 'stretch' themselves by playing larger parts in other companies would later be given priority if they were anxious to return to the National Theatre at a higher level.

The composition of the Selection Board would be left to the Artistic Director of the National Theatre. The Directors of Drama Schools would not be entitled to sit on that Board, but would propose their candidates to the Board and would be consulted by the Selection Board, if necessary, as to the relative merits of their nominees. The question of the number of applicants to be given auditions from Theatre Schools was realized to be a difficult one and the final solution was left to a later date. It was suggested, however, that perhaps only schools recognized by the Ministry of Education should be entitled to propose candidates and that in no case would applicants be considered who had not had a minimum of two years' full-time training in a recognized school.

Lord Esher suggested that at a later date an Advisory Council of School Directors should be formed to advise the Governors of the National Theatre on all educational matters. This Advisory Council would be in no way connected with the National Theatre Selection Board for apprentices.

As a guiding principle it was agreed that the question of standard should be paramount where the choice of student was concerned, but that the doors should be left wide open to all serious young men and women who had already received training and were anxious to play their part in the National Theatre organization.

X

THE GREAT DEBATE

Sooner than many of us expected, The National Theatre Bill was brought before Parliament, and having reprinted much of that earlier discussion in the House of Commons on 23rd April 1913, it seems only right that I should give the reader an opportunity to compare the two debates, and to discover why, although the first had proved abortive, the second so triumphantly succeeded in placing the National Theatre on the Statute Book. The main difference was, of course, that in the former case the question had been somewhat tentatively raised by a private member, while now at long last it was submitted and sponsored as a Government measure, with a far more instructed and favourable public opinion at its back.

The crucial debates took place on the Second Readings of the National Theatre Bill, in the House of Commons on 21 January and in the House of Lords on 17 February 1949. The operative clause read as follows: '*That, for the purposes of any Act of the present Session to authorize the Treasury to contribute towards the cost of a National Theatre, it is expedient to authorize the payment out of moneys provided by Parliament, upon such terms and subject to such conditions as the Treasury may think fit, of such contributions not exceeding one million pounds to the funds of the Shakespeare Memorial Trust, in respect of the cost of erecting and equipping a national theatre in accordance with a scheme to be submitted to the Treasury for the purposes of the same Act.*

For the following extracts from the debates I am indebted to the official reports of *Hansard*. They will be interesting one day not only from a factual point of view, but as a commentary on the prevailing public attitude towards the theatre in the middle of the twentieth century.

HOUSE OF COMMONS

Friday, 21st January, 1949

[MR. SPEAKER *in the Chair*]

NATIONAL THEATRE BILL

THE FINANCIAL SECRETARY TO THE TREASURY (MR. GLENVIL HALL): I beg to move, 'That the Bill be now read a Second time.'

This is a small Bill with a very great purpose, and I am glad that it has fallen to my lot to introduce it. It implements the announcement made by my right hon. and learned Friend the Chancellor of the Exchequer in March of last year, that Parliament would be invited to provide State assistance towards the establishment of a national theatre. That such a theatre should be established in this country, devoted to the presentation of the best plays, past and present, produced with distinction, performed by actors of merit and where the dignity of the playwright's art would be maintained in a worthy setting has long been the dream of many people in all walks of life.

National theatres have existed for many years in other European countries. In France, for example, they have had such an institution for nearly 270 years. Therefore, it is, in my view altogether fitting that we who live in the land which gave birth and language to the greatest dramatist that the world has yet seen, should now think seriously of erecting such a centre here in London, notwithstanding the fact that we are all preoccupied with other and more pressing matters.

The patronage of the Court had a good deal to do with the flowering of British Drama in its greatest period. To-day there is a sharp division of opinion as to the extent to which the State should interfere in various sections of our national life, but there is no doubt that most, if not all, of us believe that it is right and proper that the State should come to the assistance of the arts. As the House is well aware, a beginning in that direction has already been made. Although it is a comparatively recent development, the encouragement of the arts by the State is something which has met with the wholehearted approval and support of hon. Members in all quarters of the House. On the dramatic side it took, until recently, the shape of exempting from Entertainment Duty performances which could be considered as mainly of an educational character. During the war, it took a more direct form when the Council for the Encouragement of Music and the Arts—which was a war-time organization—was given a grant from public funds by, I think, the National Government in 1940. C.E.M.A. has been succeeded by the Arts Council and last year the grant to the Arts Council had risen to no less than £575,000. So far as I know, very little objection has been raised when these Estimates have been presented to the House, although I suppose that earlier generations would have considered a sum of that magnitude to be rather excessive. It is an indication of how we have advanced in our views on these matters.

The first plans for a national theatre to be built by public subscription were laid by Harley Granville-Barker, whom some of the older Members of this House will remember for the work he did at the Court Theatre, and William Archer, in 1903. Seven years later their scheme was combined with another which was already in existence to provide a national memorial to William Shakespeare. The appeal then launched by the Shakespeare Memorial National Theatre Committee attracted many distinguished supporters and some contributions. The largest contributor was Sir Carl Meyer, who made a donation of £70,000 towards the cost of building a theatre which it was hoped to open in 1916 in celebration of the tercentenary of Shakespeare's death. But war came in 1914, and it was quite impossible to carry that project to maturity.

It was not until 1937 that a site of one third of an acre in Cromwell Gardens, opposite the Victoria and Albert Museum, was purchased. Here it was proposed to erect the National Theatre for which the Committee had been collecting subscriptions. The selection of that particular site met with a very mixed reception. Some people thought that one third of an acre was not enough for a memorial of the kind which many people contemplated. Others thought that South Kensington, being as it was some distance from the centre of London and from theatreland, was not an appropriate place in which to erect such a building. It is, I agree, a long way from Shaftesbury Avenue to Cromwell Gardens, in atmosphere at any rate. Nevertheless, there were people then, and I believe that there are still some, including our greatest living dramatist, Bernard Shaw, who believe that a site such as South Kensington would be the most fitting setting for a building of this kind.

However, the discussion whether the theatre should be in South
Kensington or elsewhere can now be considered merely academic, because those who have read the Preamble of the Bill will have seen that
events have marched a good deal since the days when that controversy
raged. It has now been decided that the theatre, as and when it is built,
shall be in a more central locality. The London County Council, as the
House are aware, has for many years contemplated developing the
South Bank of the Thames, and most of us would say, 'not before it
was time'. They contemplate setting up a cultural centre in the area
between County Hall and Waterloo Bridge, and have been negotiating
with the Joint Council of the National Theatre and the Old Vic. The
negotiations have resulted in an offer by the London County Council
to exchange a site of rather more than one acre on the South Bank of
the Thames for the one third of an acre in Cromwell Gardens which
had been purchased earlier and is still in the hands of the National
Theatre Committee. Not only will there be more room on the South
Bank of the Thames, but the London County Council have intimated that they will be willing to provide approaches and roadways to the
theatre when it is built.

When they made their offer, the London County Council not unnaturally wanted some kind of assurance that the project would mature.
It would be no use their offering a site of this magnitude in the centre
of what is to be a well-planned cultural centre, unless they knew that
the money for erecting the building could be raised within a measurable
time. The Joint Council has at its disposal at the moment about
£70,000. There is no doubt that, if a public appeal were made, that
amount would be greatly increased; but it is estimated that it will cost
about £1 million to build a memorial theatre of the kind we contemplate, worthy of the name of Shakespeare and worthy of this country.
This sum is completely outside the range of the Joint Council and not
within their power to collect in a measurable time.

As the L.C.C. and the Joint Council were anxious that the project
should go forward, it was decided that the Government should be
approached to see whether Parliament would be willing to underwrite
it and to give guarantees and assurances that money up to £1 million
would be forthcoming as soon as it was possible to erect this memorial.
As my right hon. and learned Friend the Chancellor of the Exchequer
indicated when he made the announcement to the House, the Government willingly acceded to the representations which were made. They

felt sure, as I feel sure to-day, that the House will give a willing assent to this Bill and that they would agree to the proposal which is now being made.

Clause 1, therefore, provides that the Treasury may make a contribution not exceeding £1 million towards erecting and equipping such a theatre. Clause 2 is the only other operation Clause in the Bill. When this public money is advanced, it is essential that the theatre should really be a national institution and that the Government should have some control over it. That being so, Clause 2 provides that Section 36 of the Trustee Act, 1925, notwithstanding, the number of trustees of the National Theatre may be raised to seven, and that the Treasury, acting for the nation, shall approve the appointments of trustees as and when vacancies occur.

This is a non-party, non-political and I hope non-controversial Measure. It is only a two-Clause Bill and I do not want to say much more about it. However, the House will perhaps expect me to give them all the details which we have as to the kind of building that will be erected and how it will be managed.

The Joint Council of the National Theatre and the Old Vic have already appointed architects to draw up the plans and have set up a building sub-committee. Plans provide for a building containing two theatres, one seating about 1,200 people and the other about 500. There will be, we hope, and indeed there should be, special accommodation for workshops, for stores, for a conference room, for a library, for canteens, for a public restaurant and for all the other numerous offices that should go with such a centre. It is indeed intended to provide not only a first-rate national theatre in London, but a centre, in every sense of the word, for the development of dramatic art.

It is also intended to stimulate the art of the theatre through other possible and suitable means, to organize national theatre tours throughout the country and overseas. It may well be that, during the discussion, hon. Members may ask when a national theatre is to be built in Scotland and when Wales is to have one of its own. I see no reason why this project should prevent Scotland or Wales from going forward with a similar proposal, if they so desire. In fact, I think nothing would please me better than to know that Scotland, realizing that we were serious in London, wished to follow that example.

MR. EMRYS HUGHES (South Ayrshire): May I interrupt? I understand this is the result of negotiations between the London County

Council and the Government. Do I understand that this is an invitation and that if the Edinburgh Corporation came along with a similar suggestion the Government would welcome it?

MR. GLENVIL HALL: Negotiations have not taken place between the Government and the London County Council. In the first instance, negotiations took place between the Joint Council representing the Old Vic, which for many years now has watched over the Shakespearian and the more serious drama in this country, and the Shakespeare Memorial National Theatre Committee. Those two have come together, and they have been negotiating with the London County Council, and it was on joint representations from those two bodies that the Government, in the end, were brought in. If the hon. Member for South Ayrshire (Mr. Emrys Hughes) feels that a similar movement should be considered, for Scotland, and if it reaches the stage when the Government themselves might be interested—whatever Government there might be at that time—I am sure he will find a ready ear for any reasonable request that he might make.

The Bill does not go into any detail as to what management should be set up. That will have to be worked out in the interval between the passing of the Bill through Parliament and the completion of the theatre. I imagine that the trustees will probably not desire to manage the theatre themselves. They may prefer to lease it to a new *ad hoc* body which might be set up, or even to the Old Vic, which for many years now has earned the respect and gratitude of the nation. However, that is not a matter for us to consider too deeply at the moment. It is one that will have to be gone into as the building and the project mature.

Nor has provision been made in the Bill for any assistance towards the running costs of the theatre, once it is built. There will be no land charges to begin with. The land will be rent-free. Whether rates will fall on the building has yet to be seen. It may be that the committee or the trustees will find that they may be able to establish a claim under the Scientific Societies Act, 1843, and by that means avoid even the payment of rates. But if in the future some sort of assistance does become necessary, it is our view that it would be for the Arts Council to give it.

It is obviously desirable that the prices of the seats should be reasonable. I am sure all of us hope that everyone, regardless of the state of his pocket, will be able to enjoy the plays that will be put on in this theatre. I would like to see many seats sold at sixpence.

I should perhaps utter a word of warning as to when this project may begin to mature. It is quite obvious to the Government that it will be some little time before the building can be started. We take the view that we should not be justified in diverting resources of labour and materials urgently needed for housing and other constructional work contributing to our economic recovery. It is correct that plans have been laid for a concert hall on the South Bank and also to re-build the Queen's Hall. In view of this, it may well be that some hon. Members may ask why this project cannot go forward at the same time. We take the view—and I hope that the House will agree—that, desirable as it is that the National theatre should be erected as soon as possible, there are many theatres in London at the present time, whereas there are no concert halls where we can have a full scale orchestral concert production. That is a great lack which we should remedy at the earliest possible moment.

I commend this Bill to the House as one which I hope all will approve. I trust that we shall soon see arising on the south bank of the river a memorial worthy both of William Shakespeare and of the people of this country.

MR. OLIVER LYTTELTON (Aldershot): I should begin by disclosing my interest, and by telling the House that I am a 'tainted party'. I have been a trustee of the Shakespeare Memorial National Theatre for a great many years. I think I was appointed in 1936. Since 1945 I have been chairman of the joint council of the Old Vic and the National Theatre. As the Financial Secretary mentioned the subject of Scotland, and the hon. Member for South Ayrshire (Mr. Emrys Hughes) mentioned Scotland, I may say that I am half Scots myself, and that any time the Scottish nation wish to call upon my services to conduct negotiations with the Government I shall be only too ready to step forward.

MR. ELLIS SMITH (Stoke): The right hon. Member will know that there is a place called Manchester.

MR. LYTTELTON: Yes, indeed I will refer to that later on. We are on a broad national basis at the moment. My real interest dates long before this. My father and mother were both concerned with the original project nearly 40 years ago, and I am very glad to think that my mother lived long enough to know of the introduction of this Bill. So I support the Bill wholeheartedly on its merits. I support it also out of filial piety and from the association, not a short one, which I have had with the project.

The Financial Secretary has made my task very easy, because he has given the background. I should like to fill in one or two other details which I hope will be of some interest to the House. When I was appointed a trustee, the three trustees were Lord Lytton, Sir Johnston Forbes-Robertson and myself. When Sir Johnston Forbes-Robertson died, I persuaded a friend of mine, Mr. J. P. Blake, a member of the party opposite, to fill the vacancy. Mr. Blake is a devoted supporter of the drama. Hon. Members will recall that he was subsequently Chairman of the London County Council, so that at least on this occasion the Financial Secretary will agree that I picked a winner. It was also, as the Financial Secretary has said, Sir Carl Meyer, whose grandson, by the way, is at present a trustee, who originally made the donation which gave life to the project.

By the 1930's, £150,000 had been collected. In collecting these sums, and in all these matters, Mr. Geoffrey Whitworth, the founder of the British Drama League, was most active and indefatigable. In 1937 the South Kensington site was bought and, shortly after that, a suggestion was made that we should negotiate with the London County Council in order to change this site which I believe is of some importance to the London County Council under the Bressey scheme, for a site on the south bank of the river. If my memory serves me, I think that suggestion came from Mr. Blake; at any rate, it was one which I readily accepted and followed.

One of the reasons why I am going over this ground again is that I feel that it would be most unseemly if I did not say here and now how very grateful we were for the most generous attitude which the London County Council adopted. They approved the idea which underlay our proposal. It came to our knowledge that the London County Council intended to develop the site on the south bank between Westminster Bridge and Waterloo Bridge on a grand and imaginative scale. There was to be what I was sorry to hear the Financial Secretary again describe as a cultural centre. I should not like hon. Members to be turned against the project by the somewhat repellent nature of the language in which it is described. I think the French have something over us when they describe a building as an '*École des Beaux Arts*', or a ministry as a Ministry of the Fine Arts. I believe that the Muses themselves would feel a little uncomfortable in a cultural centre. Be that as it may, the London County Council had this idea, and it seemed to us, and subsequently to them, very appropriate that a national theatre should be erected on that site and as part of the scheme to foster the fine arts. The site is a very noble one of more than an acre and a quarter, and I am sure that most hon. Members will agree that it is the finest site in the whole of London we could wish for on which to erect a theatre.

When these negotiations with the London County Council were beginning, I formed the idea that it was quite wrong that two bodies— namely, the Shakespeare Memorial National Theatre and the Old Vic —should be appealing to the public and, incidentally, to the Arts Council, for what was essentially the same object. I, therefore, put down on paper a scheme by which these two bodies should act in concert. That scheme was agreed to and accepted. The committee or council which combined these interests has, of course, as hon. Members will realize, no legal existence, but it has nevertheless the force of authority, because it numbers amongst its members most of those who are, in some way or another, responsible for the affairs both of the Old Vic and of the National Theatre. I think I must say who are the members of this body. First, on the Old Vic side—if I may use that term—there are the right hon. Gentlemen the Member for Deptford (Mr. Wilmot), my hon. Friend the Member for Oswestry (Mr. O. Poole), Miss Barbara Ward and Alderman Mrs. L'Estrange Malone. On the National Theatre side there are Lord Esher, Sir Bronson Albery, Mr. J. P. Blake, and Mr. Geoffrey Whitworth. This distinguished body is under my chairmanship.

It seemed to my colleagues and me that the betrothal of these two parties was a very happy event. The National Theatre, on the one hand, had the promise of the London County Council for this site, and the Old Vic could point to a long record of successes, to the achievement of Miss Baylis's original idea in the Old Vic, and to many recent theatrical successes. It seemed to my colleagues and myself clearly right to try to combine a body whose resources could only be used for the building of a theatre, because they were limited by their trust, with that of another body which represented a company of actors and actresses, or what might be termed the living side of the theatre. So it was that this amalgamation was made, the policy governing both bodies has been agreed, and I think I may say that very happy relations have been established. Should I be pitching it too high if I said that possibly here there was a felicitous combination of private enterprise, municipal generosity and State aid? I hope not.

After this short and no doubt rather tiresome historical survey, which I hope will serve to explain the interest I have in the project, I now turn to the actual Bill. Let me state my own view quite plainly. It may be an unusual view for me to express. I hope hon. Members will not ask me to widen my remarks beyond this occasion. My view is that on this occasion His Majesty's Government have in presenting this Bill shown great boldness and imagination. I think they are to be congratulated upon these two qualities. I have often been asked, as a sponsor of this project, what is the necessity for a national theatre? This, of course, is a question which perhaps only the Secretary of the Philistine Society, if there is such a body, could appropriately ask. I usually reply in a rather conventional way by asking what is the need, come to that, for the National Gallery, for St. Paul's Cathedral, Lycidas, or the Eroica Symphony of Beethoven. These works are not necessities in the sense that the President of the Board of Trade and others use the term when speaking about clothes, food, or houses. In fact, we only begin to enter the realms of art when we begin to leave the realms of necessity.

A national theatre aims to set the highest standard of performance of the drama—just that and no more. This country has made probably the greatest contribution in modern times to the drama, and might have some claims to have made as great a contribution, not excluding Greece, to drama as any country in history. Almost all other countries which have been the nurseries of the arts and the cradles of great composers or authors have State theatres or opera houses which are assisted in some way by government funds. The most obvious examples of this policy are the ones the Financial Secretary mentioned—the Comédie Française and La Scala in Milan—but in drama, Sweden, Denmark, Germany, Finland, and Belgium, to name the first countries that come to one's mind, have theatres assisted by the State or by the municipality.

I should like to emphasize the point that these theatres with State help, such as the Comédie Française, not only set a standard for the drama but also preserve from pollution the language in which these dramatic works are played. A national theatre in Great Britain would help to keep undefiled the purity of the English language, the accents in which it is uttered, the grammar and the syntax in which it is cast, by setting a standard springing from the glorious English of Shakespeare of which we are the proud but I must say somewhat negligent heirs. But it is unfortunately the fact that if the classical drama or classical opera is to be performed and declaimed or sung by the leading artists of the day, it is most unlikely that the theatre, and quite certain that the opera house, will not be self-supporting. It is, of course, possible by private subscription, by guest artists and by cheap and improvised productions to keep classical drama in front of the public, but it is not possible without some kind of help to play the classical drama at cheap and popular prices—to which I must, in parenthesis, say I attach as much importance as the Financial Secretary—with a good standard of production. This is the fundamental reason why Great Britain should have a national theatre.

Some objections—if that is the right word; I do not think it is—have been raised to State money being devoted and destined for a national theatre in London, but I am sure the hon. Member for Stoke (Mr. Ellis Smith), when he hears what I have to say, will change his objections to enthusiasm, because I know he is in favour of the general project. I think I understand the reasons for this criticism. If this criticism of London as the home of the national theatre meant that London is to be the only centre worthy of support in the furtherance of the drama, I would agree with that criticism wholeheartedly, but a start has to be made somewhere, and a standard—the highest which we can achieve in our country—has to be set.

We should all agree at the outset that these objects can best be achieved by siting the national theatre in the capital city of the Commonwealth and Empire; but I do not go further than that, and I do not at all say that London should be the only recipient of State or municipal help in the theatre. As I say, I have already offered my services to the hon. Member for South Ayrshire (Mr. Emrys Hughes). It is part of the project of the national theatre to have stock companies travelling a large part of the year which will play in the great provincial cities, and therefore serve to stimulate the spread of this movement; and as time goes on we may hope to see other theatres with State or municipal support established outside London. I have not studied the Measure very carefully, but I believe the vehicle for carrying out the development of the theatre in other parts of the country is contained in the Local Government Act, 1948.

The next question I wish to ask and, in fact, to answer is: why do the Government bring forward this project at this time, when we are trying to struggle out of our economic difficulties and when we are admittedly living to a large extent upon aid from the United States?

The Financial Secretary touched on this question which is not an awkward one at all. It is perfectly simple, and the answer is that the London County Council, having seen the good sense as we think of having a national theatre on the south bank, naturally would require some earnest or guarantee that, having reserved the site, the funds are going to be available for building the theatre. That is the reason why, I take it, the Government are bringing forward the Measure now. It is at least doubtful whether any private individual or body in these days of taxation would ever have the resources to bring this very long-delayed project to life. It is for this reason that we who are connected with the movement approached His Majesty's Government.

The negotiations with the Government were conducted by Lord Esher. It would be most ungenerous of me not to acknowledge the greatness of the services to the cause of the national theatre which have been performed by Lord Esher, and I take this opportunity of doing so and paying a tribute to him in the warmest terms that I can command. It has not been Lord Esher's privilege or good fortune to live in an age when, as a Maecenas, he could have supported the drama out of his own resources, but within the limits of what is possible in our age no one has worked more devotedly than he.

I turn to the last part of my subject, and to answer the question whether it is wise on general or economic grounds for the Government to introduce the Bill now. The word 'economic' seems to dog my footsteps, and I cannot get away from it even this morning. I would draw the attention of hon. Members who are not particularly interested in the drama—I think there are very few of them; they are certainly not here—to the economic aspects of this question and, in particular, to the White Paper on Full Employment. This White Paper was the product of the Coalition Government in which there was a large Conservative majority, so that the party on this side of the House is even more committed to that White Paper than the party on the other, but it suffices for my purpose to say that it was a joint White Paper. The very essence of that White Paper is that in times of great trade activity when we have full employment, a Government should prepare schemes which will be to the profit or advantage of the community, and put them on the shelves so that if at any time the trade cycle should recede, and a trade depression, perhaps imported from abroad, should spread its chill hand once again upon our lives, then there should be in the pigeon-holes Government schemes and particularly building schemes ready to be put into force and to make their contribution to the re-instatement of the trade cycle and to employment.

I have tried to show that a national theatre is a scheme to which, as civilized human beings and civilized British citizens, we should sub-scribe. I would add that those who voted for the White Paper on Full Employment should also agree to the general idea of having such a scheme in the pigeon-holes of the Government on economic grounds. As the Financial Secretary has said, no building will begin until the Treasury presses the button, and no arguments therefore which seek to show that this is not the right time to build the national theatre have any validity. It is not the right time, clearly, and in fact I suppose the theatre cannot be begun until after 1951, because I believe that the site is going to be used for the Exhibition of that year.

I do not wish to be dogmatic, but I conclude by saying that those who are opposed to the national theatre of Great Britain for the plays of Shakespeare, Marlowe, Congreve, and Bernard Shaw are only fitted to be enrolled amongst the ranks of the Philistines, and I suggest that those who oppose the introduction of this Bill, if there are such, upon economic grounds are taking up a false position. I commend this Bill to my hon. Friends on this side of the House and to the House in general. I find myself in the unusual but agreeable role of congratulating the Government for imagination and audacity in introducing it at this moment, and I trust very much that it will be given its Second Reading without a Division.

MRS. AYRTON GOULD (Hendon, North): May I follow the right hon. Gentleman the Member for Aldershot (Mr. Lyttelton) by con-gratulating him on his extremely fine speech. It is a great moment when both sides of the House join in agreeing on an 'imaginative and bold scheme', as the right hon. Gentleman so rightly described this scheme for a national theatre.

This theatre is long overdue and I am divided between rejoicing, on the one hand, that a Labour Government should have the honour and imagination to introduce this Bill and sorrow, on the other hand, that the national theatre was not built long ago, when it should have been built, before the war and before there were all these difficulties about building which inevitably will mean a long delay. On the whole, I think my rejoicing is greater even than my disappointment that we have not previously had a national theatre in this country. As has been pointed out, it is a dreadful thing that in Britain, the home of Shakespeare and other great playwrights, there has been no national theatre when they have existed for so long in nearly all the countries of Europe.

I have been looking, as no doubt have other hon. Members, at the statistics of national theatres, and I find that practically every European country, certainly in Western Europe, has had one national theatre for a long time, and in some cases several. For instance, Sweden, with a population not much over one-tenth the size of ours, has three National Theatres, and magnificent theatres they are. They run opera, ballet, and drama in all these three theatres which are situated in Stockholm, Malmo and Gothenburg, three centres considerably far apart in mileage. When our theatre is built we shall have at least two theatres. We already have Covent Garden, for opera and ballet, which is doing extraordinarily well, and we shall have our national theatre for straight drama.

I think to-day is a red letter day in the history of British Government. It will go down to history as one of the days when a magnificent step forward was taken and a great scheme was promoted in a Bill by this Labour Government.

CAPTAIN BULLOCK (Waterloo): I want to ask the Financial Secretary to the Treasury if there is any thought of working with Stratford or whether Stratford will always remain something apart from the National Theatre scheme.

I agree that there should be a large proportion of very cheap seats, but I want to make the point that every seat should be a good seat. That does not apply to many of the Continental theatres where there are a great many cheap seats in which one cannot breathe, hear or see. I hope every seat in both theatres will be a good seat. One theatre which has not been mentioned is the Vienna Theatre, the Burgtheater, which has a very high tradition and which I think is better than any German theatre—better than the Berlin Theatre. It had a magnificent artistic production and it also had the two theatres scheme; it had a small theatre called the Academy Theatre which, unfortunately, was not under the same roof, consequently causing great difficulty in changing casts and scenery. Nevertheless, I hope the working of the Burgtheater will be studied because there are many points of value to be learned from that State theatre.

Speakers have referred to classical productions and to Bernard Shaw, whom I look upon now as a classic. Surely, however, in the National Theatre new plays should be encouraged. They are in France, where there are new plays by young authors. While talking of French productions I should like to say that I hope that the work done by M. Bourdet, the late director—unhappily, he is now dead—of the Française will be studied, because he revived the spirit of the Française and the Odéon, which had fallen to a fairly low level between the wars. They had a good old tradition, but needed a good deal of uplifting, and M. Bourdet threw himself into stimulating it. The productions now are of a very high level.

I should like to ask what is proposed to be done about a pension scheme in connection with the National Theatre? That is very important. I have had letters connected with people from the theatre who assure me that this country has not a tradition of a national theatre. I think that that suggestion has been answered already, and, indeed, it is answered by the fact that we had the Court Theatre of old days, and the Henry Irving productions, and, more recently, we have had the Old Vic and the provincial repertory theatres. I am sure we have the complete position of a national theatre.

As the Financial Secretary said, it is very necessary to keep party politics out of national theatres. We have not had experience of that before, but I have seen it in France. I have seen in European State theatres foreign Cabinet Ministers making little arrangements for their friends to walk on in small parts, or to be given bigger ones for which they were not fitted. I have seen it amongst the Nazis, when a tenor was removed from the Vienna Opera, and a fine actor was removed from the Burgtheater, to make room for a good party member who could neither act nor sing. That sort of thing must be avoided. It would be only too easy for the Prime Minister to do that sort of thing. I am not saying that the Prime Minister of the moment would do such a thing. However, one can imagine the kind of resignation letters that could be written, such as 'My dear So-and-so. You have done magnificently at the, say, Ministry of Food, but I have always looked upon you as a Hamlet, and your Parliamentary Secretary has to my mind been the perfect Lady Macbeth, for I have always seen her saying,

Infirm of purpose!
Give me the daggers.'

Indeed, I fear me that every Government Front Bench has many potential Poloniuses on it. So I would urge that that point be kept in mind all the time—that party politics must not enter the question of the national theatre.

MR. JOHN WILMOT (Deptford): I am sure that we would all like to help the hon. and gallant Member for Waterloo (Captain Bullock) in casting the more histrionic Members of this House for their general parts. We had a part in mind already for the right hon. Gentleman the Member for Aldershot (Mr. Lyttelton). However, perhaps it would be wiser to leave the matter for now; I, too, congratulate the Government, as all have so far done, upon their wisdom and foresight in introducing this Bill. I would also thank the Financial Secretary for the charming way he presented it to the House. I, too, have to declare my interest. I have, in one way or another, been concerned with the Old Vic for most of my life, first for many years as a patron and later as a Governor. I owe most of my love of the drama very largely to that grand old place.

I have heard a great many people say that they are a litttle worried by this project lest the ambitions and purposes of the Old Vic should be lost. They wonder whether this is really what the great founder, Lilian Baylis, had in mind as the ultimate purpose of the theatre. On that, I am happy to say we need have no doubt at all. Miss Baylis left a number of letters, to which I have recently referred, in which she expressed in the most unmistakable terms her desire that the ultimate purpose of the Old Vic should be realized by its being brought into a national theatre. She did, in fact, write to Lord Lytton, who as hon. Members know was chairman of the Memorial Theatre Committee, expressing this hope in these words:

'I always cherish the hope that eventually we might work together as one.'

She said she felt that the Old Vic, in its work, had done something to produce not only the actors and the companies which might make the beginnings of the national theatre company, but also the audiences, and those who came after them would heed, and love and use the national theatre. There can be no doubt about that, and it is very fortunate that this noble site is within a stone's throw of the old theatre in the Waterloo Road, which Hitler destroyed.

I am certain that everybody concerned with this project knows the vital importance of providing performances at prices which working people can afford to pay. That was an essential part of the Old Vic policy, and no one need have any doubt that it will be a cardinal principle of the national theatre when it is opened. As the hon. and gallant Member for Waterloo said in his most interesting and practical speech, it is extremely important, too, that the seats should be good seats. It is unfortunately true that in many of the older theatres, especially Drury Lane, many of the cheaper seats are very bad seats. I am sure that the distinguished and technically experienced architects engaged on this project will keep that point very much in mind, as will everybody concerned.

I have had a number of letters from people holding this view, which I share—the necessity of remembering that London is not England, nor Scotland or Wales. Some are critical of this expenditure in London alone. As the right hon. Member for Aldershot said in his most excellent speech, if we looked at this merely as a London project it would not stand. But of course it is not just for London. London is the capital city, and for that reason is bound to be the centre and headquarters of national movements and institutions. In the theatre it is particularly necessary to have the centre in the capital. Nothing could be more constructive in building up what I think is such an essential part of our national life, a chain of municipal and civic and public theatres in every city in the country, than to establish this centre in London from which these activities must radiate. Nor is it a one-way influence. Hon. Members may remember the very successful season at the St. James's Theatre last year, when repertory companies from Birmingham, Bristol, Sheffield, Liverpool, and Manchester presented, week after week, plays which they had performed in their own home theatres. And what a brilliant season it was; one of the best pieces of theatrical fare which has been presented to London for a very long time.

I believe it to be just as important for repertory companies of provincial cities to come and play in London as for the London companies to go and play in the provinces. The Old Vic has had some experience of that, in exchanging visits with the company which is running, with the help of the Arts Council, in that remarkably beautiful old theatre, the Theatre Royal in Bristol—probably the only eighteenth century theatre still working in this country, complete with the original stage gear and mechanism; one of the most charming relics of the eighteenth century which we possess. The theatre there is running every night, with its own Bristol Old Vic Company. That company comes to London and the London companies go to Bristol, which gives a sense of purpose and vitality in a theatrical enterprise which cannot be obtained in any other way.

I am sure it could be said that in every city and town of Britain the National Theatre Movement and the People's Civic Theatre Movement take a long step forward with the passage of this Bill; for the first time there is to be established in an Act of Parliament what ought to have been done so many years ago. For the first time the State takes its part in the cultivation of the drama as an art, just as it has for long done in painting and sculpture.

There is not very much more to say now upon this most interesting subject, save to congratulate the Government on their wisdom in including in the Local Government Act, 1948, the remarkably far-sighted Section 132, which gives to municipalities power to set up theatres, to run theatrical companies, concerts, exhibitions, and the like, and to levy an appropriate rate for the purpose. This really is a charter of the drama in the cities and towns, and the national theatre will assist in this work, and help to lift and maintain the standard. It is tremendously important that the standard should be high. These powers, if wrongly used, could do harm, just as, rightly used, they can do great good. The preparations for the use of the powers given in this far-sighted Section should begin now to take shape in people's minds and efforts, just as the plans for the national theatre will begin to be put into effect as soon as the Royal Assent has been given to this Bill.

This civic theatre movement is gathering strength and purpose, and I am glad to see that the British Drama League, which has done so much for understanding and promotion of the drama in Britain, has issued a most interesting little booklet about the powers of the Bill and how best to make use of them. I am sure that hon. Members would find that of great interest, and they should bring it to the notice of municipalities in their areas. It has been produced by a committee, on which served the indefatigable Mr. Geoffrey Whitworth, whose work for the drama is above praise.

MR. E. P. SMITH (Ashford): I should like to add my congratulations to what has been said by my right hon. Friend the Member for Aldershot (Mr. Lyttelton) as to the boldness and imagination displayed by the Government in this Bill. I should also like to congratulate the Financial Secretary on the way in which he has presented the Measure to the House. To-day it has been a case of 'roses, roses all the way' with him, and I should like to shake a few of my petals upon his reverend hairs.

When this Bill was published I regarded it with great interest—an interest which I am bound to declare—with considerable approbation, and with one or two apprehensions which have, I think, in the main been removed by the right hon. Gentleman. I regarded it with interest because, just as an admiral cannot have too many ships, so a dramatist cannot have too many theatres. How they are to be provided is not, of course, a matter of professional concern to him. I consider this Bill to be a tardy measure of justice, and I hope atonement, for the monstrous Entertainments Duty which has been levied for so many years on this living theatre. I know that this is not a subject which forms part of the Bill so I will not say any more about it because I wish to keep most carefully within the bounds of Order.

But I think I am entitled to say that in certain quarters there may be, and no doubt will be, some criticism of Parliament spending £1 million of the nation's money on a theatre project. I have not yet delved into the precise figures but I should not be surprised, and indeed I think it would be a conservative estimate, if the living theatre had not provided successive Chancellors of the Exchequer, during its long existence, with something in the neighbourhood of £30 million of revenue. The present Chancellor of the Exchequer is an austere man, more austere, for instance, than King Claudius of Denmark, but at one point he can be touched. He has a chink in his armour. Clearly

'the play's the thing wherein to catch the conscience of'—

the Chancellor. This project will cost £1 million; and, unless my arithmetic is at fault, £1 million in relation to £30 million means giving back to the theatre $3\frac{1}{3}$ per cent, which is not over-generous. When one is dealing with what has been called in this House a shabby moneylender, to get a rebate of $3\frac{1}{3}$ per cent is something—in fact, it is quite a lot. Few victims of any Chancellor of the Exchequer achieve so much.

Rather than have two theatres it might be a good thing to have three, perhaps each one bigger than the 500 capacity and slightly smaller than the 1,200. The first would be specially designed for the presentation of classical drama, not merely the ancient classics but down to Elizabethan times and even later. The second would be designed for the presentation of modern drama, and the third for the presentation of intimate opera; we have no theatre at all in London specially designed for the presentation of what I have described as intimate opera, in which we could have also ballet and the showing of special films. I beg the Government, if they can, not to be grandiose in the matter of architecture; and not to be led astray by the enthusiasm of architects, who are always prone to exaggerate the importance of their own art.

After all, aren't we all? I beg them to consider the quantity and the quality of the productions, rather than any exaggerated grandeur of the producing medium. I believe, too, that by adopting suggestions such as these we shall make the national theatre far more prosperous because, on balance, many more people will choose to go to it; and, what is of infinitely greater importance, more theatrical workers— players, producers, authors and stage staff—will find lasting and remunerative employment.

I shall not sit in this House very much longer because I shall leave its purlieus when the present Government is defeated, which will be at the next General Election. There are three of my craft in this House. We have been a pretty quarrelsome trio, but we are united, as I believe the whole House is united, in one thing and that is our genuine love for the theatre. The hon. Member for Eton and Slough (Mr. Levy) has, like myself, decided to retire. The junior burgess for Oxford University (Sir A. Herbert) has been deprived of his seat by the votes of hon. Gentlemen opposite. I am afraid that we shall not very much longer amuse the House on Budget day by tumbling into the ring and hurling custard pies at one another. Some hon. Members may think that is a loss. Others, no doubt wiser, will regard it as a gain. But, if these were the last words I should say in this Chamber, I would dedicate them as a valedictory message to my friends and my opponents to do all they possibly can, when this national theatre comes to be built, to ensure that the advantages of this Bill are given the fullest and most practical effect.

Mr. Ellis Smith (Stoke): I am in favour of national theatres, but there is no provision made in the Bill for national theatres. I approach this question in the same way as I think Lord Morley would have done. I forget his exact words on this subject but they were something like this: 'If you do a thing in a relatively small way it often prevents you from doing it later in a big way.' The taxpayers of this country are already financing activities in London, costing approximately £22½ million and which they never see. For the people in the North it has been for generations 'Work, work, work.' Now it is 'Work harder and faster than ever.' The Bill provides another £1 million. The Financial Secretary will be the first to admit that, with the increased cost of all the equipment, we shall never construct a national theatre for £1 million. In addition, the public works for the Festival of Britain will cost another £2 million; near that site a concert hall costing £1½ million is to be built, and there will also be a Festival of Britain building costing £750,000; that is another £5 million.

Where will this stop? Where does the North come in? When will the North come in? The Bill ought to have taken account of the area north of the Trent and something ought to have been provided within a few miles of Manchester, Buxton, and such places. The Austrians develop art and music throughout their country, and the same thing happens in Russia, Czechoslovakia, Poland, and even in Germany, with Hamburg, Dresden and Leipzig; but in Britain everything is still confined to London. For the North remain the black monumental areas of a hundred years ago. The Bill perpetuates that position.

Am I correct in understanding that negotiations have been opened or are to be opened with a view to the Ministry of Works taking over the lease of Covent Garden? Thousands of pounds are being given to Covent Garden and other activities in London, and that is looked upon by people in other parts of the country as a subsidy to those activities when in the main the people who attend them could easily pay much more for their seats, which others never have a chance to occupy. The Covent Garden audiences are exclusive. One has only to stand and watch the people entering and leaving to come to that conclusion.

When will this kind of activity be extended to other parts of the country? We hear a good deal about Scotland and Wales, but there are parts of England besides London. Thousands of people who have seen that greatest of films, *Hamlet*, now have a greater appreciation of the world's greatest poet, Shakespeare. Are we to cater for that greater appreciation only in London? Where is our vision and our pride in our country and our people if we allow this kind of activity to be limited in the main to the London area?

Therefore I am saying it is time that more attention was devoted not only to building a national theatre in London but to providing similar places in the great centres like Newcastle, Manchester, Sheffield, and other such places. If these centres could be used for war purposes such as the place where the Bank of England was taken, then they can be used as national artistic centres, and used also during the Festival of Britain.

Thanks to the B.B.C., thanks to recording, thanks to the development of the Hallé Orchestra and others, we are getting an increased interest in this work, and it is in order to harness and encourage that interest that I am pleading in this way. On behalf of the toiling millions of the North who have made this country great, and who are still making their contribution, I say that the time has arrived when, if we are to be worthy of them, we should be catering for them in the same way as other countries on the Continent have catered for them for so long.

MR. OLIVER POOLE (Oswestry): Two of my distinguished colleagues, the right hon. Member for Aldershot (Mr. Lyttelton) and the right hon. Member for Deptford (Mr. Wilmot) have already spoken in this Debate and I who, as the House has already been told, have the honour to be a Governor of the Old Vic and a member of the Joint Council of the National Theatre and the Old Vic, propose only to say two or three paragraphs, and not to repeat anything they have said.

My right hon. Friend the Member for Aldershot (Mr. Lyttelton) referred to the economic side of the project. Hon. Members probably are aware that on the few occasions on which I speak I do so generally more on finance than on art. Not only is the Bill a great milestone in the dramatic life of this country; this is the first time that a project has been laid before the House which is in exact accordance with the modern ideas of how budgetary influence and public works can prevent the impact of the slump and the boom upon the country. This is an aspect which we should not overlook.

It is not for me to try to put forward the views of either the governors of the Old Vic or the National Theatre, for that was done by my right hon. Friend the Member for Aldershot. But I would say to the hon. Member for Stoke and to those who think as he does that we appreciate very much indeed the points he has made and that it is our desire to try to overcome the difficulties which he can see. We urge him, however, not to say that because this job is not being sufficiently done we should not do it at all. It is far better to do one thing first, particularly in the field of art, rather than to wait until we can tackle the whole field, when it may be found that we cannot start at all.

MR. SKEFFINGTON (Lewisham, West): As one born and bred in our great city and educated in its university, and who represents a constituency on the south side of the river, I am naturally delighted to support the Second Reading of the Bill. I welcome it also as one who is very fond of the theatre and all that it means to us.

Although I occasionally go to the Old Vic in its temporary and perhaps nicer quarters of the town, it never has quite the attraction which it had for me when all the great works of Shakespeare were mine for sixpence, or ninepence if I went in at the early door. The atmosphere of the theatre seems different and now-a-days I never get quite the same stimulus. I am very glad also that in the Bill not only are steps being taken to provide for the first time a theatre really worthy of our great literary heritage, but that it is to be placed on the south side of the river.

The hon. Member for Stoke, with other hon. Members, has sometimes exaggerated the difficulties of travel for people coming to London to a national centre. The hon. Gentleman must know perfectly well, however, that if Stoke City were playing the Arsenal there would be no difficulties then about transport. We should see thousands of his friends—and should be very glad for them to be here—and they would be paying, probably, higher prices for admission to the football match than we hope they will have to pay when they come to the National Theatre. We should not exaggerate the difficulties, although I hope the hon. Member will not encourage anyone to think that we believe that London is the only place for the theatre, and the only people who want to appreciate it are in London. That is not our view at all.

I believe, as others have said, that the Bill marks a very decided change of attitude towards the theatre. As a Londoner, I am glad to welcome the Bill, for it marks a further development of the South Bank, which is once more going to come into its own. I am sure that all those interested in the theatre will give this Bill their wholehearted support.

MR. BUTCHER (Holland with Boston): The right hon. Gentleman the Financial Secretary to the Treasury seems to enjoy two experiences in this House—either the House is entirely with him all the way, and he has nothing but roses all the way, which is, perhaps, proper compensation for his other experience on Budget occasions, or he seems to have no friends at all. I would only ask him to remember on the occasion of the next Budget that on this occasion he is disposing quite easily and happily of £1 million, with a promise of more assistance to come should this national theatre when established not be self-supporting, and not to be too hard-hearted when we ask him for a remission of tax amounting, perhaps, to something like £20,000 or £30,000 during a full financial year.

While wishing to support this Bill very warmly, I think it is well worth while not to do it from any controversial point of view, but simply to raise one or two points which I believe will make the national theatre a great success. The hon. Member for West Lewisham (Mr.

Skeffington) pointed out that, for the first time for four hundred years, Londoners will be crossing the river to visit the theatre. It is nice to think that we are reverting to the customs of our ancestors, but let us examine the fact that, at the moment, the theatreland of London is a very clearly defined area, and that we are asking people to adopt new habits and to cross the river to visit the theatre.

At the moment, theatreland could be defined as being in that small area bounded to the East by Kingsway, to the South by the river, to the North by Oxford Circus, and to the West perhaps somewhere near Park Lane. In that area, almost all the cultural and theatrical enterprises and spectacles take place at the present time, and, as in all cities, there is a West End area devoted to amusement after dark. We are making a great experiment in asking the theatre-going population to cross the river in order to visit this magnificent site on the south bank.

Those who have been trained in the valuation of property know that for particular trades there are certain areas more favourable than others; one side of the road is more favourable than the other. Therefore, to suggest that the public who wish to purchase a certain article will not cross the road may sound ridiculous, but, nevertheless, it is a commercial fact that people are not prepared to do that. Similarly, a shop which is placed between two banks which are without illuminated shop fronts is of less value than one in a brightly lighted area. That being so, when we examine this theatre project on the south side of the river, we must, first of all, make sure of three things.

First, we must be certain that it is easy of access, that there is adequate accommodation for the parking of cars, for the discharge of the occupants of taxis and for the waiting of taxis for the purpose of picking up passengers, and that the theatre is on a proper bus route. Secondly, there must be adequate accommodation for meals at all prices, so as to cater for those who just want a quick snack on their way home as well as for those who wish to sit and entertain their friends after the theatrical performance. This is very necessary, because I doubt whether the time when we shall feed before we go to the theatre will come again for a very long time.

The hon. Member for Stoke (Mr. Ellis Smith) mentioned the provinces and his desire for entertainment working parties. Working parties have suddenly become fashionable in this country, but they are not the lines upon which the life of this country has developed, particularly in cultural and architectural matters. The hon. Lady the Member for North Hendon (Mrs. Ayrton Gould) said she wished that the plan had been wider in order to spread culture throughout the countryside, particularly with regard to the theatre. I agreed with her, but, nevertheless, the fact must be faced that here we do not start off with large plans and implement them on a methodical basis. We start with one obtainable objective and go on to the next. I agree with that. Therefore, this Bill must be welcomed not to the exclusion of the provinces or of anything else, but as the right, proper, and reasonable thing to do at the moment.

There is one other thing with which I wish to deal—the question of the balancing of the running charges of the theatre to which the Financial Secretary referred. He said that there would be quite a number of seats priced at 6d. That sounds admirable. The hon. and gallant Member for Waterloo (Captain Bullock) suggested that this theatre should make some contribution to the development of the tourist trade, which is equally admirable. But I cannot see that there is going to be an enormous gain in dollars if we are selling our seats at a nickel a time. Surely, the right and proper thing to do is not to require that every production should endeavour to make a profit. That, I believe, is impossible. While, perhaps, it would be impossible for the theatre to make a profit every year, I believe it should be run on the basis of the nationalized industries, and that, taking one year with another, it should not show a loss.

The price of the seats should be arranged in that way. I believe that in this National Theatre there could be a wide divergence of prices going perhaps as low as the Financial Secretary has said, though I am bound to say that to bring down the price of seeing a performance at the living theatre to the equivalent of three cigarettes seems to be bringing it lower than really need be done at the present time. On the other hand, I advocate high prices, where the best that English literature and English acting can give is expected, to our visitors from overseas, with great gain to us in every respect.

The theatre does not only consist of the building. On the whole, that is the least important matter. We have the play in this country, we believe that the plays of dramatists past and present can add to the cultural life of the community; we believe that in this country we have players second to none. Finally, we believe that given scope and opportunity the audiences will be worthy both of the play and the players.

THE GREAT DEBATE

Mr. BENN LEVY (Eton and Slough): This Debate has, as a Debate, had to labour under the burden of perhaps an excessive unanimity. I cannot find it in my heart to regret this because it is a Bill which I consider to be entirely admirable. Nor am I surprised at the unanimity after the excellent speech with which the right hon. Gentlemen the Member for Aldershot (Mr. Lyttelton) led the Opposition. But it was a little refreshing that one breath of criticism did come from my hon. Friend the Member for Stoke (Mr. Ellis Smith) and I should like to refer to it in a few minutes.

Mr. ELLIS SMITH: Constructive criticism.

Mr. LEVY: Constructive criticism. Although there has been very little criticism in this House to-day, there has, however, from time to time during the past years been considerable criticism in the country about the whole project, and it is fair that this occasion should be taken for us to try to meet that criticism here. On the whole criticism has fallen under three counts. There are those who say or have said, Why is there any need for a national theatre at all? There are those who have said, If there is to be a national theatre, why should it be exclusively centred upon London? Then there are those who say, If there is to be a national theatre, and it is to be in London, why should it be on the South Bank? I should like to say a word on each of those points.

The right hon. Member for Aldershot advanced the most unanswerable argument which, as he admitted, is also the most familiar one, when he pointed to the analogy of the National Gallery and the British Museum. I would supplement that by suggesting that the field of drama is certainly no less, possibly it could be argued an even more desirable field for that kind of institution because there is one way in which it is fair and valuable to regard a national theatre, that is as a kind of living library. It is perfectly true that plays are printed and are stored in the Library of the British Museum and elsewhere, but a play is incomplete until it is on the stage. There is no way of maintaining it, in the same way as books are maintained in a library, unless we have a national theatre. The difference between a bookshop and a public library is that a bookshop naturally concentrates for its own good on best-sellers whereas the public library concentrates on service and on providing for and thus protecting the rights of that minority whose taste may not be for the best-seller.

One would have thought that, if 50,000 people wanted to see a certain play, that was in itself a very good reason why they should be allowed to see it. But at present that is not nearly enough people to command a production. In the commercial theatre unless 300,000 or 400,000 people want to see a play it cannot be done—50,000 people are not sufficient to support it. The minority is therefore prevented by the economics of the situation from seeing the kind of play they want to see when they want to see it. But not only is it necessary for 300,000 or 400,000 people to want to see a given play; it is necessary that they should want to see it at the same time. It is no use for them to straggle in sparsely over a year or eighteen months because by that time the unfortunate manager would be in Carey Street.

These are the additional difficulties which do not apply to the publication of a book. If 5,000 people want to read a book the publisher does reasonably well. He is content and the minority is well served. The economics of the matter do not inhibit that minority from enjoying what it wants to enjoy. But when it comes to a question of 300,000 or 400,000 then it becomes extremely difficult. The extreme situation is the case of a film, for if only 300,000 or 400,000 want to see a film that number is not nearly enough. I do not want to digress into that field but that in effect is the reason why films must be best-sellers or nothing. I hope that the House and people outside will accept this as a major argument in favour of a national theatre, that it is, in short, a kind of device for keeping good plays, as it were, in print, nothing more or less, and in living print.

I know that it can be argued that there have been numerous and distinguished productions of Shakespeare and other classics from time to time without a national theatre; and it is true that we have been extremely lucky of late years in that respect. Most distinguished classical revivals have been current and abundant, but we have been lucky rather by accident. We have been lucky through the extent of the success of the Old Vic; but the Old Vic has not been a money-making concern. It is, in fact, an embryonic national theatre. In spite of the glamour of a large star company—working at far below their normal salaries—I believe that only one season made money. The others have had to be subsidized.

If one goes further back to the period when Irving produced a great number of classical productions at the Lyceum, and Tree did the same thing at His Majesty's, one will find that they too did not make money. In spite of the fact, in the case of Irving, that there were all the prestige and attraction of his own name and that of Ellen Terry, few if any of

the productions of Shakespeare at the Lyceum made money, despite
the fact that Irving also made cuts and alterations and generally cor-
seted the play into the current Victorian fashion to such a degree that
we should be shocked if we now saw his scripts. Even these essays in
appeasement were not sufficient and he had to make his money on
tour—which is a point I willingly give to my hon. Friend the Member
for Stoke—and by putting on other productions like *The Bells*, and
The Corsican Brothers, etc.

Quite clearly this is not a job which the commercial managements
can do. I say this in no disparagement of commercial management. I
wish to say publicly that, although many bricks are cast at the commercial theatre, one curious thing is true. The majority of these connected with the business side of the theatre love the theatre very deeply.
Many of them deliberately lose money on ventures which satisfy their
own artistic aspirations. Irving was one and I could quote many more.
But it is just not possible for us to rely on the good-will and sacrifice
of commercial managements and on leading players accepting salaries
far less than they could otherwise get. That is one reason why it is
abundantly clear that it is right to put this thing on the proper basis
of a national theatre.

The second criticism, which has been voiced by my hon. Friend the
Member for Stoke, raises the question of London or the provinces.
It is, of course, perfectly true that it would be very unfair if this
National Theatre were confined to London, even though London is
the capital. But, as has already been pointed out by the hon. Member
for West Lewisham (Mr. Skeffington), the plan of this National
Theatre is that London should provide the building which is, as it were,
the workshop and centre. It has never been envisaged that it shall not
be a centre from which extensive tours shall operate.

I hope, therefore, that I did not understand my hon. Friend to be
maintaining, as was recently maintained I regret to say by my friend
Mr. Ivor Brown, a distinguished critic and a man of letters, that this
project should wait until—I would emphasize until—other projects of
a similar kind have been established elsewhere. I am glad to see that
my hon. Friend shakes his head because this is surely wholly unreason-
able. He said just now that what he had in mind was constructive
criticism. I would like to reinforce that constructive criticism, now
that I gather we are not so far apart.

The hon. and gallant Member for the Waterloo Division of Liverpool (Captain Bullock) painted in his very witty speech an attractive picture of the time, now it seems not far distant, when Members of Front Benches would look forward, if they were ambitious enough, not to directorships of a joint stock bank but to the opportunity of playing Polonius in the National Theatre. That is a very attractive thought, but it has a certain symbolical significance. It may have been a light-hearted analogy by the hon. and gallant Gentleman, but it implied an enhanced dignity for the theatre. It is not wholly a joke because the importance of this National Theatre is largely a symbolical importance. It does indeed raise the status of the theatre to a dignity which all of us would welcome.

LIEUT.-COLONEL LIPTON (Brixton): My right hon. Friend the Financial Secretary will, no doubt, regard this day as one of the most pleasing and agreeable that he has enjoyed in this present Parliament because, as has been made quite clear, there is an astonishing unanimity of opinion concerning this Bill.

I rise to take part in this Debate from a rather more local angle than preceding speakers, because I have the honour to represent a Parliamentary division of the Borough of Lambeth within whose confines the National Theatre will be built and will, we hope, prosper. Whenever any Government Department, such as the Ministry of Town and Country Planning or any of the Service Departments, proposes to embark upon some activity in one part of the country or another, there is usually to be found a greater or lesser volume of vociferous local opposition to whatever plan the Government have in mind. On this occasion, if I may presume to speak on behalf of the citizens of Lambeth or in the name of the metropolitan Borough of Lambeth, I think I can assure my right hon. Friend that the idea of having the National Theatre in Lambeth will be cordially welcomed and will not be resisted or criticized by any section of the local population. After all, the Borough of Lambeth has a tradition in this respect because, as has been rightly pointed out by preceding speakers, the trail for the National Theatre has been blazed by the Old Vic, more correctly described as the Royal Victoria Hall, to give its official title.

I should like in passing to controvert the statement made by my hon. Friend the Member for West Lewisham (Mr. Skeffington), who suggested that with the initiation of the proposed National Theatre, the people of fashionable London would for the first time in four hundred years be crossing from the North to the South Bank for the purpose of enjoying theatrical entertainment. That is not correct. Very shortly after the Old Vic was established, it enjoyed a brief session of fashionable splendour when it was visited by Queen Victoria in the years just preceding her accession to the Throne, and, when accompanied by linkmen, she made her way through what is now known as the Lower Marsh to what was originally known as the Royal Coburg and afterwards called the Royal Victoria Hall.

It is therefore not quite correct to say that for the first time in four hundred years fashionable London will be going to the South Bank for the purposes of theatrical entertainment. I am quite prepared to admit that, after the brief period of social splendour to which I have referred, the Old Vic declined. As a matter of fact, it was criticized by Charles Dickens and Charles Kingsley as a sink of iniquity and a haunt of drunken hooligans. I am quite sure that that is a prospect which we need not anticipate as far as the new National Theatre is concerned.

This period of decline did not last very long because Emma Cons and Lilian Bayliss, whose names have been rightly mentioned in connection with the Old Vic, effected considerable reforms and improvements. In respect of the prices to be charged for admission to the new National Theatre, my right hon. Friend cannot possibly do better than confine the prices to what Emma Cons herself described as 'within the range of artisans and labourers'. If my right hon. Friend keeps prices of admission to the National Theatre within that range, he will ensure that the public as a whole will be able to enjoy the actual advantages of the National Theatre.

MR. EMRYS HUGHES (South Ayrshire): I can understand the enthusiasm of the hon. and gallant Member for Brixton (Lieut.-Colonel Lipton) for this Bill. As he was talking about north and south of the river I began to wonder whether people in the metropolis think there is only one river in this country. I am inclined to be more interested not in what is likely to happen on the South Bank of the River Thames but what is likely to happen on the north bank of the Tweed.

I have listened with very great thankfulness and gratitude to the Financial Secretary to the Treasury telling us that Scotland might follow the precedent set in this Bill. I have noted very carefully both the promise on behalf of the Treasury and the promise of cordial support from the right hon. Member for Aldershot (Mr. Lyttelton) when we come along, as quickly as possible, with a similar Bill to establish a national theatre in Scotland. After all, Shakespeare was indebted to Scotland——

SIR HENRY MORRIS-JONES (Denbigh): And to Wales.

MR. HUGHES: —and to Wales. The hon. Member for Denbigh (Sir H. Morris-Jones) will be able to quote his references to Wales, but I think there is no doubt at all that *Macbeth* would never have been written if Scotland had not given its co-operation to Mr. William Shakespeare. In Scotland the dramatic art and the art of the theatre is very much alive. I shall not go through the list of the great Scottish dramatists but may merely mention two of our own times, Barrie and Bridie. Throughout Scotland, even in the remotest villages of the Highlands and Islands, there is live dramatic art. Let us hope that this Bill will be the beginning of increasing its vitality. We have had some unfortunate experiences recently in attempting to establish a National Theatre. On one occasion we were offered a gift of £5,000 for a Burns Theatre from Mr. Butlin. Naturally, £5,000 does not go very far towards the cost of a National Theatre, and we were horrified at some of the plays that were produced in the theatre of Mr. Butlin—at such things as Robert Burns being made to get up off his death bed to sing *Bonnie Mary of Argyll*.

This Bill has come about, I understand, because the Shakespeare Memorial Committee combined with the London County Council in going to the Treasury about the National Theatre, so that the Treasury said, 'Very well, you shall have £1,000,000.' No doubt, in due course we from Scotland are likely to come along to ask for our National Theatre—a Burns federation in alliance with Glasgow Corporation and the Edinburgh Corporation or even the Ayr Town Council or the Ayrshire County Council to say, 'Look what support we in Scotland gave to you in England.' I hope that when I ask the Leader of the House on a Thursday when an opportunity will be given for debating the Scottish Bill the right hon. Member for Aldershot will say, 'England has had her share and Scotland ought to have her share, also.'

So I give my benediction to the Bill as one from what is sometimes regarded in this House as a hostile power. After the promises given in this House to-day I hope that when Scotland comes along—as I am sure she speedily will—to ask for some financial help—I dare not say for £1,000,000—with some modest demand, she will be considered sympathetically, and I hope that the House will then be in a similarly generous mood and say, 'Certainly, go ahead as we have done in England.'

MR. GLENVIL HALL: We get three types of legislation before this

House. The first is extremely controversial and feeling frequently runs high. The second type is that in which few people are interested so that the business almost goes through on the nod. The third type concerns some vitally important phase of our national life on which there is almost a unanimous view in favour of what is proposed. The present Bill falls into the thrid category. I have thoroughly enjoyed the Debate, which has been upon an extremely high level. There has been almost unanimous approval for the Bill.

The only real criticism came from my hon. Friend the Member for Stoke (Mr. Ellis Smith). If I understood aright what he said, his view is not so much against the proposal for a National Theatre as against its beginning in London. He thinks that we ought to begin in the provinces where the need is very much greater. My hon. Friend would probably like the first National Theatre to be built in Stoke. Quite a number of Members have replied to his criticisms. For example, my hon. Friend the Member for West Lewisham (Mr. Skeffington) and some hon. Members on the opposite side of the House have pointed out that it is natural for the main National Theatre to be built in the capital of the Commonwealth and Empire. But, as I said in my opening speech, the National Theatre will arrange tours throughout the provinces and overseas. It will be as much a national theatrical centre as a National Theatre for the capital of the Commonwealth. Quite a number of hon. Members have reminded us that there is an Act of 1948 under which municipalities can start to build municipal theatres and civic centres, so that they can receive the repertory companies and other players who will undoubtedly begin to tour from this national centre.

We all thoroughly enjoyed the speech of the right hon. Member for Aldershot (Mr. Lyttelton). It was graceful, forceful and knowledgeable and it was delivered by a man who obviously feels very strongly about the drama and the desirability of everything possible being done to fortify and assist it. He himself has done and is still doing a great deal for British drama as chairman of the Joint Council of the National Theatre and the Old Vic. Lord Esher is another great enthusiast. I should like to share in the expression of thanks to which the right hon. Gentleman and my right hon. Friend the Member for Deptford (Mr. Wilmot) gave voice and in the tributes they paid to Lord Esher. It was Lord Esher who came to the Treasury and helped considerably in the negotiations which have resulted in this Bill.

May I come to the points made by the hon. and gallant Member for

Waterloo, who made an extremely witty speech? He asked us to remember that this was not a Shakespeare Memorial Theatre, but a National Theatre and he expressed the hope that we would not think of it as a memorial to Shakespeare, if for no other reason than that there is already a memorial to the great bard at Stratford-on-Avon. I share his view. We wish to remember Shakespeare—not that we shall ever forget him—but it would be unfair to Stratford-on-Avon if the proposed theatre were looked upon solely as a memorial to Shakespeare. I hope that it will rather be one of the first of a chain of living theatres throughout the country and, in particular, around Manchester, Stoke, and the Five Towns.

The hon. and gallant Member also asked that we should make it plain that present as well as past plays would be performed. If he will look at my speech again, he will see that I emphasized that contemporary plays would be produced. Undoubtedly new playwrights arise, and we want to encourage them. Shakespeare was a young playwright once, and so was George Bernard Shaw.

I think I have covered most of the points made. There is one that has occurred over and over again and has been answered repeatedly; that is the question which it is suggested will be asked by a large number of people, why should London enjoy the expenditure of anything up to a million of the taxpayers' money when other things are much more needed and the provinces will have to go without. I do not think that argument is legitimate or holds water. I pay my wireless licence and I do not object to the fact that quite often I turn the knob and hear someone crooning. If there is anything in this world I dislike it is jazz and crooning, but I know that some people like it. I cannot understand why, but it takes all sorts to make a world. Therefore, without complaint, I pay my licence and choose my programmes. People will have to learn to do the same here. Some want Shakespeare and some want music hall. At the moment music hall is said to pay commercially, while Shakespeare, to our disgrace, does not. Here we are helping the drama in a small way. I hope it will eventually be in a big way.

On behalf of the Government, I should like to say that we are grateful for the way in which the House has received this Bill. We believe, with the hon. Members who have taken part in the Debate to-day, that this should be the beginning of something which will be of great benefit to the people of this country and to those who invest their lives in this side of its activities.

Question put, and agreed to.

Bill read a Second time, and committed to a Committee of the Whole House Monday next.'

HOUSE OF LORDS

Thursday, 17*th February* 1949

NATIONAL THEATRE BILL

THE LORD CHANCELLOR: My Lords, I rise to move the Second Reading of this Bill. I confess that the speech I have to make is more agreeable to me than the one which I had to make yesterday. Then we were treading on ground which was only a thin crust over burning fires of political controversy underneath. To-day I hope we shall not have to indulge in any controversial matter. As we always disclose interest, I ought perhaps to disclose that I am the President of the Travel Association. That is not a body which has any ulterior motive for making money, but it does try to attract foreign visitors to this country, and I think it is having a not inconsiderable measure of success. In my view, it is vitally important to push on with this all we can, and to achieve a still larger measure of success. I hope and believe that if and when this theatre is built it will be an added inducement to visitors to come to this country.

On the other hand, quite frankly, I do not support the Bill on any materialistic ground, I support it on other grounds, and for reasons which in due course I will expound. The genesis of this scheme un-doubtedly is due to the work of the Shakespeare Memorial National Theatre Committee. They worked for a long time on this project and by about the year 1930 they had amassed a sum of something like £150,000. I believe I am right in saying that the fact that they had succeeded to that extent was largely due to the tireless energy of Mr. Geoffrey Whitworth. By the year 1937 they had acquired a site in South Kensington, and thereafter a project arose for the exchange of that site with the London County Council for a site on the South Bank, in the area which is to be reconstructed. Mr. Oliver Lyttelton succeeded in amalgamating the National Theatre Committee with the Committee of the Old Vic. I think that was a very happy amalgamation, because the National Theatre Committee's function is to build a theatre and the Old Vic is concerned in the successful running of a theatre.

Ever since the days of Miss Lilian Baylis, the Old Vic have done excellent work in putting on good plays. Now the exchange of sites has been effected and that exchange, as well as the dealings with the Government which followed, have been largely in the hands of the noble Viscount Lord Esher. Apparently he knows how to handle the Chancellor of the Exchequer better than anybody else! To his efforts and to his enthusiasm a very great deal is due, and those of us interested in this project would like to pay our tribute to the work he has done.

It is at long last the intention of the London County Council to develop the South Bank—I think I may say, not a decade too soon. It is to be developed, I hope and believe, on a grand and imaginative scale. It has been described as a 'future cultural centre'. I agree with Mr. Lyttelton about that phrase. It is a phrase which fills me with gloom and despondency. It is Teutonic; it is dull; and it lacks the sparkle and gaiety which are of the essence of the whole idea. But somebody, no doubt, will invent a better and happier phrase. The centre is to have a concert hall, and those who have had to listen to music in the arid wastes of the Albert Hall will realize how much that is needed. It is to have two theatres, one with a seating capacity of about 1,200 and the other, a smaller and more intimate theatre—and that is very necessary—with seating for about 500. Here we have private enterprise, municipal enterprise, and State enterprise all working together, each playing an appropriate part.

The Bill authorizes the payment of £1,000,000 of taxpayers' money towards this project if and when the theatre is built. Some of your Lordships may ask yourselves: 'Are we justified in expending State aid on this sort of project?' Unfortunately in the conditions of to-day, Maecenas is dead, and I do not see any new Maecenas arising, unless it is the people themselves. We have to try to interest the whole people in this sort of project so that they will encourage and support it. I believe that the theatre is by far the greatest means of encouragement that exists for the mass of men to widen their horizons. The theatre is a meeting place for all types and all classes. It is the popular market-place for the exchange of ideas and, together with the concert hall, the chief centre, outside sport, for collective enjoyment. Because of this, the power for education it possesses can be a natural and an unpedantic influence, an influence that I believe to be of first importance. After all, the stage provides a world in miniature, where every form of experience and emotion can be portrayed, history revealed, poetry and satire expressed, laughter enjoyed and the power of language be immediately felt. Our English drama holds first place in the literature of the world. It is unbelievably rich and exciting and varied. Yet we have never had a National Theatre; nor have we used our national heritage to the best advantage.

I hope it will be possible to cheapen the price of seats so as to bring innumerably more people within its magic circle. Not only would the general public benefit but a new incitement to invent would be given to architects, authors, designers of scenery and properties, producers and actors, and work would be found for them. As I have said, I believe that visitors will be stimulated to visit London from all over the world. I confess that I am proud that it is under a Government of which I am a humble member that, for the first time in our history, such a plan is being realized. We have been criticized for our red tape, for our concentration on the material aspects of life, and no doubt it has done us good. But, of course, these things are the preliminary necessities, the means to an end; and that end, surely, should be the raising of the mental standards of our people. Men cannot live by bread alone, nor by comfort and health alone; nor, as the noble Earl, Lord Russell, has shown us recently, even by duty alone. Man at his best must be stimulated by his imagination. It is his great incitement to be and to do something beyond the commonplace. So we have endeavoured to improve education, and to encourage the appreciation of the arts through the Arts Council. I believe that one of the most hopeful features of our life to-day is the added interest which the people are taking in good music and in good works of art. More people than before the war are visiting our picture galleries, concert halls and museums. We now ask the authority of Parliament to allow us to finance this National Theatre, with its surrounding workshops, and to animate, by this means, further artistic achievement.

I suppose it is a fact that under existing conditions it is impossible to put on first-rate shows with first-rate actors, except by charging high prices. In such circumstances, it is only by a subsidized theatre that the best can be made available for all. I believe that what turns men's minds away from war, and from exaggerated and extreme political movements, is the opportunity for personal creation; and there we have ever been in the forefront. Perhaps Britain can now show, with the coming-of-age of her working classes, that they can emulate, and must emulate, the standards and quality and example given them by their parents and guardians, her old aristocracy. By the building of a National Theatre on the Thames side we shall, I hope, make a real contribution towards the ideal of a people's civilization.

Now, my Lords, I can avail myself of this opportunity—because no one can stop me—to add a few irregular observations, which will no doubt indicate my prejudices, and probably my ignorance. I devoutly hope that this theatre will have attached to it a really good restaurant. When I go to the theatre nowadays, not being a man who takes much exercise, I must say that my arms begin to ache with the constant passing and re-passing of cups of tea, which I think would be much better taken outside in a restaurant. Next, I would say that I sincerely hope that this theatre will be set in a district which has a life and vitality of its own. I do not want to see this National Theatre surrounded by all sorts of academic buildings and Government offices, from which everybody has gone before the theatre begins; or to drive to some place like the City, through all those ghostly habitations, as they are in the evening, peopled only by cats. If those are the surroundings in which this theatre has to work, I think it is rather a gloomy prospect for the theatre. I hope the area around it will be an area throbbing with interest and vitality.

What I have to say now is even more irregular than anything I have said so far. I hope that the area which can be devoted to this theatre will be as large as possible, if one is to have the added workshops, and so on, that are necessary. That I believe to be very important. A new National Theatre is now being built in Stockholm (of course, they have had one for a long time, because they are a highly civilized people) and I am told that they are devoting no less than two and a half acres to it. At Malmo in Sweden, which is a town only about the size of Exeter, where they are also building another National Theatre, they are devoting to it a space of two acres. I am well aware that land in London is a very different proposition from land in Malmo and I am not suggesting that we can possibly entertain a scheme on those lavish lines. But I do hope that, within the necessary limitations imposed upon us, we shall remember that it is important to get as much land as we can.

There my irregularities end, and I can only hope that no one will ever use them in evidence against me. So far as building at the present time is concerned, that, of course, is out of the question. We cannot contemplate it for some time. First of all, this site will be covered by the Exhibition, and the possibility of building will not arise until after that. Nevertheless we had to bring this forward at the present time, because if the London County Council are now making their ultimate plans they must know whether they have to provide for this National Theatre—in short, whether it is to be a reality. That depends upon whether we can provide the money to build it. And we have to answer that question to-day. Although we cannot build the theatre, we have to tell the London County Council that in their ultimate plans they should provide for it. This also must be said. When the times of depression come—and we shall be very foolish, my Lords, if we think they will never come again—we must have our plans ready (we have been discussing to-day an illustration of that) to put into force. This is one of the plans which I hope will be put into force. My Lords, I believe, on material grounds, that it is a wise thing to do; I believe, on wider grounds, that it is the right thing to do. I shall be very happy to have (as I believe I shall have) support from all quarters of the House for this project. I beg to move that the Bill be now read a second time.

Moved, That the Bill be now read 2a.

LORD SOULBURY: My Lords, I have not troubled your Lordships with many observations during the past few years, because the position which I held made it a little difficult for me to engage in controversy. I confess that on more than one occasion I have suffered in silence, and refrained even from good words. My freedom is now restored, but I am certainly not going to use it now in a controversial speech. Indeed, I feel that it would satisfy my own conscience, and your Lordships, after hearing the admirable introduction of this Bill by the noble and learned Viscount on the Woolsack, if I confined myself to the one observation that I concur with what he has said and have nothing to add to it. But perhaps your Lordships will allow me to make a few remarks in support of what the noble and learned Viscount has said.

My only regret, which I am sure your Lordships share, is that a measure of this sort was not put on your Statute Book a long time ago. If it had been, we should now possess a National Theatre which would have been built at a very much lower cost than the estimated cost of the one that is now proposed; we should have learned and appreciated a great deal more of the works of Shakespeare and other dramatists, ancient and modern; we should have had a better-educated public and a higher standard of acting. I believe it is true to say that the plays of Shakespeare provide the best training there is for the young actor. According to such researches as I have made, only once in the past thirty-six years has a serious attempt been made (apart from to-day) to achieve a purpose of this kind. That was in another place in 1913, on a Private Member's Motion, which sought to establish a National Theatre, with trustees, and to secure support and assistance from the Government of that day.

The mover of that Motion was himself a member of the Shakespeare Memorial National Theatre Committee. In those days, I believe, they had already secured about £100,000 of the £500,000 that it was estimated would be required. The object of the Motion was to persuade the Government to contribute a portion of the balance. The Government were not to be persuaded—and, surprisingly, it was a Liberal Government. But, as the old poet said:

Even good Homer nods, and long toil is an excuse for slumber.

Arguments used on that occasion—I do not agree with them—may still have some relevance in the minds of some people. One was that it would be unwise for the Government to take on the responsibility for a theatre for the production of plays if private commercial enterprise had not thought it possible to produce a profit in that way. Another argument was that the public were not educated, and that the Government ought not to step in until they were satisfied that they had an enthusiastic, interested and educated public. It was also argued that it was not the Government's business to initiate a project of that kind, but to crown it. I am very glad that none of those arguments appeals to His Majesty's Government to-day. The only offer that was made at that time was a very tentative one, that the Government would consider the provision of a subsidy, of an indeterminate amount, when— and only when—the promoters acquired the site, built the theatre, equipped it and endowed it.

That was not a very expensive form of coronation for the Government to indulge in. Of course, one has to remember that in those days, with a Budget of £190,000,000, the provision of anything in the neighbourhood of £1,500,000 was considered formidable.

In fact, the Government in those days were restrained, curious as it may sound, by the fear of losing money. It may be said for His Majesty's Government to-day that they have demonstrated on more than one occasion that they are not in the least perturbed by any such fear. The National Theatre is not, I think, likely to be a paying proposition. In the course of the debate in another place, an expert admitted that something like 300,000 to 400,000 persons would have to see a play in order to ensure its success. That means a long run. I am hoping that the National Theatre will be more in the nature of a repertory theatre, and that we may be able to see in the course of three or four years all or most of the plays of Shakespeare. Then again, I understand the idea is that the seats should be cheap, and I sympathize with that view. The figure was put at prices varying from 6d. to 2s. 6d. The noble and learned Viscount has said there are to be two theatres, one to seat 1,200 and another to seat 500. At those prices the larger theatre cannot charge much less than the theatre seating 500.

Besides the £1,000,000 initial cost, there are the running costs to provide; and may I say that I hope they will not be placed on the rates? I was attracted by the suggestion of the Government spokesman in another place that the deficit, if deficit there is, should be met by the Arts Council. I think we must face it that the National Theatre may well not be self-supporting. Personally, that does not worry me much, because, as the noble and learned Viscount has indicated, I think we shall get repayment in many other ways. Your Lordships will recollect that Demosthenes once complained of the Athenians that they were prepared to spend much more money on dramatic festivals than they were on a naval expedition. Not many people now remember, or very much care about, Athenian naval expeditions, but their drama has lived for ever. I say this to reassure the stricter economist than myself that, although there may be losses, I think it will be a very long time indeed before the National Theatre can lose as much as we have already lost in one year on potatoes.

The noble and learned Viscount on the Woolsack has informed us, quite rightly I am sure, that because of the Exhibition we shall not get this theatre before 1951. He said that it may be some years after that, and he also stated (although I do not entirely agree with him) that this delay would in some ways be excused—I will not say welcomed— because the project could be put in a pigeon-hole and brought out against a trade depression. I am not altogether enamoured of that pro-posal—and for this reason. I can foresee the time when, perhaps from one of these Benches, in reply to a request that the authorization to commence this theatre be given, a noble Lord may rise and cheerfully say that he is sorry he cannot authorize the commencement of the theatre because, to his lasting sorrow and deep regret, the slump has not yet arrived! May I ask whether, before this depression arrives, it would not be possible to give a somewhat lower priority to one or other of the Government offices in course of erection or contemplated?

I frankly admit that between the two wars the predecessors of this Government were considerably to blame in not initiating a project of this kind, and it would have been a useful step to combat the depression which was prevailing. Of course, in those days, State interference was by no means so fashionable as it has now become, and even to-day, i seems to me, one has to watch anything like State control over art with a considerable amount of suspicion and care. Such a delicate, sensitive and indefinable thing as genius does not take kindly to bureaucracy; much less can it flourish within the prescribed limits of some ideology or political or economic faith. We have seen what happened to art among the Nazis, and I make the same proviso with regard to Russia to-day, where I think it is highly imprudent, if not dangerous, for an artist to produce a play with a bourgeois or Western flavour, unt palatable to the authorities. It is a great pity that the rulers of Sovie-Russia do not refer to the works of Aristophanes, because if they did they would read what he said about the head of the Athenian State in the Pelopponesian War and yet got away with it. Had he said the same things about our Prime Minister, I think he would have spent the rest of his time writing his plays in the Isle of Man! Yet the theatre of Athens was a public institution, and the State was entirely and completely responsible for Athenian drama.

In Clause 2 of the Bill, the Treasury are given a voice in the appointing of additional trustees for this theatre. That is inevitable. Public money is being spent, and the public must have a voice. To that extent we are admitting a Trojan Horse into the Borough of Lambeth; but I do not think we need fear the Treasury in this case, even when bringing gifts. The most important proviso is that the private management should consist of those who know something about managing theatres, and of the people of the profession, and not people selected from gifted amateurs or aesthetically-minded politicians. The Government's spokesman in another place said that it was too soon to consider the question of management, and I think he is probably right. But it is a vital point, and I for one would be happy if it were left in the hands of the Old Vic.

I noticed, also, that in the debate in another place, a suggestion was made that there should be a Minister of Fine Arts. I hope there is nothing of the sort. This gentleman, it was said, would stand apart from Party politics. A Minister, whatever Government appoint him, cannot usually stand apart from Party politics, and such a political hermaphrodite is unknown to our mythology.

There are few more points with which I want to trouble your Lordships. The noble and learned Viscount mentioned the site, and I think your Lordships agree that the new site is preferable, both from historic associations and, I think, from its proximity to the great centres of population. I share his views in regard to the term 'cultural centre'. To me it is too redolent of earnest-minded, professional zealots and long-haired intelligentsia. Like all your Lordships, no doubt, I should welcome an invitation to dine at the National Theatre, and see a play; but if I were asked to attend the 'Lambeth Cultural Centre' I should have a vision of nut cutlets and a lecture on eurhythmics. I entirely agree with the noble and learned Viscount on the Woolsack with regard to the environment: I think it is most important that it should not be austere and highbrow. After all, Piccadilly Circus, Leicester Square and Shaftesbury Avenue at present form our cultural centre; and although it may not be possible or desirable to imitate all the intimacy and irregularity of that area, at any rate I hope that a new lay-out will try to develop something of the charm and, if you will, the romance which have endeared that part of the world to Londoners for generations.

When the new scheme is complete, I think its benefits will immensely outweigh its cost or any possible losses that may accrue. After all, it will do a great deal to preserve the English language—and that is certainly in need of preserving. It will improve the spoken word; we shall be able to hear English pronounced as it ought to be pronounced by people who have studied the subject. It will set a standard, much as the Comédie Française has set a standard in France. It will provide further inspiration for our great creative dramatic genius. It is of much more value to hear poetry spoken—and particularly dramatic poetry—than it is to read it. There were few books in ancient Greece, and few people read or could read Homer; but thousands upon thousands heard him recite his poetry and knew his lines by heart. No one can estimate the colossal contribution that those poets made to the poetic and dramatic genius of the Greeks. With ourselves, the Bible has played a similar part—I wish I could say it still played that part. In past times, I imagine, the majority of the population regularly heard passages from the Bible; and there again, nobody can estimate the contribution that the Bible and its translators have made to our literature. The plays of Shakespeare himself were written not to be read but to be heard and seen; and hearing and seeing them will, I am certain, prove one of the greatest inspirations to thought and literature in the world.

The National Theatre should provide a very valuable stimulus to the dramatic profession. Dramatic actors and actresses in the provinces may graduate to the National Theatre, and the competition which would result would do much to ensure a high standard. I believe that is the practice in Sweden to-day. Then there is the question of employment; it should be possible to subsidize the theatre to provide employment. There are at present many actors and actresses, especially younger ones, who are constantly out of employment.

Finally, the National Theatre must not be regarded as being for Londoners only—nor indeed for the United Kingdom only. It is in London because London will be a centre for the whole of the Commonwealth. Nor must the theatre itself be solely a memorial to Shakespeare. There is no other land in the world so rich as ours in either the quantity or the quality of its dramatic art; and we can now look forward to the time—and I hope it will not be far ahead—when the National Theatre will be presenting to visitors from all over the world examples of our dramatic art from the sixteenth century to the present day and onwards.

VISCOUNT ESHER: My Lords, I have been connected with this project for more years than I care to remember, and it gives me the greatest pleasure to know that this measure is at last going to reach the Statute Book. For many years I have belonged to a small band of enthusiastic people working in that obscurity which always seems to be the lot of people who are active in a popular cause. We were united in a conviction that it is a disgrace to this country, which has perhaps the greatest dramatic literature in the world, that we should be the only civilized country in Europe without a National Theatre. Nevertheless it seemed an impossible thing to achieve, and for a very long time we made no headway at all. I sometimes think there are certain tides in politics, when you can succeed at one moment and fail at another. No one can account for those tides. For instance, your Lordships will remember the case of slum areas in our urban towns. For about a hundred years people lamented the existence of those slums, and all through our richest hour they said it was impossible to do away with them. Now they cannot leave them standing for another minute—when we are poorer than we have ever been in our lives before. It is curious how at one moment no one will listen to what one has to say, and the next minute it becomes quite easy to carry a thing through both Houses of Parliament without any opposition at all.

This, of course, is a great day for all of us who have struggled to see the accomplishment of a National Theatre in England. We are also very gratified that a pleasant link with the London County Council has been forged and that we are to be part of their noble plan for reconditioning the South Bank of the Thames. Another question arises from that. All my life I have heard people lament that the South Bank of the Thames is a disgrace to an imperial city such as London. People used to come back from Paris saying how beautiful and wonderful was the lay-out of the Seine and how marvellously it has been incorporated into the city. So far as London was concerned, nothing was done in the time of its greatest wealth; it is only now that we are determined to sweep away the ugly slums on the South Bank and create a noble lay-out there. The London County Council have been very friendly to our idea from the start and the exchanges that we have made with them really amount to the fact that the London County Council provided £185,000 as a contribution to the cost of the National Theatre.

The noble and learned Viscount on the Woolsack has referred to the approaches which I have made to the Government. My colleagues were not hopeful of those approaches—not as hopeful as I was myself. But I was surprised at the warm welcome I received from Mr. Dalton when I saw him about this measure. Then, almost immediately, Mr. Dalton fell into misfortune and I had to begin again with a new Chancellor of the Exchequer whose formidable austerity had been rubbed into me by every newspaper in the last five years. I imagined that he was going to be rather like that Puritanical Roundhead, Prynne, who during the Commonwealth wrote a pamphlet and succeeded in getting the theatres closed during the whole of the period of Cromwell's reign. I did not find Sir Stafford Cripps in the least like that. On the contrary, I found he was just as cordial about the idea as Mr. Dalton had been. I think your Lordships will agree that it is not the sort of thing that one would have expected to have appealed to this Government.

The theatre is essentially an individualistic profession. There are good parts and high salaries for some people, and bad parts and small salaries for others. Your Lordships will have observed the grossly unfair advantage that pretty women have over plain ones in the theatrical profession. Nevertheless, in spite of all that, this idea has received the cordial and enthusiastic response from the Government, untainted by a theoretical equalitarianism. It only shows that the Government are in much closer touch with public opinion than many people think. That is shown by the unusual debate which took place in another place, where there was a debate of several hours and there was no opposition to this measure at all—which I have been told is an almost unprecedented event in that place.

I share the optimistic view which the Government have of the future. This country has had a great loss of military power and of wealth. These things have passed to those two remote monsters who live to the East and West of Europe. Their way of life, though very different one from the other, has no real appeal to us. But I am convinced that Shakespeare's countrymen are about to enjoy an Athenian summer of great interest and charm. The Arts Council and the B.B.C. have created and found vast new audiences who are keen and vitally interested in all these artistic questions. It is true that they are not yet educated. I have the greatest admiration for Mr. Oliver Lyttelton, who has given long service and loyalty to this cause, but he is terribly afraid of this expression 'cultural centre', a fear which apparently is shared not only by the Lord Chancellor but also by the noble Lord, Lord Soulbury; but no one ever produces another phrase for it. The other day I was talking to a woman who lives in Battersea, where they have just made a cultural centre. She was extremely proud of the fact that her community had a cultural centre. She said, in fact, that it was going to be opened shortly by Mr. Edgar Wallace! I was not priggish enough to insinuate to her that he was not the sort of man I should have selected to open this cultural centre. I only pointed out to her that he had been dead for many years, and it was really extremely unlikely that he would be opening the centre. She said: 'Oh, then, it must be Shakespeare who is coming!'

It seems to me to show that cultural centres are necessary in some districts of England. Mr. Oliver Lyttelton and the Lord Chancellor do not reach for their revolvers when they hear such words; they reach for their satirical witticism, which is a much more dangerous weapon in this country. It is all very well for them to do that, but I do not think they realize what an important work these centres accomplish in districts where there is enthusiasm but not sufficient education. I myself have found a universal appreciation of this movement. Those who are in contact with the new democracy know that it is alive with genius. I have perfect confidence that it is going to produce a civilized life equal both to the aristocratic life enjoyed in the eighteenth century by the great families, and to the middle-class civilized life which was produced in the nineteenth century.

I have no anticipation that I shall myself live to see the National Theatre built, still less to see the chain of civic theatres which will bring the drama to the starved provincial towns. I should like to congratulate the Government upon their courage and imagination in bringing in this measure. Nearly everything that Governments do is inevitably, perhaps mercifully, forgotten. The political and economic issues about which we fight get out of date, lose their virulence and become un-important. But what we are building to-day will stand for ever as a lasting monument to this Administration.

LORD BLACKFORD: My Lords, I should be sorry to strike any dis-cordant note in the spirit of harmony which prevails at this moment, particularly as all my life I have been a great lover of the theatre. Probably I have seen as many plays and films as any member of your Lordships' House. When Mr. Oliver Lyttelton said, as he did in the debate in another place, that the object of the National Theatre was to set the highest standard for the drama, those words expressed my sentiments entirely. But this is a Bill which involves extra expenditure. It seems only fair to remind ourselves that all the bankers have recently issued their annual pronouncements. They are unanimous on one point —namely, the overwhelming necessity to ease the burden of taxation. The only way of easing the burden of taxation is to reduce expenditure. Therefore, any Bill which seeks to increase expenditure, however small it may be in comparison with the gigantic expenditures which are made in other directions, must surely receive a careful scrutiny. We should assure ourselves that the two theatres which are envisaged in this Bill are necessary.

The first thing we must remember is that the expenditure on this project will by no means be confined to the £1,000,000 envisaged in this Bill. The noble and learned Viscount the Lord Chancellor made that clear in his speech, when he spoke of wishing to add a restaurant and to build the theatre with workshops in an area of some two and a half acres, and when he expressed the hope that prices of between 6d. and 2s. 6d. would be the highest prices paid by the spectators. Obviously, any such project would entail a heavy annual subsidy, and we must be prepared to face that. Then, in regard to this theatre, would it, in fact, be a National Theatre? That certainly was not the unanimous opinion of speakers in another place. One of the Members from the North of England said that up in Manchester they were tired of paying taxes, or their share of taxes, for projects from which only Londoners reaped the benefit. Another, from Wales, said that his idea was to have a National Theatre in Wales, and if this Bill passes he would approach the Treasury for a grant in order that his country should have its own National Theatre. A third Member, from Scotland, said exactly the same in respect of his country, and Mr. Oliver Lyttelton in his closing speech in that debate offered his services to back him up in obtaining a grant for Scotland to have its own National Theatre. Let us therefore not be under any delusion that the amount of finance involved is confined only to the not considerable sum which is asked for in this Bill.

I wonder whether we are right in thinking that the South Bank of the Thames is an ideal place to construct this national theatre, if indeed it is decided to construct it. If that is so, how is it that every other theatre is on the North Bank? How is it that no theatre, except Miss Baylis's effort, has ever flourished on the South Bank of the Thames. I venture to think that Miss Baylis's effort should not be taken as a precedent. She was a lady of great ability and personality, who created a vogue and who carried on her theatre—although not everybody will admit it—on the lines of presenting the drama in its highest standards. She did wonderful work, but she did not do such work as would be required of a National Theatre. I am very doubtful, therefore, in spite of the eloquent testimony of Lord Esher and the Lord Chancellor, whether in fact, from the long-term point of view, a site on the South Bank of the Thames will be successful.

Am I not right in thinking that Lord Esher is also a sponsor for the creation of a highly important music centre in the area of Portman Place, which would surely be a strong competitor with a similar cultural centre on the South Bank?

VISCOUNT ESHER: There is no proposal whatever to build a theatre in the Regent's Park area; that is merely in connection with music.

LORD BLACKFORD: But a concert hall is to be built there, I think, and at Portland Place there will be the counter-attraction to that which it is now sought to have on the South Bank.

Lastly, in that connection, are there not enough theatres already for the presentation of drama? In these hard times, before we commit ourselves to the construction of two new theatres, would it not be wise to make quite certain that there is a demand for a permanent National Theatre Company in London? Surely it would be possible, if such a plan were considered desirable, to start away with it straight away. What is the matter with the Gaiety Theatre? It has been empty for some years. It is true that the lease on the theatre has recently been taken up by Mr. Lupino Lane, but I have no doubt that as he is not at present able to obtain a licence to repair it he would be willing to lease it for such purposes as this. It would appear to me that the Gaiety Theatre offers many advantages. It is in a good traffic centre; it is in the middle of theatreland; the road amenities round it are good, and it was run very successfully for about twenty years. If a small theatre is desired quite close why not lease the little Kingsway Theatre? I have been to many good shows at the Kingsway Theatre in my time, and I do not know why it has been neglected in the last few years. There seems to me no reason why a short lease should not be taken of that theatre in order to try out this proceeding without committing the country to a heavy capital expenditure.

My Lords, this Bill deals only with the actual building, and I submit that the construction of a building is not at present advisable, for the reasons I have stated. But, surely, the more important things about a National Theatre are the play and the players. Buildings are no good without the men and women who write the plays, and those who produce and act in them. Surely, we are already doing a great deal to propagate the drama in that respect. We are, to the best of our ability, taking the drama to the people. I have no doubt that many of your Lordships have read the last annual report of the Arts Council. It seems to me that the Arts Council are doing a fine job at very little expense. Its chief work in London is to subsidize the Old Vic Company. What is the Old Vic Company if it is not a National Theatre Company? For the last four years it has been producing repertory at the New Theatre, with the very best actors and actresses, and with the very best producers. Yet according to Mr. Benn Levy, speaking in another place —and he ought to know all about it—in only one year out of the four during which the Old Vic Company has been performing at the New Theatre has it broken even; in all the other three years it has required a subsidy from the Arts Council. Whenever I have been to the New Theatre it has always been full to capacity. If that is the position, it only shows what a grave loss would be suffered if an attempt were made to produce national drama at prices from 6d. to 2s. 6d.

T 289

But in addition to the Old Vic Company in London, there is a small theatre called the London Masque Theatre, also subsidized by the Arts Council and carried on in the nature of a repertory theatre. It has produced one highly successful play called *The Linden Tree*, and two or three others of a cultural value without the same box office appeal. In addition to that, the Arts Council entirely run three repertory companies in the country, at Bristol, Coventry, and Salisbury; and they are interested in, help the finance of, no fewer than thirty-one companies all over the country, including Scotland and Wales. I have not worked out the number of plays which were put on by those thirty-one companies during the year 1947–8 which is the year with which the report deals, but it is well over 150. All this has been achieved at a cost of £63,000—£56,000 being for England and £7,000 for Scotland. I see that the Lord Chancellor is shaking his head. It is true to say that the total grant to the Arts Council was £428,000, but much the greater part of that was spent on art exhibition, music, ballet, and so forth. The actual expenditure on the drama was only £63,000 for this last year, and I maintain that a great achievement has been accomplished by the Arts Council at that very small expenditure.

I am in favour of increasing those efforts because I believe that that is doing a great deal more good than would be done by erecting a building in London. Quite apart from that, however, it seems to me inconsistent that we Conservatives, who are always blaming the Government for their excessive expenditure, who are at this very moment moving in another place a vote of censure on the Government for the gigantic miscalculations of such gargantuan wasters as the Ministers of Health and Food, should in this small matter be persuaded by the eloquence of the Lord Chancellor and the attraction of the project to depart from our consistent principle—namely, only that reduction of taxation, among many other things, can save this country from the economic blizzard which will one day come upon it.

THE LORD CHANCELLOR: My Lords, I have little to add to what I have previously said. I was sorry to note that the noble Lord, Lord Soulbury, did not much like my remarks about trade depression. I rather agree. I did not much like them myself, but I put them in to try to get over the sort of difficulties which we have just heard enunciated. However, as they obviously have not got over those difficulties, I withdraw them. Of course, I entirely agree with what the noble Lord said about management. It is obvious that it is necessary that the management should be in the hands of someone who is an expert and skilled manager. I hope to goodness that no Government, whatever their complexion, will be foolish enough to think that they should concern themselves with managing a theatre.

The noble Viscount, Lord Esher, expressed surprise that this Government should entertain such a project. After all—and I do not want to strike a controversial note—this Government have a very good record in these matters. There has never been a Government before which contributed something of the order of between £400,000 and £500,000 a year to the Arts Council. We believe that in these directions we are spending the taxpayers' money in a very useful way. I am afraid that I should never convince the noble Lord, Lord Blackford, but he has had his say and 'got it off his chest', so to speak; and I hope that, having done that, he will be good about it in the future—indeed, I think that he will. He says that we really cannot afford this expenditure. I cannot help feeling that it was just that sort of attitude—if I may use Lord Esher's illustration—which kept those slums with us for so many years. If we had only made up our minds that we would afford it, and we had afforded it, we could have got rid of those slums years ago at about one-tenth of what it would cost now. We should have eliminated a vast amount of human misery and human suffering if we had made up our minds that we were going to afford it, and had afforded it. We should, moreover, have had a National Theatre at somewhere about the same time that Louis XIV gave France a National Theatre. It was always the 'cannot afford it' attitude that stood in the way.

I am not saying that the situation to-day is one in which we can be permitted to indulge in any wild extravagance. But I do not believe this is wild extravagance. I believe that anything which is going to contribute to the moral, spiritual and mental welfare of the people is very wise expenditure—expenditure which we not only can but ought to afford. Therefore, I disagree with the noble Lord with regard to his other suggestion. Particular theatres were mentioned. The noble Lord will realize that some of those theatres would be quite inappropriate to the project we have in mind. To play repertory in some of the theatres would, of course, be foolish. I am grateful for the reception which this Bill has received. Though I have not quite succeeded in convincing Lord Blackford, yet I think he realizes there is something to be said for the project which I have brought before your Lordships.

On Question, Bill read 2a, and committed to a Committee of the Whole House.

T*

XI

PENULTIMATE

The immediate effect of the passage of the National Theatre Bill through Parliament was to spur the Joint Committee and the London County Council to go ahead with the planning of the theatre and with the preliminaries for the exchange of sites; for the way of advance was now clear of obstacles, subject only to the word 'go' from the Government, as witnessed by the terms of the Act:

WHEREAS arrangements have been made between the Trustees of the Shakespeare Memorial Trust (in this Act referred to as 'the Trustees') and the London County Council for reserving to the Trustees as a site for the erection of a national theatre by way of memorial to William Shakespeare, certain land in the Borough of Lambeth belonging to the Council and for transfer to the Council of certain land in the Royal Borough of Kensington previously acquired by the Trustees for the purpose aforesaid:

And whereas it is expedient to make provision for authorizing the payment out of public funds of contributions towards the erection and equipment of such a theatre by the Trustees:

Be it therefore enacted by the King's most Excellent Majesty by and with the advice and consent of the Lords Spiritual and Temporal, and Commons, in this present Parliament assembled, and by the authority of the same, as follows:

I. *Upon the submission to the Treasury of a scheme satisfactory to them for the erection by the Trustees of such a theatre as aforesaid on the site reserved to them for the purpose in accordance with the said arrangements, and for the equipment and management thereof, the Treasury may undertake to make, and may make out of moneys provided by Parliament, upon such terms and subject to such conditions as they may think fit, such contributions to the funds of the Trustees as they think fit (not exceeding one million pounds) in respect of the cost of erecting and equipping the theatre in accordance with the scheme.*

II. (1) After the commencement of this Act no person shall be appointed as a new or additional trustee of the Shakespeare Memorial Trust unless his appointment is approved by the Treasury.

(2) Notwithstanding anything in subsection (6) of section thirty-six of the Trustee Act, 1925, the number of trustees of the said Trust may be increased by virtue of appointments made under that subsection up to seven and appointments may be made thereunder notwithstanding that the number of trustees of the Trust for the time being exceeds three.

III. This Act may be cited as the National Theatre Act, 1948.
Presented by Mr. Glenvil Hall, supported by Mr. Silkin and Mr. Hardman. Ordered by The House of Commons, *to be printed,* 18 November 1948.

At that date, we must remember, a contribution of a million pounds had been held sufficient for the erection of the twin stages under one roof. The respective uses to which they should be put had not, however, been defined; though it was commonly assumed that they would follow the lines laid down in Granville-Barker's book. It seemed likely, however, that this arrangement would be called into question, and before finally instructing the architect as to the precise form of the smaller theatre, the Building Committee desired that its membership should be widened so as to give expression to a larger range of professional opinion. This was made known to the Joint Council who, early in 1950, agreed to seek the co-operation of Sir Lewis Casson, Sir Laurence Olivier, Mr. John Gielgud, Lt. Col. Stanley Bell, and Mr. Donald Albery. Together with Mr. Llewellyn Rees, as Administrator of the Old Vic, and Mr. Hugh Hunt as Director of the Old Vic company, these gentlemen (with the exception of Mr. John Gielgud, who was abroad) duly met the existing Building Committee and approved the plans and model for the larger theatre submitted

293

by the architect. But they left the problem of the smaller theatre for further consideration; and this was just as well, for at about the same time, Mr. O'Rorke felt it necessary to inform us that owing to the rapid rise in the price of building, the million pounds previously estimated as adequate for the erection of the two theatres would now suffice for the larger one only. The smaller would cost a further £200,000 at least.

To ask the Government to increase their grant would now be clearly out of order. Resourceful as ever, Lord Esher came to the rescue, saying that the dilemma might be solved if the Old Vic were, for the time being, adopted as the second theatre, to be served by the one National Theatre company, thus preserving the flexibility of programme and acting *personnel* which had always been envisaged under the twin-stage plan.

The Joint Council, the S.M.N.T. Committee, and the Old Vic Governors gladly agreed to the compromise, albeit the S.M.N.T. stressed its temporary nature, and added a resolution to the effect that they would welcome any suggestion whereby the additional sum for building the smaller theatre might be raised. This, you may say, in present circumstances, was crying for the moon. Indeed, the likelihood of private munificence on such a scale must be minute compared even with what it was in the golden days. Yet here and there great fortunes do persist, though they are no longer reflected in great incomes, and may even be an embarrassment to their owners now that capital realization offers the only outlet for the personal disposal of wealth.

However this may be, the more I think things over, the more persuaded I become that the old conception of the twin stages under one roof will ultimately be found to be crucial to the full development of our National Theatre. In the last resort two separated theatres can only complicate the problems of management, as emphasized by Captain Bullock in his speech in the House of Commons reported on page 255. Working costs would certainly be greater and the integrity of both enterprises seriously imperilled.

PENULTIMATE

From both the moral and economic standpoints one hopes that the period of bifurcation may be short and sweet.

Having plunged so rashly into the expression of a purely individual opinion, may I hazard one further point about the use to which the smaller theatre should be put when once it has been built? All who have seen Mr. O'Rorke's model for the interior of the large theatre are unanimous in believing that he has triumphantly solved the problem of providing an 'all purpose' playhouse with a stage that can be swiftly adapted for the production of classical and modern plays alike. This suggests that the smaller theatre might well be more specialized in type. There are many who hope for something 'modern', harmonious with the tendencies of the hour that swing now towards a freer style of stage presentation than has been customary hitherto. But on a long view I would plump unhesitatingly for a conventional picture-frame stage. The time will come when historic justice will demand that the drama of creative realism which illumined the great period of European theatre from the emergence of Ibsen to the death of Bernard Shaw, shall be performed in surroundings similar to those which conditioned and inspired it. Years hence, I contend, the picture-frame stage will be held to be as desirable for the realistic play as the open stage is now held to be so for the production of Shakespeare. By the same token, intimate comedy or farce will always be most effectively enjoyed by a small audience in a small setting. Nor let us too easily take it for granted that a National Little Theatre need confine its activities to the performance of naturalistic plays. I can foresee a drama so spiritual in theme, so subtly imaginative that, well nigh asphyxiated as we are by the global ordure of these years of disgrace, we cannot credit the loveliness that may be in store. Such a drama will need a remoteness of vision that can only be attained at one remove from the spectator, and within a frame that marks the magic line between the reality and the dream.

But enough of this. The ultimate decision will be made, no

doubt, by the Board of Governors which will eventually take the place of the present Joint Council. At the moment, it falls to the Joint Council to draw up a Constitution for the theatre which will be embodied in the Royal Charter for which application must soon be made. According to the National Theatre Act, not more than seven new Trustees may be appointed in whom ownership of the site will vest. They in turn may become *ex officio* members of the Board, which can include eminent representatives of various national, provincial, educational and theatre interests, together with (in the first instance) some members chosen equally from the vanishing S.M.N.T. Committee and the Old Vic Governors. This implies a fairly numerous body who may feel moved to nominate a small Executive to meet more frequently and advise on the running of the theatre. As for the Director, it has been agreed that he should have full managerial powers, including the engagement of artists and technical staff, subject only to the general policy, financial and otherwise, laid down from time to time by the Board, whose primary concern will be the financing of the first productions during the formative period of the theatre's life.

And now the reader may feel himself cheated to find our narrative abruptly concluded before its proper climax, the opening night of the theatre itself. But as things have turned out, this would entail yet another chapter, and perhaps another hand to write it. So I have thought it best to finish with this Festival year of 1951, whose high-light for us will surely be the laying of the theatre's corner stone by the King. When first I made bold to suggest that this symbolic rite might be linked with the Festival of Britain, the idea was warmly welcomed by the Joint Council, and in due course our Chairman was able to inform us of His Majesty's gracious consent, and of his choice of a day in July as the date for the ceremony.

That the recent death of J. P. Blake, the only begetter of the South Side plan, will deprive us of his presence, is a cause of profound regret; and we must likewise acknowledge that common sense, if not piety, forbids over-confidence in the future. Yet if Providence see fit to give us peace in our time, the walls of the National Theatre will surely arise, and we shall soon be set the final task of realizing on the stage some of those ideals towards which have been directed the hope and effort of a century. To adapt the words of the poet:

> Let there be nothing common done or mean
> Upon that memorable scene.

Failures yes, and there may be many; but they need not be ignoble if only our high ambitions hold and the future keeps faith with the past.

Glancing back over these pages, I am struck by the relevance to the present situation of so many of the early arguments for a National Theatre—particularly on its creative side. Times indeed have changed, not always for the better, but seldom has our stage been so prolific in talent as it is to-day, whatever the croakers may tell us. Yet along with much that is admirable, there is a new restlessness that springs not only from the spiritual *malaise* of our age, but also from more mundane factors such as the growing distractions of cinema, broadcasting, and television, and from the ambassadorial voyages dutifully undertaken by our premier companies to the uttermost parts of the earth. Dare one also, despite the enticing brilliance of our newer playwrights and their interpreters, dare one hint that there is danger of a too easy reliance on the plaudits of a public more intelligent perhaps than of yore, but quite inexperienced in playgoing and apt to confuse the pleasures of surprise with more solid satisfactions? A glittering surface is all very well in its way, but will never suffice to restore to a still younger generation the ability to appreciate and enjoy the essential values of dramatic art.

This is why the country needs, and needs more than ever, at least one exemplary playhouse where permanent standards prevail and where the will to perfection can live on, despite the lures of an easy popularity. For this reason I would deplore the sending of a National Theatre company abroad till it has got thoroughly into its stride. We shall start, I know, with the incomparable asset of a living organism which has long proved its worth. But the whole ethos of a National Theatre offers a very special challenge. In a sense it will mean a new beginning, and if it starts with the backing of a fine tradition it will no less require to establish a new one.

And here one calls to mind that wonderful creation of an English school of ballet under Dame Ninette de Valois. It has always seemed to me that there is something reserved and cloistral about the régime at Sadler's Wells—something almost domestic. Would that that atmosphere could be repeated on the South Bank, as already to a large extent at Stratford-on-Avon, for the actor surely deserves a serene and peaceful home for the practice of his art, and from home all the best things come.

APPENDIX

STATE SUPPORT FOR SOME FOREIGN NATIONAL THEATRES

THE following information as to the amounts of State subsidy now being granted to some of the leading National Theatres abroad has been supplied by the British Centre of the International Theatre Institute, 7 Goodwin's Court, St. Martin's Lane, London. Secretary: Kenneth Rae.

FRANCE

The combined subsidy received by the Comédie Française and the Odéon for the year 1950 was approximately £235,000. The Théâtre National du Palais Chaillot, where large spectacular productions are staged, receives a subsidy of £27,500. The Opéra and Opéra Comique, according to information recently received, also receive a subsidy of over £715,000 annually.

BELGIUM

The State Theatre in Belgium is composed of two sections, the French and the Flemish. The former is situated in the Théâtre de la Résidence, Brussels; the latter in a fine theatre in Antwerp. Each receives a Government subsidy of approximately £35,700.

HOLLAND

The Government and Municipalities give subsidies amounting to £73,300, spread over the annual deficit of the State-supported theatres at Amsterdam, Rotterdam, the Hague, Utrecht, and Haarlem. The deficit on these five theatres amounted to £77,067 for the year 1948–9, and the figure given above goes to paying this off, so that they are still left with a deficit of £3,759.

DENMARK

In Denmark the Government contribute £210,500 towards two State Theatres in Copenhagen. It should be noted that in Denmark, State Theatres give opera and ballet as well as drama.

NORWAY

The National Theatre at Oslo receives an annual grant of over £20,000 which keeps its 150 players and technicians in employment throughout the year.

APPENDIX

SWEDEN

The Government grant to the Royal Dramatic Theatre which belongs to the State and is let free of rent, is just over 25 per cent of the turn-over. The latter is approximately £150,000, so that the subsidy comes to £45,000. This, however, does not derive from public funds in the ordinary sense of the words. There is a State lottery, the profits from which are devoted to the support of cultural activities. From this source comes the Government subsidy to the National Theatre which pays no entertainment tax either to the State or to the Municipality of Stockholm.

HUNGARY

The first Hungarian National Theatre was opened in 1837. In 1903 the Government declared the building obsolete, and planned to erect a new National Theatre which it is hoped will be completed in 1953-4. In the meanwhile the National Theatre functions at the renovated Folk Theatre at the corner of Rakoczi Street. Here there are a larger theatre and a smaller theatre under one roof. This, and the other State-supported theatres in Hungary, operate on a highly developed system of *abonnements*, which, together with the normal box-office takings, provide some 50 per cent of the costs. For the remaining 50 per cent the Government is responsible.

NATIONAL THEATRE COMMITTEES
1st January 1951

Shakespeare Memorial National Theatre

Trustees: The Rt. Hon. Oliver Lyttelton, D.S.O., M.C., M.P.
The Rt. Hon. The Viscount Esher
Sir Anthony Meyer, Bart.

Executive Committee

Chairman: The Rt. Hon. The Viscount Esher

The remaining two Trustees	St. John Ervine, LL.D.
Sir Patrick Abercrombie	Mrs. Elsie Hulbert
Sir Bronson Albery	H. Hamilton Fyfe
Sir Kenneth Barnes	Sir Barry Jackson
Sidney L. Bernstein	S. R. Littlewood
Sir Lewis Casson	R. A. Scott-James
Ashley Dukes	Dame Sybil Thorndike

Hon. Secretary: Geoffrey Whitworth, C.B.E.

APPENDIX

JOINT COUNCIL OF THE NATIONAL THEATRE AND THE OLD VIC

Chairman: The Rt. Hon. Oliver Lyttelton

Sir Bronson Albery
The Viscount Esher
Mrs. L'Estrange Malone, J.P.

Oliver Poole
Miss Barbara Ward
Geoffrey Whitworth, C.B.E.

The Rt. Hon. Lord Wilmot, P.C.

Old Vic Executive Committee

Chairman: The Rt. Hon. The Viscount Esher

Sir Bronson Albery
The Lady Violet Bonham Carter
Mrs. L'Estrange Malone, J.P.

Oliver Poole
Miss Barbara Ward
The Rt. Hon. Lord Wilmot, P.C.

Building Sub-Committee

Chairman: Sir Bronson Albery

Donald Albery
Lt.-Col. Stanley Bell, C.B.E., A.F.C.
Sidney Bernstein
John Burrell
Sir Lewis Casson
The Viscount Esher
John Gielgud

Hugh Hunt
Michael MacOwen
Norman Marshall
Sir Laurence Olivier
Llewellyn Rees
Richard Southern
Geoffrey Whitworth, C.B.E.

Secretary to the Joint Council and Sub-Committees:
Kenneth Rae

301

BIBLIOGRAPHY

A National Theatre: Scheme & Estimates, William Archer and H. Granville Barker. Duckworth. 1907

The Foundations of a National Drama, Henry Arthur Jones. Chapman & Hall. 1913.

The Exemplary Theatre, Harley Granville-Barker. Sidgwick & Jackson. (Chatto & Windus. 1922.)

The National Theatre, Harley Granville-Barker. Sidgwick & Jackson, 1930.

The Theatre of My Heart, Geoffrey Whitworth. Revised edition. Gollancz. 1938.

The Theatre and the Nation, Geoffrey Whitworth. (Lecture to the Royal Institution). Quality Press. 1939.

Drama, (The Journal of the British Drama League). July and December 1924.

INDEX OF NAMES

INDEX OF NAMES

INDEX OF NAMES

INDEX OF NAMES